PRODUCING A QUALITY FAMILY HISTORY

Patricia Law Hatcher, CG

Hatcher, Patricia Law.
    Producing a quality family history / Patricia Law Hatcher.
       p.   cm.
    Includes bibliographical references and index.
    ISBN 0-916489-64-7
    1. Genealogy–Authorship. 2. United States–Genealogy–Handbooks, manuals, etc. I. Title.
    CS16.H36 1996
    808' .066929–dc20   96-8240

MS-DOS is a registered trademark and Windows is a trademark of Microsoft Corporation.

Macintosh and TrueType are registered trademarks of Apple Computer, Inc.

ATM and Adobe Type Manager are trademarks and PostScript is a registered trademark of Adobe Systems, Inc.

Hammermill Laser Plus is a trademark of Hammermill Paper Company.

Century Schoolbook is a registered trademark of Kingsley-ATF Corporation. CG Times is a product of Agfa Corporation. Times, Times Roman, and Univers are registered trademarks of Linotype-Hell AG. ITC Zapf Dingbats is a registered trademark of International Typeface Corporation. Courier is a registered trademark of Smith-Corona Corporation. Other fonts mentioned are the trademarks or registered trademarks of their respective companies.

EcoFLEX is a trademark of Johnson Printing Service.

GBC and Velo-Binding are registered trademarks of General Binding Corporation.

Scotch, Magic, and Post-it are trademarks of 3M Co.

HP, LaserJet, and PCL are registered trademarks of Hewlett-Packard Company.

DocuTech and Xerox are registered trademarks of Xerox Corporation.

Other products mentioned are the trademarks or registered trademarks of their respective companies.

© 1996 Patricia Law Hatcher
Published by Ancestry Incorporated
P.O. Box 476
Salt Lake City, Utah 84110-0476

Author photograph (back cover): Barbara Roberts Baylis

First printing 1996
10 9 8 7 6 5 4 3 2

Printed in the United States of America

Characteristics of a Quality Family History

✓ A quality family history presents quality research—research that is thorough, new, and based on a variety of primary sources.

✓ A quality family history is well-organized, understandable, and attractively presented.

✓ A quality family history uses a recognized genealogical numbering system.

✓ A quality family history documents every fact and relationship fully.

✓ A quality family history expresses information accurately, indicating the likelihood of conclusions.

✓ A quality family history goes beyond records, placing people in context.

✓ A quality family history includes illustrations such as maps, charts, and photographs.

✓ A quality family history has a thoughtful and thorough index.

Acknowledgments

Thank you to my colleagues and friends in Instructional Communications who taught me most of what is in this book.

Thank you to the genealogists who asked questions, forcing me to put into words what I know about writing, editing, and publishing.

Thank you to my friends who took the time to review and comment on this manuscript.

Thank you to my class for their interest.

Contents

Publishing Family History in the 1990s

As recently as two decades ago genealogical publishing was accessible primarily to the affluent—and the process was overseen by genealogy and publishing professionals. In the 1990s word processors and laser printers put the power of publishing—information transfer—into the hands of most of us. With attention to standards we can produce professional-quality publications.

Who can benefit from this book?

Anyone publishing his or her family history.

➤ Those who want to publish "just something for my family."

➤ Those who want to publish a professional-looking family history.

➤ Those who want to publish a quality family history.

What does this book do—and not do?

Genealogists put much time and effort into their research. Then they put substantial time and money into publishing. The end-product should be useful, attractive, and understandable. Their family histories should reflect the quality of their research.

The purpose of publishing is to convey information to those who do not have the information. This book shows you how to convey information efficiently and effectively.

This is not a step-by-step cookbook. Instead it is a guidebook, explaining what you need to know—and what decisions you need to make—in order to produce a quality family history.

This book does not tell how to buy or use hardware or software. It assumes you already have—and use—a laser printer or ink-jet printer and word-processing software. It also assumes you know how to do genealogical research—and have been doing it for some time.

Publishing family histories

Self-publishing with modern technology and tools is easier than it has ever been and accessible to more people than anyone could have imagined only a decade or so ago. Many genealogists have the power to publish their family histories. But with power comes responsibility: responsibility to disseminate quality research, responsibility to follow standards of presentation, responsibility to document, even responsibility to create something you and your family will be proud of a decade from now.

There is a trend away from publishing straight genealogy and toward publishing family history. Genealogies of the past were apt to be compilations of names and dates (similar to many of today's genealogical name databases).

Family histories are more apt to tell the stories of our ancestors' lives, to attempt to create people from those names and dates and bits of paper. They are more likely to share stories and more likely to contain information describing our research.

Why has the focus changed?

Both research and publishing have changed.

➢ We have a broad audience: our family, other genealogists, even researchers in other fields who are drawing on our research. Each seeks certain things in our text. For example, family members want to learn about the people and their lives; genealogists want to know about the research.

➢ Standards for research are high. A publication should not be a rehash of published material. It should be thoroughly documented.

➢ Many modern genealogists are researching ancestors who are relatively recent immigrants, landless, illiterate, living on the frontier, or migrating. There seems to be a trend away from idealizing our ancestors. (My-ancestor-was-more-important-than-your-ancestor is out. New bragging rights may be my-ancestor-was-harder-to-find-than-your-ancestor!)

> We often don't find a single document that explicitly states relationships. The problems we tackle are more complex. Often our "proof" for a relationship relies on building a case for its likelihood from a multitude of documents. We must present that argument in our publications.

> Our ancestors were people who lived in specific times and places. Their world differed from ours. We try to understand their world in order to do quality research. We share that understanding with our readers to make our ancestors' history interesting.

What makes a quality family history?

Browse through family histories at your library to see what you do and do not like. Read the critical book reviews (not book notices) in journals to see what the reviewers did and did not like about specific family histories. Generally, a family history with the following qualities receives good reviews.

> *It presents quality research—research that is thorough, new, and based on a variety of primary sources.*

> *It is well-organized, understandable, and attractively presented.*

> *It uses a recognized genealogical numbering system.*

> *It documents each fact and relationship fully.*

> *It expresses information accurately, indicating the likelihood of conclusions.*

> *It goes beyond records, placing people in context.*

> *It includes illustrations such as maps, charts, and photographs.*

> *It has a thoughtful and thorough index.*

This list is also printed at the front of this book. You may wish to photocopy it and place it next to your computer as a reminder.

How has technology changed publishing?

In addition to changes in expectations for *what* we publish, technology has greatly changed *how* we publish. Today's tools are easier to use than those of the past. They cost less, are more accessible, and offer more variety.

Today's tools aren't magic wands, however—they still require skill and knowledge to be used effectively.

What does it take to publish a book?

Publishing a quality family history requires research, tools, skills, and knowledge.

In the past the individuals involved in the *traditional publishing* process provided the tools, skills, and knowledge. Often they also reviewed the author's research.

Today, with the exception of the printing and binding, often a single individual is responsible for the creation and production of your family history—you. You own the tools. You may need to acquire the skill and knowledge to use them effectively. You also are responsible for the quality of the research.

What is the traditional publishing process?

The traditional publishing process has always been an extremely linear function with various individuals (such as writer, editor, and typesetter) taking ownership of the manuscript in discrete phases. It is characterized by manual activity, paper copies, transcription or retyping of text, and explicit checkpoints. As a result, traditional publishing is both extremely tedious and extremely time-consuming.

Who prepares a book for publication?

In the traditional publishing process there are a number of roles—or functions—involved in book preparation.

➢ The writer
➢ The content editor
➢ The typographer
➢ The typesetter
➢ The copy editor/proofreader
➢ The graphic designer
➢ The indexer
➢ The layout/paste-up person
➢ The printer
➢ The publisher

In traditional, linear publishing, these roles were (and often still are) performed by different individuals.

In genealogical publishing, which is self-publishing, often all roles are performed or overseen by the genealogist.

How do these people learn their jobs?

Historically individuals trained in their roles through apprenticeship. You may have encountered apprenticeship agreements in guardianships or deeds in your research, "*binding him until he is age 21 to learn the trade, art, or misterie of . . .*" In recent times writers, editors, typesetters, and graphic artists have learned through formal education plus that old stand-by: hands-on experience.

The purpose of this book is to teach you some of the "art and misterie" of writing, editing, typography, and graphic layout. That—along with lots of hands-on experience with your own software and printer—will help you prepare a quality family history.

What is the modern publishing process?

Today many of us find ourselves in a publishing environment that is almost seamless and does not have a linear structure. This is certainly true in two worlds in which I function: technical writing and genealogy. We type words only once, often in the exact form in which they will appear in the final printed version—including typeface, point size, page layout, and any special treatments.

It is literally possible in this environment to produce a book without *ever* producing an intermediate black-on-white printed page of *any* kind. Reviews can be done in electronic form. Technologies are available (and routinely used) to produce high-resolution camera-ready art, film negatives (single page or fully impositioned signatures), printing plates, and printed pages or signatures directly from electronic files.

Many of us identify "brave new world" with Huxley's brooding, pessimistic novel, but I am often reminded of the optimistic tone of the source of that phrase—Miranda's awe-struck statement in Shakespeare's *The Tempest*: "O brave new world, That has such people in 't!" (She was commenting on her first sight of the handsome, shipwrecked sailors.) Where Huxley saw a dismal future, Miranda saw a wondrous one. I agree with Miranda.

Publishing has entered a brave new world. We can produce work of quality in this new environment if we are willing to recognize the challenge. This book was written to help.

What are the advantages of the seamless approach?

An important advantage of technology and the new "seamless" approach—especially for genealogists—is that no piece of information need ever be retyped. This means that no new errors are introduced into the manuscript.

In the traditional linear approach, *proofreading* generally meant comparing the source copy to the retyped copy for errors. In the modern seamless approach, review effort can focus on reviewing the *content* of the original manuscript, thereby improving the overall quality of the publication.

The use of laptop computers to abstract, extract, or transcribe source material can increase accuracy dramatically. Their use encourages more thorough abstracting, more complete documentation, immediate review for transcription or typing errors, and—most important—more thorough analysis while the original document is at hand.

Using copy/paste, insert, or import commands in our word processors to copy abstracted, extracted, or transcribed text removes any possibility of errors being introduced during retyping. The text of an ancestor's will that was typed on a laptop computer and proofread while viewing the will on microfilm, for example, can be copied or inserted into the appropriate place in a family history without a single character being retyped.

What are the disadvantages?

There are two potential pitfalls. You can avoid both.

➢ The individuals involved in book preparation provided both expertise and a fresh eye. When outsiders are no longer a *required* part of the structured process, it is tempting to omit them entirely. Don't!

You can acquire some (but not all) of the expertise. If possible, obtain some professional advice. You certainly should arrange for a fresh eye to look at your book. See DEVELOPING AN EDITORIAL EYE for suggestions.

➢ With the loss of linearity comes the loss of *checkpoints*. Force yourself to establish at least two review times: one early in the process when you (and someone else) review your manuscript for organization and quality of content, and a second review *before* you prepare the camera-ready art when you (and someone else) review your manuscript for grammar, typos, inconsistencies, and everything else you can think of.

What is self-publishing?

Genealogy is a field in which *self-publishing* is considered the norm. In other fields self-publishing (or *vanity publishing*) is what authors resort to when no publishing house will buy their efforts. There is an inherent tinge of "not quite good enough" to a book (and its author) that is self-published. Sometimes this is unfair, as certain types of books (genealogy, for example) are niche books, more easily marketed directly by the author. In fact, often the author has the best access to his or her markets.

In self-publishing *you* are responsible for financing, marketing, distributing, and all of the business arrangements of creating a book. You should assume other responsibilities also. In particular you should arrange for quality control. Someone should review the first draft for content, and someone should proofread the final draft.

This book describes the many tasks of self-publishing.

What is desktop publishing?

When the term *desktop publishing* (or *DTP*, for short) was coined, it referred to the concept that with computers and page-layout software, individuals would be able to publish multiple copies of things like newsletters from their desk tops.

It didn't take long for most users to recognize that it was more efficient to use these tools to produce camera-ready art to take to a print shop. But the term continued to be used, albeit with a new meaning of "preparing camera-ready art."

What is camera-ready art?

Camera-ready art—also known as *final copy*—is what you provide to the printer. With the possible exception of photographs, it looks just like each page that will be in your book. The printer uses the camera-ready art to prepare the negatives and plates from which the book will be printed.

What are the tools of desktop publishing?

The introduction a few years ago of high-quality, relatively affordable laser printers and quality fonts makes it possible for us to produce books that truly look professional. The quality has continued to improve.

Once upon a time there was *word-processing software* and there was *page-layout software.* The differences were clear-cut and distinct. Word processors handled words well, but were inefficient at handling graphics (if they accepted them at all). The opposite was true of page-layout programs.

That is no longer true. Now both types of software match features almost item for item. In practice some features are more robust in one program than in another, but most often the choice is a matter of personal preference.

Genealogists who have not settled on the program they plan to use to prepare their book (and who have a choice) should investigate the newest Windows-based (or Macintosh) word-processing software. Their font-management and typesetting capabilities make them considerably easier to use than older DOS-based software. Pay particular attention to the indexing features. (What's a genealogy book without an index?)

Many tools that formerly required separate software, such as a font manager, indexing program, spell checker, grammar checker, thesaurus, and drawing program, are now included in many word-processing packages.

You must invest some time and effort in learning to use these tools. How? Take a class (or hire an experienced user as a tutor for a few hours), read the user's guide, and practice, practice, practice.

But I can't understand my computer manuals

To unlock the power in your software and printer, you *must* read the user's guides—and probably buy an after-market user's guide or two. Browse through the user's guide to see how it is laid out. Look for tutorials. If you are just beginning, buy a getting-started book. After you are more advanced, look for an unlocking-the-power book. Use them in conjunction with the user's guide.

Periodically reexamine the material in the books. As you use the software, gain experience, and try new things, sections that were at first meaningless will become meaningful. Use the table of contents and the index to locate information. If the user's guide isn't close at hand, use the on-line help system for the software.

How does this book help me create a quality family history?

➤ WHAT TO WRITE; WHEN TO WRITE IT discusses quality research, how the writing process can be a valuable part of the research process, and types of family histories.

➤ YOU MUST HAVE STYLE discusses creating a style guide and explains many of the decisions genealogists must make.

➤ WRITING discusses the writing process and presents guidelines and tips to help.

➤ UNDERSTANDING TYPE AND FONTS discusses why there are so many fonts and helps you choose and use them effectively.

➤ BOOK DESIGN discusses the parts of a book and page size.

➤ PAGE LAYOUT AND FORMATTING discusses using formatting and paragraph styles to make your book attractive and readable.

➤ ORGANIZING AND PRESENTING FAMILY INFORMATION discusses types of family histories, how a genealogical numbering system helps convey information to the reader, and the numerous typesetting decisions involved.

➤ HOW DO YOU KNOW? discusses documentation, explaining why documentation is more than citing sources.

➤ TURNING PAPER INTO PEOPLE discusses context and offers suggestions for finding contextual information and incorporating it into your family history.

➤ ILLUSTRATIONS, CHARTS, AND PHOTOGRAPHS discusses ideas and techniques for adding graphic interest to your book.

➤ DEVELOPING AN EDITORIAL EYE discusses ways to assure that you can be proud of both the content and appearance of your family history.

➤ OPENING THE DOOR TO YOUR BOOK discusses what and how to index for genealogists (who read books from back to front) and for your family (who are interested in the stories and pictures).

➤ PREPARING CAMERA-READY ART discusses the nitty-gritty of getting ready for the printer.

➤ TURNING CAMERA-READY ART INTO BOOKS discusses the many printing options available and offers advice on choosing and dealing with a printing firm.

➤ OPTIONS FROM TECHNOLOGY discusses nontraditional publishing options such as printing directly from computer files.

➤ Self-Publishing discusses the tasks that you as the publisher need to do and offers helpful hints.

➤ Resources provides information about places to turn for additional help.

➤ Index lets you find related topics quickly. Read the introduction at the front of the index for a list of major topics.

How can I get the most from this book?

Read What to Write; When to Write It. Then skim the remaining chapters, stopping to read when you recognize an issue you need help on now. The new seamless approach has blurred the chronology of publishing considerably. It is no longer possible to present a step-by-step 1-2-3 approach to publishing.

Return to the book whenever you have a question, using the index to locate the appropriate section.

If this is your own copy of this book, highlight any information that is new to you or that you don't want to forget, and then periodically review the highlighted text. Genealogists are usually so careful not to mark in books, we tend to forget that sometimes it is OK.

This book uses several techniques to help you find information.

➤ At the end of each chapter is a section on Getting help that directs you to publications and other resources related to the chapter.

➤ Each chapter concludes with a useful Checklist.

➤ The chapter Resources near the end of the book contains detailed information on resources that may be mentioned throughout the book: bibliographic entries for publications, addresses and phone numbers, and other resources.

The typesetting features discussed in this book are found in most full-featured word-processing and page-layout software for Windows™, Windows 95, and Macintosh®. The same results can be achieved with DOS-based software, but the mechanisms are different.

Getting help

To produce a professional book, do as the professionals do and surround yourself with reference and resource material—and with models. You should have all the items on the CHECKLIST at the end of this chapter *within reach*. Many can be found in used-book stores. See RESOURCES and other chapters of this book for specific recommendations.

These resources won't help if you don't use them. Every time a question arises, research the answer. Make use of sticky-notes or flags to mark pages so you can refer to them again easily. Use a highlighter to mark important passages.

Checklist for reference works

- ☑ A good dictionary
- ☑ A style manual
- ☑ A grammar guide
- ☑ Guidelines/examples of genealogical numbering systems
- ☑ Guidelines/examples of proper documentation
- ☑ Guidelines/examples of good indexes
- ☑ Examples of attractive typography and layout
- ☑ Examples of quality family histories
- ☑ Software user's guide and printer user's guide
- ☑ This book

What to Write;
When to Write It

The quality of a family history is evaluated in two areas—content and presentation. Poor presentation can diminish good content. Good presentation can never compensate for poor content.

What is a family history?

People research and publish their family histories for varied reasons and in varied ways. Some researchers concentrate on a single surname. Others seek to identify ancestors on all parts of their pedigree. Within those two broad categories there are almost as many variations of purpose, interest, and focus as there are researchers.

This variety is not a problem for publishing. Structurally, two classes of publications—*descendants-of* and *all-my-ancestors*—can accommodate many variations. We'll look at those in detail later in this chapter. First let's look at some changing trends.

Traditional genealogies

The traditional descendants-of genealogy usually begins with the immigrant and follows descendants for some number of generations. Often they have a paternalistic bent and follow only male descendants who bore the surname. This form was most popular in New England in the latter nineteenth century and early twentieth century, but it was used across the country and is still seen today.

Early genealogies tend to focus on names and dates. They may note other records created by the individual, such as deeds, but the overall reliance is on vital records, wills, and family-supplied information. Documentation, if it is included, is often a simplistic reference to a town vital record.

These genealogies do little to place the individuals in ethnic, geographical, historical, political, religious, or social context. They simply list names, rather than describing people.

Modern family histories

One significant change in research and publishing is the move toward family history. Placing people in context both helps in our research and makes the published results more interesting to our audience. In other words, we are transitioning from publishing *genealogy* to publishing *family history*.

A second trend we see in modern publications is an increased emphasis on fully documented information from a variety of sources. More people are researching ancestral lines in times and places where vital records are insufficient, inadequate, or nonexistent. Documentation today is often more than citations. It may require an analysis of the reliability of the record. Sometimes there isn't a document per se, but the presentation of a complex argument as to why we think John Jones is the son of William Jones rather than Thomas Jones.

A less-apparent but growing trend is an understanding of the importance and influence of female lines. People lived as families, not surnames, and often the maternal family ties were stronger than the paternal family ties. In the future we hope to see less short-changing of maternal lines and collateral lines in published material.

Fortunately, the traditional descendants-of structure can accommodate these new trends quite well.

Organization of descendants-of books

Descendants-of publications are organized generationally and chronologically, beginning with the oldest (furthest back) generation. We research from present to past, but we write about our research from past to present. Each generation is presented as a separate chapter.

The first generation presented is that of the immigrant. Many of us haven't gotten that far. If that is the case, begin with the furthest-back person you have identified. The initial individual in this country is known as the *progenitor.*

In the first chapter (The First Generation), include a brief listing of the children of the progenitor, but save details and expansion on the children for the following chapter (The Second Generation). The proper format is described later in ORGANIZING AND PRESENTING FAMILY INFORMATION.

The second chapter presents the children of the progenitor, with summary information for the grandchildren. The third chapter (The Third Generation) expands upon the grandchildren, and so forth. This means that the chapters grow in size as the generations progress.

What about leftovers?

If you're stuck with several individuals of the surname who you feel are related but you can't seem to tie together with proof, you have two options.

➤ If you have a hypothesis and some evidence as to where they belong, include them in the family, but clearly indicate the tentative nature of the assignment and describe your research and reasoning.

➤ If you are unsure where they belong, consign them to an appendix (Persons Named Smith Who Could Not Be Placed in the Family).

When you have done substantial and meaningful research on people you can't tie into the family, *don't leave them out.* Your research may provide valuable information to other researchers. Those researchers may possess the missing link that will allow you to attach the mystery people to the appropriate place in the family—but you won't know that unless you print what you have.

Variations on descendants-of

Single-line descent. Notice that the organization described above would work equally well if you were tracing only a single line of descent. Each chapter would treat only the direct-line family (and therefore all chapters would be roughly the same size), but the structure and presentation would remain the same.

Several surnames in one book. Suppose you want to publish your findings on several lines together. For the organization and numbering, think of each family as a separate book within one cover. The families should be presented alphabetically so that the reader can move easily from one section to another. (Sometimes there is a primary family, which can be presented first.) The index, however, should be a *single* index covering *all* families.

This is a good time to remind you that although you may have families organized in your mind by who-married-whom, the same cannot be said of your reader. Family members not involved in genealogy and not familiar with our pedigree organization find it much easier to access information in ways they understand: alphabetically and by generations.

Up-and-down presentation. In this method of presentation for descendants-of material, each line is followed down until there are no more descendants, and then it back-tracks until a line is reached that wasn't followed down, and then it is followed down.

This method is favored by many new writers because at first glance it seems to keep families together. It's fine if you are descended from the first son of the first son, but becomes increasingly cumbersome to use the further away you are from that line. It is extremely difficult for outsiders to use. (Just look at how difficult it is to explain!)

All-my-ancestors publications

For those wanting to prepare an all-my-ancestors book, there are basically two alternatives: pedigree or expanded descendants-of. The volume of information that you have to present usually determines the choice.

Expanded descendants-of

The several surnames in one book descendants-of format described above is a popular way of presenting all-my-ancestors research. There are two caveats.

➢ Make your decision about the order in which the families are presented based on what makes it easiest for the reader to find and understand the information. There are three possibilities (the first two are preferable): primary family first with the rest in alphabetical order; all families in alphabetical order; some form of structure based on familial relationships.

➤ Consider how much information you want to present. Can you cram the contents of four file drawers resulting from 15 years of research between the covers of a 250-page book? Should you? How can you adequately cover those 315 ancestors bearing more than 100 surnames? Must you revert to a names-and-dates genealogy rather than a family history in order to do so?

After considering the second point, some family historians are choosing to publish in smaller pieces.

Ancestry of . . . books

Preparing separate books on the ancestry of each of your eight great-grandparents may be a better plan. Getting an eighth of your research prepared for publication seems a more reasonable goal that will allow you to focus on *quality*, not *quantity*.

Warning: As you write, you will uncover omissions that require further research, and your book will grow—even though it covers only an eighth of your ancestry.

Alternately, you might choose to do four books on the ancestry of each of your grandparents or 16 booklets on each of your great-great-grandparents. Look at your pedigree chart and your research to see if one break is more logical than another.

Organization of ancestry-of books

Suppose you want to publish a book on the ancestry of your great-grandmother Sarah Smith titled *The Ancestry of Sarah (Smith) Jones (1860–1925) of Podunk, Iowa*. How might you organize it?

Part I: Sarah Smith
    The Life of Sarah^3 Smith (1860-1925)
    Stories of Podunk
    Children and Grandchildren of Sarah (Smith) Jones
Part II: The Smith Family
    Possible English origins for Stephen^1 Smith
    Stephen^1 Smith (1790-1838) of Marblehead, Massachusetts
    Samuel^2 Smith (1822-1888) of Springfield, Illinois
Part III: The Adams Family
    Adam^1 Adams . . .
      . . .
Part IV: The Brown Family
      . . .
Index

The first part is a personal history for Sarah; the second is her descent in the surname family; her other ancestral families follow in alphabetical order; and finally there is a combined index. Within each family part there are subdivisions. You can see that this structure is both well-organized and flexible.

Pedigree (ahnentafel) numbering system

A *pedigree* (from the French for crane's foot, because of its shape) and an *ahnentafel* (German for ancestor table) are ways of charting names and vital dates for ancestors. They use the same numbering system. Each individual has a unique number.

#1   You
#2   Your father
#3   Your mother
#4   Your paternal grandfather
#5   Your paternal grandmother
#6   Your maternal grandfather
#7   Your maternal grandmother
#8   Your paternal great-grandfather
#9   Your paternal great-grandmother
    and so on

To obtain the number for the father of an individual, double the number of the individual. Thus males (other than possibly yourself) are always an even number. The number of the mother is one greater than that of the father. Simple math lets you follow the trail up and down a pedigree or ahnentafel quite easily.

Pedigree (ahnentafel) format

To publish using a pedigree/ahnentafel approach, simply expand upon the amount of information presented in a chart. Present the family information generationally from yourself backwards, presenting the individuals in numerical order. For each individual you may include as much information as you want.

What the pedigree numbering system does not have is an established way to present individuals who are not a part of the direct ancestral line (more popularly known as "the rest of the family"). It is highly recommended that when publishing in a pedigree format, you also include a children-of section for each individual. Use the model for the children section described in ORGANIZING AND PRESENTING FAMILY INFORMATION.

The pedigree presentation method is perfectly acceptable. It is not, however, seen much in hard-bound publications. It works best when the information to be presented is limited. (If the publication is limited because not much research has been done, it probably wasn't time to publish anyway.)

A pedigree format *does* work well when the limitation is generational. For example, if you wish to prepare a book on the generations back *through* your eight great-grandparents, the pedigree format is fine.

The information may be voluminous, presenting family stories and many photographs, but it focuses on only 15 individuals and their families (if you count yourself). It isn't likely that your readers will be confused about who is who.

If the family in question uses *patronymic naming*, such as a Scandinavian family, the pedigree format may be preferred. Because the surname changes with each generation, the surname-based descendants-of format doesn't work well.

Overview

Creating a family history follows these general steps:

1. Define the project. Decide what to write, when to write, what to publish, and when to publish.

2. Do a literature search. You don't want to waste time and money replicating what is already in print. If you disagree with what is in print, you must present substantive evidence for your case in your book.

3. Begin writing by focusing on one family unit (father, mother, children). Just as every journey begins with a single step, every family history should begin with a single family.

4. Review your research on the family unit. Is each document as close to the original as possible? Have you established the fact of the marriage and that the couple are the parents of the children?

5. Write the narrative on the parents. Document every fact.

6. Write the information on the children. Document every fact.

7. Once you have created the basic structure of the family, it is time to incorporate contextual information and describe what their lives were like.

8. Define index entries and generate the index. It is best for the first-time indexer to wait until the text and pagination is final before working on the index.

9. Add illustrations. Because files containing graphics are much slower and more cumbersome to work with, save this step until last.

Choosing what to write and what to publish

Be realistic. Tackle a project that you can complete *without sacrificing quality*. A small volume presenting top-notch research is always a greater contribution to genealogy than a large volume regurgitating published secondary material.

As suggested earlier in this chapter, you may want to plan a separate volume on the ancestry of each of your eight great-grandparents, for example.

Although you can postpone the final decision, do some preliminary investigation and decide what size and type of book you plan to publish. BOOK DESIGN discusses page size; TURNING CAMERA-READY ART INTO BOOKS discusses binding and printing options.

Choosing when to write and when to publish

Be aware that if you want your book in time for, say, Christmas or a family reunion, you need to send camera-ready art to the printer well in advance. Depending on the options you have chosen, such as paper size, binding, printer, and photographs, this *lead time* (*in-house* time) could range from one week to three months.

However, any time is the right time to write. You can write when all your research is done. (If you can tell when that is—some of us never feel as if we are done.) Or you can write as you do your research. There are many advantages to the write-as-you-research approach.

Writing as a research tool

One thing that professional writers know very well is that if you write clearly you are forced to write accurately. The clearly written word does not lend itself to covering up faulty or fuzzy reasoning.

If you write clearly, your reader can understand and evaluate your reasoning. The reader can go back and refer to facts you've used to build your case, and they can reread your conclusions.

But even more important, *as you write*, you will find yourself analyzing, rereading, and reevaluating. Our research skills grow and develop as we research. Our knowledge of the individuals we are researching grows. Our understanding of the records, the locality, and the social context grows.

It is often the writing process that triggers our analytical skills. Questions almost invariably come to mind as we write up research we did years ago. In fact, it is rare if questions do not come to mind as we write up research we did merely hours ago!

Writing (and the associated mental activity) is the most valuable research tool you can use.

Tips for using writing as a research tool

As you write, use the word processor's tools to highlight sections of text that you are concerned about and to write notes to yourself about your concerns and items to check. This places the facts, research, documentation, comments, and strategy together.

Depending on which techniques you use, you can control whether those notes to yourself are displayed only on the screen or if they also are printed. Here are a few ideas you might try. Read the user's guide to learn which of these features are available and to learn how to use them if they are new to you.

> ➢ *Color.* Technical writers sometimes use color (usually red) to flag text that we think is OK and reads as if it is final, but has not yet been verified against the final product. Genealogists can use the same technique to flag a sentence in which there is ambiguity. When the text is printed on a laser printer or ink-jet printer, it may be printed in black or in gray, depending on your software and printer option settings. (If you have a color printer, it is printed in color.)

> ➢ *Underline.* Underlining is not used in typesetting, so you can use it for the same purpose as color. It is available in even the simplest of word processors. You can use the search function to search for underline. This lets you review your text quickly for outstanding issues that you still need to research.

➤ *Hidden text.* Hidden text (available in some word processors) is for writing notes to yourself. You can choose to display it on the screen—or not. You can choose to print it—or not. This is a good way to list ideas for further research and to point out discrepancies (??? Surely the first and second child were not born five months apart ???).

Use hidden text to annotate information about sources, such as call numbers or your evaluation, that you don't want to appear in the final printing (FHL# 976.999 X2222—full of errors).

➤ *Annotations.* These are used for the same purpose as hidden text, but work quite differently. Investigate the user's guide.

➤ *Searchable characters.* Choose a string of unique characters, such as ***, ???, or xxx, and place them at each end of your comments to yourself. (xxx Check this marriage record. There is a conflict. Is this date for the license, marriage, or recording? xxx) This technique is available on any word processor. You can search for the special character string to locate your problems.

Both prepublishing and writing in pieces have benefits

With today's technology, publishing needn't wait for that thick, hardback tome.

➤ Write up your research as you go. Document it properly. Exchange it with others researching the same line. It's a wonderful way to network.

➤ Don't publish everything at once. Instead of writing about *all* your ancestors, focus on *one* surname or *one* individual. Then you can focus on quality.

➤ Prepare holiday or reunion booklets, sharing what you've found. Tell family members that you are working on a book and ask them to provide any additions or corrections they may have. They may even offer to loan you a photograph of your great-grandmother as a child for inclusion in the final publication.

➤ Write an article for an appropriate periodical correcting an error in print. Depending on the editor and the periodical, you may get invaluable (and free!) advice on further research and on improving your writing. Or the article may be read by another researcher who has a letter that contains a critical piece of the puzzle.

➤ Publish just a few copies initially. It can be an 8½"×11" photocopy with a paper cover, or use the DocuTech technology described in OPTIONS FROM TECHNOLOGY.

When writing and publishing in small pieces, follow the standards. Document completely, use a recognized numbering system, and be as critical as possible. It's OK to be frank about doubts you may have. In fact, it's useful.

Do a literature search

Undoubtedly one of the most frequent criticisms found in book reviews is related to material already in print. The criticisms fall into three broad groups.

➢ The author has relied almost entirely on published secondary sources. (This is known as "they killed a tree for nothing.")

➢ The author has republished known erroneous information for which the correction is in print, because he or she did not find the correction. (This is known as "now it will take another 50 years to stop this error from circulating.")

➢ The author has done original research, but has arrived at exactly the same conclusions published fifty years ago. (This is known as "don't reinvent the wheel.")

All three of these criticisms might be avoided with a good literature search. This is especially true for corrections.

Genealogists are gaining access to new records every day. More genealogists are researching, and more genealogists are publishing the results. Often corrections are published as articles rather than in books.

Surveying what is already in print early in the research process lets you focus your own research in the most productive direction. At the minimum, a basic literature search requires checking two resources. One is for books; the other is for periodicals.

There are many additional resources you might—and should—check, but these two encompass the broadest scope of published material.

Some additional finding aids are listed in RESOURCES under LITERATURE SEARCH. A search on important collateral names may be valuable also.

Family History Library Catalog

The Family History Library (popularly known as "Salt Lake City"), which is operated by The Church of Jesus Christ of Latter-day Saints (LDS), contains the largest collection of genealogical material in the world. This includes many published family histories. The *Family History Library Catalog*™ (FHLC) is available across the country at the family history centers (FHC) of the LDS church in both microfiche and CD-ROM formats. (Visitors are welcome.) The microfiche version can be purchased (in whole or in part) for home use.

The catalog is in four basic parts: Surname, Locality, Subject, and Author/Title. (Only the surname section is described here, but if you are not using the other sections, especially the Locality section, as a research tool, your research is probably not as thorough as it should be.)

When the library receives a family history, the book is reviewed and a brief paragraph is written describing the contents: progenitor, locality, and *some* of the other surnames included in the book. The primary surname and the other surnames become individual entries in the FHLC. Thus, some collateral lines are listed, and some are not.

The Surname section of the microfiche is arranged alphabetically by the keywords, and the descriptive paragraph is shown. Simply scan the descriptive paragraph for all the books under your surname. On the computer you can use specific words to limit your search. For example, you can search for Hutchinson entries that contain "Massachusetts" in the descriptive paragraph.

If you find a book that you think might be about the line you are researching, locate the book. Check at your local library and the FHL (some—but not all—books have been microfilmed, and you can rent the microfilm to read at a FHC), hire someone to check it for you (see PROFESSIONAL GENEALOGISTS in RESOURCES), or—best of all—plan a research trip to Salt Lake City.

Periodical Source Index

The Allen County Public Library (popularly known as "Fort Wayne") has the largest genealogical periodical collection in the world. To make the contents of this wonderful collection accessible to their users (they have closed stacks) and to others, they created the *Periodical Source Index* (PERSI), a massive computer-generated index that currently contains almost a million entries in twenty-five volumes.

They examined every article in every periodical in their collection. For each article, they assigned a keyword describing the primary topic of the article (such as the surname). The listing is sorted by keyword and gives the title and journal volume, date, and page. Major sections include Names and Locality.

Annual indexes covering the current periodicals acquired during the previous year have been issued each year since 1986. Additionally, an on-going retrospective project is indexing all issues of genealogy and local history periodicals.

You can find PERSI in many genealogical collections. To see what has been published on your family, look in the Names sections in each of the annual publications (nine at present) and each of the retrospective series (four at present). (That's thirteen volumes to check through 1994, but it's easy and quick to use.) Plans are underway for a merged version, possibly in 1997, on microfiche and CD-ROM.

When you find a likely article, attempt to locate a copy of the journal. (Don't be surprised when a great article on a New Hampshire family is published in a Michigan periodical, for example.) If you have difficulty obtaining a copy, you can order one from the Allen County Public Library through your library's Interlibrary Loan program. There is a basic service charge per request (but you can request several articles at once) and a per-page photocopying fee.

And, as with the FHLC, if you are not using the Locality section of PERSI as the powerful research aid that it is, you're probably missing out on something.

Begin with a single family unit

Now that you've defined your project and done your literature search, it's time to dig in. Focus on a single family unit. Often it is easiest to begin with the one furthest back in the primary surname line, especially if your family history is in a descendants-of format.

Dig out all of the information you have found about the individuals in that family: father, mother, and children. Begin by arranging the information in a single chronological sequence, merging the research on the children. Place a completed family group sheet at the back.

Sit down in a quiet place with the chronologically arranged research material and a pad of sticky notes. You are going to review the stack of research papers several times.

Review your research for quality

Quality research is research that is based on a *variety* of *primary* sources.

> ➢ *Review for primary sources.* It isn't necessary for us to get bogged down in a discussion of primary versus secondary versus tertiary sources (several books listed in DOCUMENTATION AND EVIDENCE in RESOURCES discuss the subject in detail). Try this instead. As you look at each sheet, ask yourself:

Is this the original? If not, can I get closer?

If your sheet refers to a published abstract for a will, for example, use a sticky note to write yourself a reminder to examine the will book and also to find out if there is a probate packet. Attach the note to your sheet.

> ➢ *Review for reliability.* The quality of a source depends on more than whether it is primary or secondary. Factors such as the reliability of the information provider, the care of the information recorder, and the condition of the record all enter in. So ask yourself:

Do I have any doubts about this source?

If the ink was seriously faded, or the writing hard to decipher, or there was no dower release when there should have been, or the author provided absolutely no sources for his or her "facts," make yourself another sticky note. You'll want to include this information about your evaluation of the source in your book (see HOW DO YOU KNOW?).

> ➢ *Review for variety.* Now that you've been through the entire stack, consider whether or not you have used a variety of sources. If you've relied almost entirely on census records and a few published genealogies, you may be in trouble.

In particular, for most American ancestry you need to explore land records (and tax records where possible). You also should have located every census for every family member (especially the later years where elderly parents might be living with grown children).

Review for reasonableness

Now go through the sources again, evaluating them for reasonableness. The chronological arrangement aids this task greatly. Ask yourself:

Is this reasonable?

For example, a marriage record in Georgia probably does not belong to a man who has been actively engaged in farming in Missouri for ten years, even if he once resided in that Georgia county. It isn't impossible, but it is unlikely, and therefore requires additional proof.

Watch for such things as a man with a wife Mary, then a wife Sarah, then a wife Mary, then a wife Sarah. Or someone residing and farming simultaneously in Kentucky and Indiana. In either case, you've probably tried to merge two separate men into one.

Look at the timing of significant events. Investigate:

➤ Any marriage before age 21. (Was there a marriage permission?)

➤ Any marriage after age 30. (Was there a prior spouse—and is he or she dead?)

➤ Any birth before marriage or less than one year after. (Of course it sometimes happened, but check your dates.)

➤ Any death after age 70. (Do you have good evidence for the birth date and that the records belong to the same person?)

➤ Any births when the mother was under 21 or over 40. (Scrutinize late-life pregnancies carefully—there may be two wives.)

➤ Any births that are abnormally close (if closer than 18–24 months, there may be an error in a date) or widely separated (if more than three years, there may be a second wife).

➤ Any adult activity before the mid-twenties, such as buying land or holding a public or military office.

All of these are possible, but they were not the norm in *all* localities in *all* time periods. They should be flags that you may have merged records belonging to two different individuals—or you may have overlooked additional records.

Review for relationships

At the bottom of the stack we placed the family group sheet. Put it on top. Ignore the dates and places. Look at the wife's name and (recalling the sources you have just reviewed) ask yourself:

Have I proved that she is the wife of this man?

A marriage record between John Jones and Mary Miller isn't sufficient unless you have reason to believe that he is *your* John Jones. If the answer is "yes," put a check mark next to her name. If the answer is "no," it's sticky-note time.

Now look at each child's name and ask yourself:

Have I proved that he or she is the child of this man and this woman?

If you found, for example, a wife Mary named in a deed and a will, you might write yourself a note, "Children #5-8 are the children of the Mary named in the deed and will. Children #1-4 are *probably* the children of Mary also, because there is no large gap between any of the births."

Create a narrative

Now it's time to write. You have several options for presentation. See ORGANIZING AND PRESENTING FAMILY INFORMATION for details on writing and formatting family information.

The simplest way to write a narrative is to present your research chronologically, creating a biography for the family. The chapter WRITING offers some suggestions for ways to keep your book from sounding like a boring repetition of your research notes.

Another way to organize is topically. If your ancestor was a merchant, for example, you may choose to have separate sections on his mercantile activities, his growing family, and his military career and pension. Variety in the narrative is good.

Expand with context

Read your narrative. Close your eyes and try to imagine your ancestors' lives. What was their world like—food, clothing, buildings, travel, crops, tools, military, neighbors, church, schooling? List several topics that interest you—and make a note to learn as much as you can about those topics as they applied to your ancestors' time and place. TURNING PAPER INTO PEOPLE offers many suggestions on finding and incorporating contextual information.

Create the index

A genealogy book without an index is not a genealogy book. The index is not optional. Furthermore, the book is only as useful as the index is good. If you have information in the book that isn't in the index, you might as well not have written it. OPENING THE DOOR TO YOUR BOOK contains suggestions on constructing a useful index.

The index should be created near the end of the project, but do not leave it until the last minute. It requires time and thought to create a good index. It also turns out to be a useful research tool, helping to make connections and point out problems.

Add illustrations

Show a family history to a family member, and he or she will turn immediately to the photographs. Show it to a genealogist, and he or she will go to the charts and maps (after checking the index). ILLUSTRATIONS, CHARTS, AND PHOTOGRAPHS offers advice on illustrations for family histories.

Although you can select photographs and illustrations as you write the book, for practical reasons you should not incorporate them into the computer file until very late in the process.

When you embed graphics, it takes the software exponentially longer to load a file and to display a page on the screen. You'll be able to open and close the file and move from page to page *much* more quickly if you wait to include the graphics until the book is written.

Getting help

In RESOURCES, the section STANDARDS FOR GENEALOGICAL PUBLISHING lists several items with helpful ideas for organization and presentation.

The sections EXAMPLES: BOOKS and EXAMPLES: JOURNALS in RESOURCES lists several award-winning books and outstanding journals. In addition, you can browse the bookshelves at the library with a critical eye.

Checklist for preparing a family history

☑ Decide what and when.

☑ Do a literature search.

☑ Focus on one family unit at a time.

☑ Review your research on the family unit.

☑ Write the narrative on the parents.

☑ Write the information on the children.

☑ Incorporate contextual information.

☑ Define index entries and create the index.

☑ Add illustrations.

You Must Have Style

In nonfiction writing (and genealogical writing certainly should not be fictional writing), organization, attention to detail, and consistency are far more important than creativity and imagination.

What is style?

Most simply stated, *style is consistency*. Style covers typography, grammar, spelling, punctuation, and layout. Wise style decisions are based on standards—standards in writing and standards in genealogy.

In writing and typesetting, there is no single right way to do things. There are many times when you must choose from several equally correct options. That choice is your style.

Why style?

Readers find it easier to read and comprehend the printed word when the unexpected does not occur. Just think how discombobulating (what a wonderful word!) it would be if the size of the print changed with each line in this book.

We don't want anything to interfere with the smooth transfer of information from the printed page to the reader's mind. Nathaniel Hawthorne defined it most eloquently.

The greatest possible merit of style is, of course, to make the words absolutely disappear into the thought.

Let's look at an example. It is correct grammatically to put a comma before "and" or "or" in a series—or to leave it out. It is a matter of style that you choose one way and stick to it.

If you switch back and forth, readers occasionally find themselves rereading a sentence because the meaning wasn't clear. Usually they won't even know why (all of this is processed in our wonderful subconscious).

Style manuals and guides

Almost all publication groups have a *house style*. This is a collection of decisions the group has made concerning style. When assembled together in a printed form, those decisions are called a *style manual* or *style guide*. When decisions apply only to a single publication, they often are called a *style sheet*.

The *Chicago Manual of Style* is recommended by many genealogical editors. *Chicago* (as it is generally called) contains the decisions the University of Chicago Press made about the style *it* wants for *its* books.

Published style manuals are not all inclusive. Each may discuss several—but not necessarily all—options. For example, *Chicago* does not offer advice on how *much* to indent the beginning of a paragraph, because the University of Chicago Press *never* indents the beginning of paragraphs.

Do you need to buy a style manual?

Until recently genealogists did not need to buy a style manual. The manuals' focus on production and typesetting was helpful only to those preparing *camera-ready art*. But there are many genealogists in that category now—and the number is growing.

If you are preparing a book for publication, buy—and use—a style manual (see STYLE MANUALS, GRAMMARS, AND TYPESETTING GUIDES in RESOURCES). If money is a concern, you can buy a used copy, as much of the information does not go out-of-date.

Begin your own style guide

Your family history is a publication. You need your own style guide. Begin it right now. In big letters on the front of a blank notebook, write "Style Guide for My Family History." At the top of the first page, write "Punctuation."

Do you want to use a comma before "and" and "or" in a series? Decide now—and write it down. You've begun building your style guide. You'll be coming back to it often to add decisions on punctuation, spelling, and format as you make them—and to refer back to those decisions as you write.

Creating your own style guide is important for genealogists. It isn't merely an exercise to make you feel like a "real" writer. Your style guide should never be more than two feet away from your computer. It is a valuable tool for preserving your sanity.

Choose a title

Use some thought in your choice of a title. Family histories should include who, when, and where in the title.

Some Descendants of
Andrew Harper (1699–1755)
of Harvard, Massachusetts

Reserve catchy phrases for the subtitle. Often only the title (not the subtitle) appears on the spine of a book, in computer catalogs, and in other listings. *Northern Roots and Southern Branches* is clever and may be descriptive of your family. But the second cousin (the one with the family Bible you don't know about) won't recognize that your book is about her family, too.

A long title may not fit as a running page header (see PAGE LAYOUT AND FORMATTING). Determine what wording you wish to use for the title in the header.

On a page headed "Title" in your style guide, note the title, the subtitle, and the title text to use in the page header. This may sound pretty elementary, but instances in which the cover title does not match the header title (or the title page or the copyright registration or the page header) are fairly common.

You might also note everywhere you actually use the title—in case a last minute discovery lets you move the progenitor back one generation and changes the title. (Search-and-replace helps, but if you have one little word or letter off in one occurrence of the title, you'll miss it entirely.)

Make typographic, formatting and layout decisions

Create pages in your style guide headed Fonts, Formatting, Page Layout, and Numbering System (or choose headings you prefer). Read UNDERSTANDING TYPE AND FONTS, PAGE LAYOUT AND FORMATTING, and ORGANIZING AND PRESENTING FAMILY INFORMATION.

As you read about each option, make your choice and enter your preference in your style guide. Do not assume that you'll remember them. (This will also be a useful reference for future publications.)

If you change your mind after you've begun writing, make the changes *immediately* in *all* existing files, *and* change the entry in your style guide.

Style for genealogists

There are five areas in which genealogists must make a significant number of decisions related to style (and standards). These decisions encompass both decisions of content and decisions of format.

➢ Genealogical numbering system

➢ Names

➢ Dates

➢ Transcripts and quotations

➢ Documentation and citation

The style and standards decisions related to numbering systems are discussed in ORGANIZING AND PRESENTING FAMILY INFORMATION; documentation is discussed in HOW DO YOU KNOW? Style and standards for the other categories are discussed below.

Spelling of names

For our ancestors spelling generally didn't count. A name often was spelled several ways—even within the same document. In a publication, however, spelling does count. Choose a preferred way to spell each surname. Select a single way to spell each individual's name. Record the choices in your style guide under "Names of People."

One option to handle variant spellings is to discuss them in a special section in the book. This approach provides a place to explain to your family that the concept of consistency in how a name is spelled is fairly recent. If you have a document in which two family members managed to spell the surname five different ways, use it as an illustration.

You may instead (or additionally) point out specific spellings where you think it is important. Often this is done simply by putting the variant spelling in quotation marks. (Thomas "Aldmand" was taxed in 1770.)

Women's names

Think about the women in your book. How should you refer to them? The most commonly used method is to put a woman's maiden name in parentheses.

For example, we might call a woman "Martha Ann (Brown) Cook" in our Cook family history. But that wasn't her name when she was born. And suppose she was always known as Marnie and married three times? It seems odd to say "Martha Ann 'Marnie' (Brown) Cook Davis Evans was a tiny baby, supposedly weighing only four pounds when she was born."

The most interesting writing isn't formulaic. We don't want our family history to read as if it fell out of a computer onto paper. We want to write about *people* not *names*. Women (and men) are known by different names during different phases of their lives. Try to preserve that.

> Martha Ann Brown was a tiny baby, supposedly weighing only four pounds when she was born. Perhaps "Martha Ann" was too big a name for her. She was called "Marnie" all of her life, even in most legal documents. Marnie Brown spent her first fifteen years on the small farm in Kentucky. One week after her marriage to Hiram, Marnie Cook left her parents and younger sisters and moved to Illinois to begin a new life.

If your research is in a culture where a woman used her birth name (maiden name) after marriage, do not refer to her by her husband's surname. You may add "(wife of John Jones)" or "[Jones]" to help your reader. And this cultural difference is an interesting fact for you to point out to your readers.

Nicknames

By all means include a person's nickname. It is, after all, one of the most personal things about him or her. You could put the nickname in parentheses, but that doesn't work well if you put a woman's maiden name in parentheses also. Quotation marks are preferred.

Often the nickname simply follows the name (James "Jimmy" Johnson), but your book will be more interesting if you can comment on the nickname. (James Johnson was called "Jimmy" to differentiate him from his cousin "Jim" Johnson).

Name modifiers

Do not routinely use name modifiers such as Jr., Sr., II, or III unless they truly apply to that individual—for all of his or her life. Until the twentieth century such modifiers had nothing to do with the name of one's father. They were used to describe relative ages within the community at a specific time. We should not artificially assign them to our ancestors to make it easier for us to tell them apart.

Explain this in your book so your family will understand why the "John junr" who bought land and the "John senr" who sold it were the same man.

Likewise, use title modifiers such as Reverend and Captain only when they are appropriate. It is inaccurate to say, "In 1752 President George Washington surveyed land in the Northern Neck of Virginia." He was not president until 1789. In 1752 he was Mr. George Washington.

Which brings up another point. Mr. and Mrs. were titles with particular meanings in the seventeenth and eighteenth centuries. Don't add them if they weren't used—and don't ignore them if they were. (And, yes, tell your readers all about it.)

Place names

Not only was spelling creative for names of people, it was dynamic for names of places, too. Geographic features bearing Indian names were often wildly phonetic.

Some places were known by different names at different times— or even at the same time.

Select a preferred name and spelling and record it in your style guide under "Names of Places."

If it is helpful to your reader, add the alternate name or spelling in parentheses. Within a quotation or transcript, use square brackets instead. If you know when or why the name was changed, your readers might find this information interesting.

Date formats

The most widely accepted format for presenting genealogical dates is 12 September 1873. Never give the month as a number, and never shorten the year to two digits (12/9/73). The problems therein are obvious. (Is it 12 Sep 1873 or 9 Dec 1773?)

You may prefer a traditional date format for your family history (September 12, 1873). That's fine. Notice that when the date appears mid-sentence, the year requires commas both before *and* after it (born September 12, 1873, in Ohio).

You may use a shorter form for the month. Do you prefer Sep, Sep., or Sept.? All are accepted in genealogy. Make your choice and record the abbreviations for all months in your style guide.

You may use different styles (preferably not more than two) within different types of text. For example, you might choose a traditional style for narrative text, but an abbreviated style for the children section and notes. Record your date decisions in your style guide.

Use a hard space to avoid breaking up dates

You can use a *hard space* (*nonbreaking space*) between the day and month to avoid an ugly line break that leaves them on separate lines. (A *hard space* is a character the word processor doesn't know is a space, so it doesn't break apart the words on each side of it onto two lines.)

You also might wish to use a hard space between the month and year. If you fully-justify text, using hard spaces to keep dates intact can result in equally ugly white space between all words on the line, which reduces readability.

Preserving original date formats

If the date in a source appears in anything other than a straightforward manner, include the original form somewhere in your publication. This makes it clear to other researchers that you have correctly interpreted (translated) the date.

Researchers using computer databases should be especially conscientious to differentiate between the original date and the interpreted date. Usually you must record the original wording in the notes.

In your book you may use the original form in the text with the interpreted form in parentheses or square brackets.

They were married on the "20th day of the 11th month [January] 1732[/3]."

You may prefer to give the original text as part of the note. (You needn't be consistent about this choice. Choose the option that fits best with the narrative in each case.)

They were married on 20 January 1733.[1]

> 1. The marriage entries are chronological. On "ye 20th day of the 11th month 1732" the marriage was performed by . . .

Some particular instances of date formats are discussed below, but there are many others. (If any of these date formats apply to your research, you may want to discuss them in your book.)

➤ *Calendar change.* Prior to September 1752 the American colonies were still using the Julian calendar, which began its year on March 25. Much of the rest of the world had switched to the Gregorian calendar, which began its year on January 1. This is why September (seventh), October (eighth), November (ninth), and December (tenth) are now the ninth through twelfth months.

Double-dating was one recognition of this problem. You may find a document that says "January 15, 1741/2." But if your document says "January 15, 1741," do not "fix" the date. If the context or other information makes it clear that the year is 1741/2 rather than 1740/1, use "1741[/2]," "1741 OS" (for Old Style; NS is New Style), or even "1741[/2?]" if you aren't absolutely certain.

➤ *"Quaker" dates.* Because Quakers did not believe in assigning pagan names to months or days of the week, they typically referred to them ordinally. Hence, "first month" was January, except prior to 1753, when the "first month" was March. Ordinal dating for months was not used solely by Quakers.

➤ *Church calendar.* Some dates, especially in other countries or in colonial times, were given in relationship to the church calendar. Payments might be due "on the feast of St. Michael the Arch Angel" or a baptism performed "on the second Sunday after Trinity [Sunday]." Either within the text or in a note, preserve this wording, and then translate the year for your readers.

➤ *Regnal years.* In old documents you may find the year given as "in the third year of Edward" or "in the seventh year of our Independence." Putting the year in square brackets is a good method of presenting such dates.

Date modifiers

Often we cannot find precise dates for an ancestor's birth, marriage, or death. When you can't find a precise date, provide either estimates or boundaries for the vital event. Don't ask your reader to keep track of records and events mentally. We have several useful ways of expressing imprecise dates.

➢ *Calculated.* Use calculated or calc. (in parentheses) when you have a complete age (such as on a tombstone) and are subtracting to calculate the birth date. "John Jones was born 13 January 1813 (calculated from tombstone)."

Be especially circumspect when dealing with precise birth dates for a life that spanned the calendar change. Not only did the "year" change for January through March, but 11 days in 1752 (September 3-13) never even occurred. Some people adjusted their "birth day" and some did not—and you can't be sure without a birth record.

➢ *About* and *circa.* Use *about* or *circa* (Latin for about or approximately) when you can place an event within a year or so, as when you find an age on a census, deposition, or tombstone. For example, if John Jones is listed as 37 on the 1850 census, you might say, "John Jones, born *circa* 1813," or "John Jones, born *circa* 1812-13." Note that "in the third year of his age" is the same as "at age two."

You can use *circa* for a marriage year if you have identified births for the first several children, allowing you to project the marriage date. If you have identified only one or two children, it might be better to use one of the less-specific modifiers below. Set *circa* in italics and avoid the abbreviation *ca.*

➢ *Say.* Use *say* (with a comma before and after) when roughly estimating a date (estimating the year of birth from a deed or marriage, for example). Usually the year is divisible by 5. "John Jones was born in, say, 1815."

➢ *By, before, between, after.* Often we have an exact date or dates that are boundaries for vital events. For example, the first wife died *before* the date of the husband's second marriage; she died *after* the date on which she released dower on a deed; she died *between* the date of the dower release and the date of the second marriage. Frequently we can say, "John Jones died between 15 November 1868 when he made his will and 13 March 1870 when it was probated."

Watch for events that had legal age limits, such as marriage, purchasing property, apprenticeships, and choosing a guardian. When using such events, mention in the text or notes the basis for your calculation. "When a child reached 14, he or she could choose his or her own guardian. On 1 July 1840, John chose his uncle Thomas as his guardian, so he was born by 1 July 1826."

➢ *Related events.* Be extremely conscientious about identifying the precise *event* when stating vital dates. Is the date for the birth or baptism; the marriage, license, bond, or return; the death, burial, writing of the will, recording, probate, or inventory?

Decisions about numbers

Genealogists rely on dates and numbers. There are several style concerns in addition to those discussed above. Make your choice and record it in your style guide.

➢ *One or 1, twenty or 20.* Should you spell out numbers? Yes and no. Everyone is agreed that you spell out the numbers from one to nine. Some style manuals spell out all numbers through 99; others do not. It's your choice. Within a sentence however, be consistent. "The children were between eight and thirteen." Numbers from twenty-one to ninety-nine are hyphenated.

➢ *19th century or nineteenth century.* You may refer to a century using either numerals or words—but not both. Be consistent. Writing the word out is more graceful.

By the way, when modifying a noun, "nineteenth century" is hyphenated. When it stands alone, is not. "According to a nineteenth-century document, he was born at the beginning of the eighteenth century."

➢ *23, 23^d, 23rd, 23d or 23rd.* Although it is not often done anymore, you may want to refer to dates ordinally. If you do, pick which version you want and whether or not you want to superscript. See also the discussion on superscripts below.

➢ *1700s and 1860s.* Note that there is no apostrophe when referring to centuries and decades with numerals.

Abbreviations

Genealogists use abbreviations a lot—for events (b., bp., m., d.), for places (Co., Cem., Cr., Mass.), for months (Sep., 1st m.), and for other terms (ca., lic., prob.).

All those periods, commas, and little short words create choppy text. Look at the previous paragraph. It isn't very inviting, is it?

A more important consideration is that abbreviations don't read well. In fact, we really don't read them, we translate them. Each time we encounter an abbreviation, we quit thinking about the idea for a fraction of a second in order to figure out what the abbreviation means. By the way, did you think "prob." in the first paragraph was for "probate" or "probably"? If you guessed wrong, you might end up rereading the sentence.

Yes, but . . . You were going to say abbreviations save space, right? Sure they do. Some. But not as much as you think. Replacing common genealogical abbreviations with spelled-out words does surprisingly little to increase length, even of long genealogical manuscripts. This is because typeset (proportionally spaced) text is very efficient in its use of space.

It is acceptable to choose different styles for abbreviations in different *types* of text within a publication, but you must be consistent within the type.

If you aren't ready to drop all abbreviations, try a compromise. Spell out all words in the narrative, but use abbreviations in the notes. Or perhaps you could choose to avoid all genealogical abbreviations (b., bur., prob.), but retain those that are familiar to your reader (Co., Dec., Mass.). Just remember to record your decision in your style guide, and then be consistent.

While we're on the subject of abbreviations, let's look at initials, acronyms, and modifiers also.

➢ Initials always have a period and a space after them. If there are two initials, they do not get shoved together (J. F. Kennedy, not J.F. Kennedy).

➢ Acronyms (the initials of organizations and such) have no periods and no spaces (FHL).

➢ Jr. and Sr. should have commas around them (traditional style) or use none at all (modern style). It is incorrect to have a comma only in front.

Abstracts, extracts, and transcripts

There are several schools of thought on how much (if any) to modernize the wording and punctuation of documents. The advantage is that the modernized documents are more readable. The disadvantage is that you lose both accuracy and charm. There are a number of separate decisions to make. Whatever your choices, define them in the introduction to your book.

Base your decision on your audience, how extensively your family history includes extracts, and your personal preference. If you are publishing a diary of an ancestor who used what can charitably be called creative spelling, try putting a few samples in the introduction, but modernizing the lengthier transcript.

➤ *Spelling.* From a practical point of view, it seems wise to preserve the original spelling somewhere in the publication. Old documents are frequently difficult to read, use a variety of unfamiliar letter forms, and are occasionally open to interpretation.

If we "fix" the spelling, we obscure the possibility of alternate interpretation or future corrections. However, modernizing spelling (for publication purposes, never for your research abstract) is not considered incorrect, as long as you indicate that you are doing so.

➤ *Capitalization and punctuation.* Capitalization and punctuation was a seemingly random thing for our ancestors. Standardizing capitalization and adding punctuation are the most widely accepted modernization techniques. Some genealogists add punctuation only if it is enclosed in square brackets (see below). However, this is so intrusive that it does not help readability.

➤ *Contractions, abbreviations, and superscripts.* You can, if you wish, expand contractions and abbreviations (with or without the use of square brackets). You can lower superscripts. Some writers expand with square brackets. The concerns expressed above under spelling apply here. Consider how you would prefer to see Wy^m (Willyam or William), p (poles), or—here's a tough one—$Eliz^a$ (Eliza or Elizabeth).

The decision about superscripts may well be a technical choice. If the superscripted letters would be too small or too close to the preceding line, choose "sd" instead of "s^d."

➤ *Y^e, y^t, and other thorny matters.* "Ye Olde Curiosity Shoppe" is pronounced with a "th." That isn't really a Y at the front, it is an archaic English letter called a *thorn*, which is pronounced "th." It was used frequently in old documents at the beginning of certain words. Should you render "y^e" in a document as "y^e," "ye," or "the"? Should "y^t" be "y^t," "yt," or "that"?

Before making your final choice, consider how you would handle the archaic characters in ffoster (Foster), ℘ son (person), or ℘ cell (parcell). (In the latter two, per and par were often written using a special character somewhat like a p. That character isn't available in typesetting, but we picked an approximation. Do you think that is acceptable?) Again, make choices that are appropriate for your publication and the capabilities of your software and printer.

> *Square brackets.* Square brackets indicate added information that was not in the original. If you have chosen not to modernize spelling, punctuation, or contractions, you can use this device where appropriate. "The s[ai]d p[ar]cell of land[,] which is located . . ." It isn't pretty, but it is accurate. Some editors subscript and reduce the point size of the brackets for punctuation: [,]

Even if you modernize punctuation, use square brackets when you add commas in a series of names, such as in a will. "To my daughters Mary[,] Jane[,] Emily[,] Ann[,] and Sarah." This makes it clear that *you* decided there were five daughters rather than three or four, and that there were no commas in the original document.

> *Ellipsis points.* An *ellipsis* is something left out. *Ellipsis points* are how you indicate that something has been left out. They are wonderful for retaining accuracy and voice in an original document while eliminating all the boring stuff.

Ellipsis points (. . .) are three dots (periods) with a space before, a space after, and hard spaces between the dots. (A hard space is a special character that prevents the word processor from breaking apart the three dots onto two lines as if they were separate words.)

A second, more complicated, style includes retaining punctuation such as periods and commas that occur before the ellipsis. If you prefer this style, consult a style manual for details.

> *Sic.* People make mistakes. To acknowledge that you recognize possible errors, follow the word or number with [sic] (square brackets, *sic* in italics). For example, "Mary, bornd 31 [sic] April 1813." This says, "I know that this is wrong or that it looks really strange, but this is what is written there."

Presentation of transcripts and quotations

Undoubtedly there are instances in which you want to include words in your family history that were not created by you, such as an ancestor's will or text from a published book.

> An *abstract* is a document that pulls the important elements from a document, not necessarily in the order or format in which they appear. An abstract is a research tool; it generally would not be directly quoted in a family history.

> A *transcript* is a verbatim (word-for-word) listing of a document. When a transcript of an entire document is used in a family history, it is often presented in an appendix. Transcripts of portions of a document add interest to a family history. It is thoughtful to include a transcript if you are using a document image as an illustration.

➤ An *extract* is a transcript in which all of the boilerplate elements are replaced by ellipsis points (see above). This is an extremely useful format for family histories, highlighting the important information while retaining the "feel" of the original document.

➤ A *quotation* as used here means text from a published source.

In text, set off brief transcripts, extracts, and quotations within quotation marks. For quotation marks within quotation marks, use single marks for the internal quotation. (The diary says, "We named the farm 'Hilly Haven.'") Use "curly quotes" in both cases (see UNDERSTANDING TYPE AND FONTS).

Place all commas and periods inside the closing quotation mark. Place exclamation points and question marks belonging to the sentence rather than the quotation outside. Place note numbers outside the closing quotation mark.

When a quotation or extract is part of the flow of the sentence, there is no special punctuation, but introductory words such as "said," "wrote," and so forth are followed by a comma. (In his will he stated, "I give to my wife . . .").

Set off lengthier quotations or extracts from the text as indented paragraphs. Make your choice based on which method is more appropriate and effective for the particular quotation.

The text in indented quotations is generally one to two points smaller than normal text. Because you expect your reader to *read* quotations, care must be taken to assure that the point size used is large enough for readability (at least eight or nine points).

Additionally, you can use other typographic treatment for emphasis, such as italics or a different font. (Some fonts can provide a feeling of "old" to a transcribed document such as a newspaper obituary. Just take care to choose one that is also readable.)

Indented text should align with the indent at the beginning of normal paragraphs if paragraph indents are used. It should have line space above and below if paragraph spacing is used. Although most style manuals do not recommend indenting on the right also, readers seem to prefer it.

Copyright

The issue of copyright—of reproducing someone else's words or creation within your own book—is important for genealogists. It is federal law. *Don't violate it!* Copyright is a complex subject. Although it is legislation, interpretation of its scope is derived primary from case law.

A number of books in Resources under Copyright, Publishing, and Style manuals, grammars, and typesetting guides discuss copyright in more depth. Major changes occurred in the copyright law effective in 1978. Additional changes were made in 1989. Future changes are expected.

Just because your book is primarily for your family, or because you aren't printing many copies, or because it won't make any money, or because it is mainly educational does not mean that you can copy someone else's creation, and it does not—repeat *not*—exempt you in any way from the copyright law. Abide by it.

What follows is this author's understanding of what copyright means to genealogists, expressed as simply as possible, and is offered only as a guideline.

What and how much can I copy?

"Fair use" does not have a quantitative measure. It is evaluated qualitatively, based on how much *of the original* you are quoting, *how important* that part is to the original, and purpose (for *criticism, comment, scholarship,* or *research* only). Some suggested guidelines have been 25 words, 100 words, one paragraph, and three paragraphs. Less is better than more.

Thus, you might use a few sentences from a social history that describe a particular farm activity such as threshing or that contain facts or numbers from the author's research, but you would not quote four pages describing many aspects of farm life.

Indicate clearly that you are quoting and attribute the source.

How do I know what has copyright protection?

The present-day status of material is summarized below.

> ➤ *Anything published more than 75 years ago.* Material published more than 75 years ago is definitely out of copyright, and you may quote from it (or reproduce illustrations) without permission. Of course, you *will* include full credit and citation.

➤ *Anything copyrighted less than 75 years ago, but before 1978.* These works had a copyright of 28 years that could be renewed for 28 years, which was automatically extended to 47 years (total of 75) by the new law. If the work was/is renewed, it has 75 years protection. If it wasn't/isn't renewed, the protection expired/expires after the original 28 years.

Chances are a book that wasn't reprinted by the original publisher did not have the copyright renewed, but you should investigate. The Copyright Office will check for you, but there is a search fee. (See COPYRIGHT in RESOURCES.)

➤ *Anything published after 1978.* Most works fixed in tangible form after 1 January 1978 are copyrighted for 75 years—even if there is no copyright notice or copyright registration.

➤ *Anything created entirely by the Federal government.* Publications of the Federal government are in the public domain, except for any portions of them that may have been copyrighted individually. Material produced by many other governmental entities is also in the public domain (check for copyright notices).

➤ *Newspapers and magazines.* Many newspapers and some magazines are not copyrighted as a whole, although some individual articles may be. Look for a copyright notice. Most of the newspaper material genealogists use (obituaries, wedding notices, reports of legal actions or neighborhood activities) is not copyrighted.

➤ *Unpublished material.* This is the bad news, because it covers many of the archival materials with which genealogists work. We aren't talking about *records*, but about things that are considered *creative works*. This includes such things as *diaries, letters,* and *memoirs.* The copyright on *letters* is considered to belong to the creator (the writer), not the recipient or current owner.

Although the new law defined the copyright for unpublished material as the life of the author plus 50 years, there was a kicker. Even if the author has been dead for over a century, any unpublished work created before 1978 is protected through 2002.

This means that if you want to quote from an unpublished letter, diary, or account book, you *must* obtain written permission from the owner and from the copyright holder, and you must cite the permission in your book.

This can be difficult, but you *can* use the *information* you find—you just can't quote more than a small part of the text or reproduce an image without permission. So the easiest solution is to paraphrase.

➤ *Pictorial and graphic works.* Maps, photographs, and drawings have the same copyright protection as literary works, as outlined above.

Permissions

Fortunately, copyright owners, whether publishing companies or archives, are often willing to give reasonable permission (usually without a fee). Just send a short, simple letter to the Archivist or Permissions Editor with a self-addressed, stamped envelope. (If someone else holds the copyright, the letter will be forwarded to the appropriate person, so be patient.) You may use the following as an example:

Dear Permissions Editor,

I am publishing my family history. I would like to use the map of Alabama Baptist churches from *Baptist Churches in Alabama*, page 167, by Rev. Right. I want to circle the locations of the churches where my family attended.

I am attaching a draft of the pertinent pages and the citations that I would like to use. May I have permission to use the material? Is the attached citation/permission acceptable, or do you have preferred wording?

Thank you for your help.

Getting help

As always, a variety of aids are listed in RESOURCES. This is a good time to go to the library and browse through the journals listed in EXAMPLES: JOURNALS. With paper and pencil or your style guide in hand make detailed notes about what you do or do not like about how each journal presents information. Make photocopies of good model pages.

Checklist of major topics in a style guide

☑ Title

☑ Organization and content

☑ Numbering system

☑ Documentation

☑ Names

☑ Places

☑ Dates

☑ Abbreviations

☑ Transcripts

☑ Fonts

☑ Formatting

☑ Page layout

☑ Index

Writing

The foremost goal of writing is to convey information. To do this well, the writing must have structure, it must be interesting, it must be easy to understand, and it must be grammatically correct.

Putting pen to paper (or fingers to keyboard)

In any publication, someone is responsible for stringing words together one after another in logical order and format. That person is you. But first, you must *prepare to write*. (No, you don't just sit down and start writing.)

The OVERVIEW in WHAT TO WRITE; WHEN TO WRITE IT glossed over some organizational and detail steps. It's time to look at them in greater depth.

Identify your audience

The first step for a professional writer is to identify the primary target audience for the book. Even when a variety of people will use the book—people with different backgrounds, ages, educational levels, and reasons for reading—the writer still identifies the main target audience.

Many writers actually choose one individual in the target audience to write for—maybe a real person, maybe someone imaginary. Although it seems like a contradiction, writers have found that they address everyone's needs better if they write for only one person.

Is your primary audience your immediate family, the broader family, other genealogists researching this surname, or genealogists in general? Take a few moments to think about it. If you understand to whom you are talking, writing flows more easily.

Create an outline

Begin by creating a top-level outline of the book, just parts (groups of chapters, if you are using that division) and chapters. Review Organizing and Presenting Family Information for ideas.

Now add detail to your outline. What will be included in the front matter and back matter? (See Book Design.)

How do you want to organize each chapter? By its nature, a family history has a certain amount of enforced order. (Although we've all seen some that managed to defy any sense of order!) You have some options, though. Do you want an introductory or scene-setting section in each chapter, for example?

Do you want the genealogical summary before or after the expanded discussion of the family? (See the discussion in Organizing and Presenting Family Information.)

Will you intersperse photographs and illustrations throughout the text or group them together? (See Illustrations, Charts, and Photographs.)

Record your organizational decisions in your style guide.

Five characteristics of good nonfiction writing

Professional writers keep guidelines in mind at all times as they write. You can benefit by doing the same. A popular set of guidelines for writing lists the five criteria used to judge and evaluate nonfiction writing. They provide excellent guidance for genealogical writing also.

Good nonfiction writing is:
Clear
Concise
Correct
Consistent
Understandable

You will find that these guidelines are not restrictions, but rather aids in helping you decide how to express a thought, construct a sentence, lay out a page, or choose a font.

Pat's Maxim and Corollary

Years ago, I developed a single guideline that has served me well in every publishing decision I make, from sentence structure through sizing an illustration.

Pat's Maxim: The purpose of nonfiction writing is to convey information to the reader.

Corollary: Anything that helps convey that information is good. Anything that detracts is bad.

Everything you read in this book is based on that maxim and corollary.

Importance of writing

Words are the only tool you have to persuade your reader that the information you are providing about your family is true. Choosing the word that says exactly what you mean is important. When writing is clear, concise, correct, consistent, and understandable, information flows smoothly and effortlessly from the paper into the readers' thoughts.

Making writing interesting

You might notice that "interesting" is not one of the five criteria. It is inherent. (Perhaps "not uninteresting" would be more accurate.) If you cannot hold the attention of your audience, you cannot convey information.

The two biggest stumbling blocks that keep much genealogical writing from being interesting is that it is either formulaic or pompous.

Genealogical writing needn't be a recitation of facts—and you should not try to make it sound scholarly. Pompous-sounding language is often boring and imprecise.

Writing gracefully

Although written language is different from spoken language, one cure for awkward writing is to turn your back to the computer and say what you have to say out loud. Then turn back to the keyboard and type what you said. This trick may help you learn to avoid writing sentences that would be unnatural for you to speak.

One of the most difficult things about making your family history interesting is trying to keep every sentence and every paragraph from sounding the same. It's very easy to fall into the rut of beginning each sentence with the equivalent of "In 1813 John Smith . . ."

➤ Look at ways to rearrange the parts of a sentence to add variety, such as moving a prepositional phrase or clause to the front or back of the sentence.

➤ Within a paragraph, try presenting the background information first, followed by the specifics about the ancestors. This technique offers more options for sentence structure.

➤ Although we suggested earlier that the easiest way to write is to narrate the events chronologically, sometimes presenting the information topically (land, military, children, farming) is more interesting and better accommodates contextual information.

➤ Some types of contextual background require that you write one or more paragraphs on the subject. Look also for ways in which you can interweave the contextual information with the facts.

Shorter is easier to understand

To improve the readability of your writing, shorten your sentences. Be more concise or break up long complicated sentences into two shorter sentences.

Studies have shown that reading comprehension starts to fall when a sentence has 20 or more words. (Sentence length does not have any effect on comprehension when sentences are below 20 words in length.) The effect is dramatic. The 90 percent comprehension rate for a 19-word sentence drops to 31 percent for a 31-word sentence!

The same principle applies to paragraphs. Long paragraphs can be intimidating, especially when small type and long line lengths are used. Look for paragraphs with, say, 10 or more lines and see if there is a logical place to break one paragraph into two paragraphs.

And remember, periods and paragraph breaks are your friends.

Pitch the pomposities and prune the padding

When we speak, we often fill our speech with unnecessary words to allow ourselves time to organize our thoughts and to frame our next sentence. When we write, however, the purpose (and result) of unnecessary words is just the opposite—to disguise and hide what is being said.

There is a pitfall in genealogical writing. Because our research (we hope!) is indeed scholarly, we are tempted to use scholarly-sounding articles as models. Avoid the temptation. Your purpose isn't to impress your reader. It isn't to obscure or hide your research.

Your purpose is to help your reader understand your research as accurately—and as painlessly—as possible. He or she should not have to wade through a quagmire of unnecessary words. Examine the following examples for ideas about how you can painlessly prune your own words.

it is contained in	it is in
they make the assumption that	they assume
it is within the realm of possibility	it is possible
born in the state of Kentucky	born in Kentucky
the church's early beginnings were in	the church began in
John of Kentucky is one and the same as	John of Kentucky is
due to the fact that	because
moved at the time of	moved when
demonstrates that he was	demonstrates he was

Avoid passive voice

Active voice says who did what. *Passive voice* says what was done to whom—and sometimes the identity of the doer isn't even revealed. Passive voice bogs down the action, but it is often appropriate in family histories. For example, we say "Mary Miller is buried in Pineland Cemetery" because "The Pineland Cemetery caretaker buried Mary Miller" puts the focus on the wrong individual.

On the other hand, "The local farmers built the school" is livelier and two words shorter than "The school was built by the local farmers." To spot passive voice, look for *be* verbs such as *is, are, was,* and *were* and for the preposition *by*. Grammar-checking software is very useful for highlighting passive voice.

Past or present tense

A greater problem for the genealogist is tense. Is "the will says" or "the will said" correct? Here's the rule: people *did* (they are dead now, so they can't do), but documents *do* (they are still around, so they still have the same words now that they did on the day they were created).

> John Jones *made* his will on 1 November 1840. He *left* his land to his eldest son Josiah. *The will is* difficult to read due to mouse munchings, but *it identifies* the land as being a parcel *he won* in a poker game from Frank Farris.

Grammar

The rules of grammar are not arbitrary. They aid us in writing in a consistent and understandable manner. Correct grammar conveys information correctly; the same cannot always be said about incorrect grammar. Incorrect grammar almost always bogs down reading.

Don't get hung up on what is correct or proper grammar—but don't ignore it either. You will have a few readers who are very conscious of bad grammar—and for them it can get in the way of the information.

Put modifiers as close to the modified as possible

Misplaced modifiers can sometimes be funny, as in "Abraham Lincoln wrote the Gettysburg Address while traveling from Washington on the back of an envelope." But for genealogists they can be a serious matter.

We discuss the use of evidence-evaluation modifiers such as *probably, possibly, likely,* and *maybe* in HOW DO YOU KNOW? Which of these sentences about your ancestor would be correct?

1. He probably was born in Ipswich in 1740.
2. He was born probably in Ipswich in 1740.
3. He was born in Ipswich probably in 1740.
4. He was born in 1740 probably in Ipswich.

If you guessed 2, 3, or 4, you're correct. Is the uncertainty about the place, the date, or both? The position of the word "probably" in that sentence tells the reader the result of hours and hours of your research.

If you guessed 1, you're wrong. The one thing we do know for sure is that your ancestor was born!

Parenthetical elements—parentheses, dashes, and commas

A parenthetical element breaks the continuity of a sentence and isn't required for the sentence to be true and complete—it merely provides additional information. The phrase can be extremely brief (like a person's name) or quite long (it can even be a full sentence). Because the phrase is optional, we separate it from the rest of the sentence with punctuation.

There are three punctuation marks we can choose to separate a parenthetical element depending upon how closely we think it should be tied to the sentence. Parentheses and dashes (in typesetting we use an *em dash*), as shown in the paragraph above, indicate a very loose tie. Commas, as is shown in the previous sentence, bind the information more closely.

In addition, parentheses and dashes are useful alternatives to commas in sentences that are already loaded with commas. Omit the second comma or dash if it would occur at the end of the sentence. You always must have matching parentheses.

If you get confused as to whether you need a comma at a certain place in a sentence, look to see if there is a parenthetical element involved. In other words, could you take the phrase out entirely—or maybe put it in parentheses? If so, you need a comma at each end.

Consider the following incorrectly punctuated sentence:

Her mother Jane Smith was born in Little Gap, Kentucky to a poor family of cordwainers, leatherworkers.

Jane Smith and *leatherworkers* are parenthetical. We can even think of *Kentucky* as parenthetical to help us avoid another common punctuation error. (The names of states have commas before and after them.) Try the sentence with parentheses:

Her mother (Jane Smith) was born in Little Gap (Kentucky) to a poor family of cordwainers (leatherworkers).

In fact, try omitting the phrases entirely:

Her mother was born in Little Gap to a poor family of cordwainers.

The sentence is still true, isn't it? So how could we punctuate it?

Her mother, Jane Smith, was born in Little Gap, Kentucky, to a poor family of cordwainers (leatherworkers).

We used commas before and after *Jane Smith* and *Kentucky* because they are factual, albeit optional additions, but used parentheses around *leatherworkers*, a definition added to clarify a term that might be unfamiliar to the reader.

Jane Smith is parenthetical because someone has only one mother. But suppose the sentence were "His wife Jane Smith was born . . ." Does that need commas?

➤ Yes—if he was married only once, because the sentence is true without her name.

➤ No—if he was married more than once, because the identification of which wife is not optional.

Grammar gripes

The following types of errors are commonly marked by editors (and aren't covered elsewhere in this book).

➤ *Commas in a series*. In YOU MUST HAVE STYLE, we mentioned the decision about using a comma before "and" or "or." You either do or don't—consistently. There is another option you occasionally might find useful. When the elements of a series need to have commas within them, use a semicolon to punctuate the series. (She bought red, white, and blue bunting; green, lilac, and blue calico; and white lace.)

➤ *Subject-verb agreement*. You wouldn't say "they is" or "he are," right? You know they are incorrect, so you already understand the principle of subject-verb agreement. When we get into trouble with singular subjects and plural verbs (or vice versa), it's usually because there are other words in between.

Don't go by what "sounds" correct—use your thumb to cover up the words between the subject and verb, and then see if the subject and verb match.

> *Parallel construction.* Our minds can organize what we read more quickly and efficiently if we find what we expect to find. For example, if the first element in a series begins with a verb form, we expect the rest of them to. (Not: Her day consisted of *picking* berries, *clothes* to be washed, and *dusty* roads. Instead: Her day consisted of *picking* berries, *washing* clothes, and *walking* dusty roads. Or: Her day was filled with *juicy berries* to be picked, *filthy clothes* to be washed, and *dusty roads* to be walked.)

Other places to watch for parallel construction are *either/or* pairs, *both/and* pairs, and bulleted lists (which aren't used often in family histories).

> *Compound sentences.* If you have two stand-alone sentences connected with *and*, you need a comma. Cover the *and* with your thumb. If there is a sentence on each side, add a comma. If the word on the right of your thumb is a verb, drop the comma. (He plowed one row, and the horse quit. She washed clothes and hung them up.)

If you want to tack two very closely related sentences together, use a semicolon. (He made his will on Monday; he died that night.)

> *That, which, and who.* There are actually two problems here: which word to use and how to punctuate the sentence.

Which is parenthetical (nonrestrictive or nonessential). The phrase that follows is not required to make the sentence true. *Which* always requires commas. ("Use the index, *which is on the table*." There is only one index in the room; I'm just helping you find it more quickly.)

That indicates the next phrase is required to avoid ambiguity (restrictive or essential). It never uses commas. ("Use the index *that is on the table*." There are several indexes in the room, and you need to use the correct one.)

Who refers to people. (*That* also is used occasionally to refer to people.) *Who* can be either parenthetical or restrictive. Its meaning determines whether or not commas should enclose the phrase.

> *Compounds and hyphens.* Words beginning with "non," "re," "multi," and many other prefixes are not hyphenated unless the second part is a proper name. "The nonconformists were mostly non-English."

An adjective-noun pair *preceding* a noun is hyphenated ("log-cabin life in seventeenth-century Virginia").

Aside from that, compounds and hyphenation gets complicated. Refer frequently to the dictionary. In general, compound word pairs begin as two separate words, eventually become hyphenated if they are used together often, and finally merge into one word. This evolution sometimes takes centuries.

The Chicago Manual of Style has an indispensable multipage table "Spelling Guide for Compound Words and Words with Prefixes and Suffixes." If you own *Chicago*, put a bookmark in that section and refer to it often. Locate any similar sections in whatever style manual or grammar guide you are using, and mark and use them.

Use spell-checking software

Use the special dictionary feature of the spell checker. As soon as you begin your book, create a special dictionary just for that book. This gives you a place to store the odd names, abbreviations, and misspelled words from documents that are correct for this book, but incorrect elsewhere.

Make it an automatic routine to run the spell checker each time before you print. This habit will help you avoid some—but not all—last-minute typos.

Use grammar-checking software

Use grammar-checking software. It can point out not only grammatical errors, but also cumbersome or colloquial writing. Many newer word-processing programs have built-in grammar-checking software. You can buy separate software if your word processor doesn't include a grammar feature.

After you have written *one* chapter, run it through the grammar checker. (This takes a fair amount of time, so use the grammar-checker as a learning tool, not a repair kit.) Select strictest rules and a sentence length of 20 words if you have those options. As the software highlights text and makes suggestions, try to identify your bad habits so you can avoid them in the future.

Three or more prepositional phrases in a row are difficult for the reader to follow and sound sing-song, so they are generally highlighted by grammar checkers. They are, however, difficult to avoid in genealogical publications: "John was married to Sarah on 1 July 1860 at the Baptist church in Boston by Rev. Smith."

Be aware that the software can't really read and comprehend your words, so sometimes its suggestions are bogus. But it is still a helpful tool. Seriously consider its comments.

Reading level

In addition to highlighting potential punctuation and grammar errors, most grammar checkers calculate reading level scores describing the education level needed to comprehend your text, arrived at by considering the length of the words and how many words are in a sentence.

These scores vary widely by scoring system, depending on which text is included or excluded in the calculation and the weight given to word length versus sentence length. (For example, three separate systems scored a portion of this book at 8.1, 10.5, and 14.3.) Because of abbreviations, dates, and long proper names, it is especially difficult to define a target for genealogists.

Instead, aim at lowering the number—whatever it is—by about half a grade. For example, if you have a chapter with a score of 12.0 (twelfth-grade reading level) try to reduce it to 11.5.

➤ Look for puffery and phrases that are unnecessary or that can be replaced by a single word.

➤ Set the grammar checker to highlight every sentence with more than 19 words. Is there unnecessary wording that can be removed? Can the sentence be broken into two simple sentences? Balance long sentences with short sentences.

➤ Look for unnecessarily long words. Some instructors advise that we replace long words with short words. Don't. If the longer word best says what you want to say, use it. Make the change only if the shorter word is as accurate as the longer word. If you used the long word merely to sound impressive, replace it.

Getting help

Professionals weren't born with all the rules memorized. Most of us refer frequently to several of the books in RESOURCES. When a problem is pointed out to us, we read up on it—and flag the page in the reference book so we can go back to it easily until the grammar rule finally becomes second nature to us.

Checklist to improve writing

☑ Identify your audience

☑ Get organized

☑ Use your style guide

☑ Be concise

☑ Avoid passive voice

☑ Choose the best word

☑ Place modifiers correctly

☑ Watch punctuation

☑ Use a spell checker

☑ Use a grammar checker

Understanding
Type and Fonts

Typesetting is the activity of assembling letters into text on a page, whether that activity is done with moveable type or the technology of a word processor. The terminology of computer typesetting is founded in the historical mechanics of moveable type.

History of type

Johannes Gutenberg's invention of *moveable type* changed the world forever. The process (which varied somewhat over the years) went something like this. Letters of lead type were *composed* (arranged) in rows on a composing stick to form words and lines.

Extra pieces of lead were placed between words (or even letters) to *justify* the type against the edges and hold it tight. *Leading* (a thin strip of lead usually 2 *points* high) was placed between each line. The type was then transferred to a *galley tray*. When the tray was full, a *galley proof* was printed for *proofreading*.

After corrections, the type was placed in a metal tray that contained the illustrations, page headings, page numbers, and other nontextual elements. Then a *page proof* was printed and proofed for *broken type* or *pitted type*. When everything was correct, the tray (or trays if several pages were printed at once) was *impositioned* or *registered* to place it properly in relationship to the paper. Finally, the page was printed.

Then came the significant part. Once sufficient copies were printed, the letters of type could be returned to their proper places in the *type case*, ready to be reused in the next printing job.

This flexibility meant that ideas and information could be printed and disseminated relatively quickly. Computers, word processors, and laser printers have magnified that revolution.

Technology changed the process, but the terminology survives.

Typographers and type foundries

There are thousands of tiny decisions and details involved in designing a *typeface*. Someone has to define every curve and stroke of the capital letters, the small letters, the numbers, the punctuation, and the special characters. And then there are the styles or attributes: bold, italic, and bold italic.

That individual is called a *typographer* or *type designer*. We are familiar with many of the past greats, because their names— Claude Garamond, John Baskerville, William Caslon, Frederick Goudy, Giambattista Bodoni, Herman Zapf—have been preserved in the names of the fonts they created as long as 350 years ago.

Back when type was made out of lead, it had to be cast by *foundries*. A few of those foundries that produced large quantities of crisp, quality type are still around—it's just that their business has changed, first into phototypesetting equipment, and then into computer-based composition equipment, and finally into supplying fonts to computer users.

There are currently over sixty type foundries, many of them using computers to create decorative and novelty fonts for the graphics art industry. And yes, they are still called type foundries—an interesting contrast between the heavy metal casting industry and the computer world of typographic software and Bézier curves.

You'll sometimes see the name of a foundry as part of the name of a font in your font list, BT (Bitstream) or ITC (International Type Corp.), for example.

It is important to understand that fonts are property. They were created by someone, and the specific definitions of a font (the exact curves and sizes that make up the letters) are owned by someone.

In order for you to have a font on your computer legally, you have to buy it (unless it happens to be public domain, and there aren't many of those). It is not legal for you to copy a font from someone else's machine. The cost of good fonts is low.

You undoubtedly received some fonts as part of your computer operating system, more came with your printer, and even more with software that you've purchased (especially drawing packages). You may even have purchased a disk or CD-ROM containing dozens of fonts.

Fonts and typefaces

Historically the term *typeface* had a very broad meaning, and the term *font* had a very specific one. A font was defined by its typeface (a name such as Times New Roman), a point size (10 point), and its style and/or weight (such as bold, italic, condensed). The typesetter or printer had to purchase the lead letters of each specific size and style in the font he wanted.

With the growth of word-processing-based typesetting and scalable fonts, the terms became almost interchangeable. Unlike the typesetter of the past, the purchaser of a scalable font (as most fonts today are) gets all incremental sizes in that typeface. The resizing is done through computer algorithms.

Likewise, if the font doesn't include definitions for bold, italic, and small caps, those styles can be created by software. (The result doesn't look as nice as if they were designed by the typographer, but some of them are acceptable.)

Types of fonts

Fonts fall into one of three basic categories:

➤ Decorative (novelty)
➤ Serif
➤ Sans serif (gothic)

Decorative fonts include script, calligraphic, and novelty type. In a family history you might use a decorative font for the title page, dedication, and chapter titles but not elsewhere, because they are not very readable. (You also might use them in the flyers and advertising for your book.)

The difference between *serif* and *sans serif* (*sans* is French for *without*) type is best shown by example. The extra little strokes at the base and ends of the crossbar of the T on the left are *serifs*.

Tag
serif

Tag
sans serif

The strokes at the lower right of the *a* and top right of the *g* are also typical of serif letters, as is the significant variation in weight between vertical and horizontal elements of the letters.

Sans serif fonts, on the other hand, are often *gothic*—all of the strokes have equal weight.

Serif fonts and readability

We know from numerous studies that readability and comprehension is higher for serif fonts than it is for sans serif fonts. What we aren't quite so certain of is how much of the readability is due to the serifs and the weight variations that help our eyes track across the line and how much is simply a matter of familiarity. It's probably some of both.

We do know our minds have memorized the general shape of common words such as "the," "an," "can," "is," "be," and so on. In those words, we never really read the letters. (In fact, we mostly read just the *tops* of the letters.) And because we learned in school to read a serif font (it's even called Schoolbook), that's what our minds recognize most quickly.

Because of this, a serif font is preferred for *body text* (the basic text used in paragraphs).

Using sans serif fonts

Sans serif fonts are used for *display type*. Display type includes such things as titles, headings, and brief captions that we read at a glance. In many instances, display type is a large point size.

It used to be taboo to mix typefaces on a page, certainly it was frowned on to mix serif and sans serif type. However, between advertising art and I-just-got-a-laser-printer publications, our eyes have become accustomed to a mixture. Try to keep it down to two typefaces on a page, though.

Uppercase, lowercase, capital letters, and small caps

The *type case* mentioned earlier where the printer put the individual letters between printing jobs had two parts. Guess where he put the capital letters? Yep! In the *upper case*. Likewise, the lower case contained the *lowercase* letters.

Today we use UPPERCASE to refer to words set *entirely* in capitals. Capitalization means that the first letter of the word is a capital. SMALL CAPS means that letters normally set in lowercase are set in uppercase in a smaller point size.

Uppercase is hard to read

When looking for special typographical treatments, avoid uppercase if possible. It is more difficult to read since our mind processes it letter-by-letter rather than recognizing the overall shape of certain words and letter combinations.

Genealogists sometimes use uppercase to emphasize the names of people in family histories. In most *proportional* fonts (where the letters have varying widths) uppercase letters are very wide, so a name like CORNELIS VAN COUWENHOVEN seems to go on forever (over half a line, here). Try font treatments such as bold or small caps instead.

Type styles

A basic font family includes roman, italic, bold, and bold italic versions of the typeface. There are additional variations, which are sometimes considered a style variation and sometimes considered a separate font within the typeface family.

We call normal type *roman* or *upright*.

Aldus Manutius invented *italic* type. However, it wasn't quite what we are used to today. He invented only the lowercase letters! The capitals were set in roman type. Today we use italic type for emphasis and contrast, but Aldus was creating a compact type for hold-in-your-hand-not-lay-on-a-table editions of the classics, hoping to encourage fireside reading. We know italic is not a very readable style and would not use it for that today, but we're grateful to Aldus anyway. *Oblique* type is similar to italic.

Most of us are familiar with *bold* type, a slightly heavier casting of the basic roman style. We use bold to emphasize text. (In a good typeface, bold italic is designed as a separate font to keep the type clear.) There are also specially designed heavy fonts referred to as *black* and lightweight fonts referred to as *light*.

Traditionally, *small caps* weren't merely capital letters in a smaller point size, but special versions of them. That is no longer true in word-processing-based typesetting. Now they are normally set with uppercase letters about 2 points smaller, which is done automatically by your computer.

Most word-processing and page-layout software has small caps as a *text attribute* or *text style* option. Many people have trouble creating small caps. The secret is to enter the words as you would normally type them ("John Jones"). Then apply the small caps attribute to the text to change it to "JOHN JONES."

Typeset text is never *underlined*. One reason is that the underline would cross the *descenders* of letters such as jpgqy.

Condensed or *narrow* fonts are nice when you must squeeze something into a small width without making the letters too small (genealogical charts, for example). *Extended* fonts or *wide* fonts are proportionally wide.

Pitch, points, and proportional fonts

Most typewriters type in *fixed pitch*; every letter is the same width. There are two basic styles: elite (12 characters per inch) and pica (10 characters per inch). In typesetting we use fixed-pitch fonts (called *monospaced* in typesetting) only for special purposes (such as certain types of charts). The most commonly available monospaced font is a form of Courier. Letter Gothic is another popular monospaced font.

The letters of *proportional* fonts vary in width. This allows many more letters in a line. Almost all typesetting is done with proportional fonts. We measure the size in points.

Point size

There are 72 *points* in an inch. However, today's word processors virtually remove any necessity for you to know this.

We think of point size as "how big" a font is. That isn't accurate. Point size describes how *tall* a font is from the top of the tallest letter to the bottom of the longest letter. Usually all capitals are the same height. Often all letters with *ascenders* (b, d, f, h, k, l, t) are the same height as each other and the capitals, but that isn't necessarily true. In the serif font in this book, for example, h is a little taller than the capitals and much taller than t.

Point size does not describe the relative height or width of the letters. This is why 11-point type is a bit small for elderly eyes in one font—and so big it's downright childish looking in another.

The way to determine the correct point size is to look at a sample. But it isn't enough to look only at the type. Other factors must be considered, which are covered in the next chapter. However, as a starting point, you might try an 11-point serif type for the paragraphs in your family history, and adjust up or down from there in half-point increments.

Type managers

One of the most useful features provided with Windows (and with the Macintosh) is the type manager.

➢ A type manager means that instead of each piece of software (and you, the operator) struggling to understand which fonts you have, a centralized program can handle much of that detail for all of your Windows software.

➢ If a font is a TrueType font (and most of them are now) it is scalable. The font manager automatically displays it properly on the screen and prints it properly on the printer.

➢ ATM (Adobe Type Manager) is the type manager if you are using a PostScript printer and Type 1 fonts. Most genealogists do not have PostScript printers, so ATM is not discussed here.

Yin and yang

Typesetting is a matter of balance. Good typesetting properly balances the black of the ink with the white of the paper in a way that is aesthetically pleasing and best conveys information to the reader.

Look at the words below. Notice that the letters are defined not only by the black that creates them, but also by the white that frames them and separates them from adjacent letters.

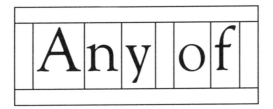

The white space before the A and after the y tells us that Any is a word. The strip of white (leading) above and below the line keeps our eyes on track as we read.

This black and white must be carefully and harmoniously balanced to create an inviting page that is easy to read and that promotes comprehension.

The overall amount of black versus white within a paragraph (how gray it looks if you squint) is called the *type color* (even though it's black and white). Type color affects your reader's subconscious feelings about the page. Black or dark paragraphs feel weighty, heavy, serious, even uninviting. On the other hand, white or light paragraphs may say "don't take me seriously."

Type color is affected by the thickness of the letter strokes and by the spacing between letters within words (*letterspacing*), words within lines (*word spacing*), and lines within paragraphs (*line spacing* or *leading*).

The effect of type color is moderated somewhat by the amount of white space around it: the spacing between paragraphs, the margins, and any paragraph offsets.

If your family history looks too serious and weighty, consider a lighter font, a bit more leading, greater paragraph spacing, or shorter line lengths. Try one adjustment at a time. It isn't necessary to try them all. PAGE LAYOUT AND FORMATTING gives more detail about letterspacing, word spacing, line spacing (leading), paragraph spacing, paragraph offsets, and margins.

Kerning

When typeset, some character pairs are set so close together that part of one character intrudes into the space of the other. If you look carefully at "Ty," you can see that the "y" is actually under the right crossbar of the "T." This is called *kerning*.

Typesetters used to have to be concerned about kerning, but most newer word processors handle it quite well with most fonts, and you'll never have to make an adjustment. If you spot a letter pair that is kerned too much or not enough, consult the user's guide for instructions. It is likely to be a problem only in very large point sizes, such as on a title page.

Choosing a font

Fonts are often described in language similar to that used to describe wine. Each font has character, personality, and a proper use. For a family history, you want a serif font that is dignified, respectable, and—above all—readable. (You certainly don't want one that is fun, frivolous, and difficult to comprehend.)

Many people prefer a font based on Times Roman because of its familiarity. Originally designed for a newspaper, its style has become widely used. (Look for the word Times or Roman in the font name.) Fonts such as Bodoni, Schoolbook, Garamond, and Goudy have remained popular over time simply because they are readable. All are worth considering.

Types of fonts

You may come across the following terms in relationship to fonts.

> *Scalable fonts.* A scalable font is defined by mathematical formulas that describe its outline. When you request a certain point size, the formula determines the size and shape of the letter that is sent to the screen or printer. TrueType fonts are scalable fonts.

> *Bit-mapped fonts.* Bit-mapped fonts, on the other hand, are created by the equivalent of coloring in the little squares on a sheet of graph paper. They are rarely of as good quality as scalable fonts. Often you can actually see the stair-step edges of the curves.

> *Downloaded fonts.* These fonts must be sent by the computer to the printer. This takes time and uses memory, but is very flexible. If you don't use many different fonts on a page, don't have lots of graphics on a page, and have ample printer memory, this is the way to go.

> *TrueType fonts.* TrueType fonts under Windows (you may see a double-T icon by the font name) are downloaded fonts. The display on the screen and the printed page are almost the same.

➤ *Internal (printer) fonts.* Printer fonts (you may see an icon by the name—it's supposed to look like paper sticking up from a printer) came with your printer. You can neither remove nor add printer fonts. You do not have to wait for the font to be downloaded to the printer before it can print. Printer fonts do not use up any room in your printer's memory. Some printer fonts are scalable, and some are a specific point size. They may or may not be displayed accurately on the screen.

➤ *Font cartridges.* Some printers allow you to insert a cartridge containing fonts into the printer. Cartridges are faster than downloaded fonts, slower than internal fonts, and do not use any memory. Some cartridge fonts are scalable.

Special characters make the difference

One of the things that differentiates "typeset" text from "typed" text is the use of special characters. Some special characters—em dashes, en dashes, curly quotes, and apostrophes—are basic to any typesetting job. Their proper use is discussed below. Special characters (such as £, ¢, ½, and ¼) and foreign characters (such as â, é, ö, ñ, and ß) occur frequently in genealogical works.

The special characters within a font may vary. In some fonts the special characters are not very attractive. Not all fonts have all special characters (especially decorative fonts). You can always change fonts just for the special character, and then return to the normal font. (If you do this, proofread a *printed* copy carefully to assure that all font changes were made correctly.)

Accessing special characters

You must learn to use the special character or symbol feature of your software. Look in the software user's guide *and* the printer user's guide for tables showing special characters. You can use only the characters that your software, your printer, and your font "know."

Easy access to special characters is a main feature of current software and hardware. Spend some time and learn to use them.

If it is cumbersome in your software to access a frequently used special character, set up a macro or keyboard shortcut to help. For example, you can create a macro that with a single keystroke types "" and positions the cursor between the quotation marks, ready to type the quote. Keyboard macros for en dashes and em dashes are also popular. (An alternative is to create a separate document containing the special characters you use, and then copy-and-paste through the Clipboard.)

Windows special characters

If you transfer text created in a DOS-based word processor to a Windows-based word processor and the text includes special characters, such as the less-common foreign characters and a special ff or *ff* character (as in ffoster or *ff*oster), look it over very carefully.

DOS uses ASCII character sets for special characters, and Windows uses ANSI character sets. (ASCII and ANSI are both standards, but they aren't in total agreement as to where specific special characters belong.) This means that some special characters, most notably accented foreign characters, may not be correct on converted files. Problems may also occur with special characters if you move files between software.

The ff and *ff* characters above were created by reducing (condensing) the letterspacing between the two letters. Look in the user's guide for instructions if you need to do this.

Hyphens, em dashes, en dashes

It sure was easy with a typewriter. There was one all-purpose key, just to the right of the zero. We used it for a hyphen, a minus, and a dash. Sometimes we got fancy and hit it twice for a dash. But that simply won't do in typesetting.

There are three basic characters (the hyphen, the en dash, and the em dash) that replace that all-purpose key. Each has specific use, explained below. The difference in their width is considerable.

- -   hyphen
- –   en dash
- —   em dash

Em dashes

A *dash* is a separator. It separates elements in a sentence that are not closely related. In typesetting, a dash is created with the *em dash* special character. The em dash originally was as wide as the point size of the font—or about the width of a letter m. Today it varies considerably from font to font.

Notice that there is no space before or after an em dash. Some fonts have em dashes that do not include any white space around them, so the dash sometimes touches the letters before and after it. If this is the case, you may find it necessary to add a bit of white by increasing the letterspacing. (See the user's guide.)

Genealogists have come up with an additional use for the em dash. We use it to say "unknown," as in "Mary (–) Brown," "Mary (——) Brown," or "Mary (–?–) Brown." (Underscores, "Mary (__) Brown," are also used.) Which style do you prefer? Note your preference in your style guide.

En dashes

An *en dash* means "through." It is a dash half the width of an em dash or about the width of the letter n. Genealogists need en dashes frequently, especially in citations. Two uses are shown below.

Court Records (1791–1793), pages 101–104.

Use the en dash whenever you need a minus or negative character also. The hyphen is simply too narrow.

Hyphens

The hyphen is very narrow, as is appropriate for a character that is used to tie two words together or to tie the broken parts of one word together. Some guidelines for hyphenating two words are given in YOU MUST HAVE STYLE and DEVELOPING AN EDITORIAL EYE.

We also use a hyphen when we break a word onto two lines. There is a strong trend away from breaking words. Do it sparingly. Sometimes, however, hyphenating a word is needed to reduce the white space between words in justified text or the white space at the end of a line in nonjustified text.

In word processing, there are three forms of hyphens: ordinary hyphens, soft (optional hyphens), and hard (nonbreaking) hyphens. Read the user's guide to find out how to enter the hyphens and set any manual or automatic options.

➤ An *ordinary hyphen* always prints and always breaks if it occurs at the end of a line.

➤ A *soft (optional) hyphen* indicates that *if* it occurs at the end of a line, it will be printed and the word will be broken. Otherwise, it's invisible.

➤ A *hard (nonbreaking) hyphen* always prints and never breaks if it occurs at the end of a line. We don't often use it (t-shirt, I-beam, and CD-ROM are the only examples that come immediately to mind), but you should know it exists when you need it.

Curly quotes and apostrophes

On typewriters, we have one style of quotation mark ("). In typesetting we have two (" "), called *curly quotes* or *typographic quotes* to differentiate them from *straight quotes*. Notice the difference below:

The name was spelled "Almond" or "Almand" in Virginia.

The name was spelled "Almond" or "Almand" in Virginia.

The same is true of apostrophes and *single quotes* (used for quotes within quotes). Again, notice the difference:

She said, "John's son was called 'Billy' or 'Willy' as a baby."

She said, "John's son was called 'Billy' or 'Willy' as a baby."

Some, but not all, software automatically uses the curly apostrophe and curly quotes. You may have to select an option. Check the user's guide.

The straight quotes and apostrophe are not obsolete. We still use them to indicate feet and inches.

Superscripts

Superscripts, whether note numbers, generation numbers, or abbreviations such as s^d, are raised above the *baseline* (an imaginary line on which most of the characters rest) by several points and are several points smaller than the base font. They should not be too small to read, nor should they touch any characters with *descenders* (such as g, j, or y) in the previous line.

Some software will automatically adjust line spacing to allow *extra* room for superscripts. You do *not* want this. The uneven line spacing is unattractive, distracting, and hard to read. Either turn this option off, or use fixed line spacing throughout.

Getting help

This chapter should be read in conjunction with PAGE LAYOUT AND FORMATTING and DEVELOPING AN EDITORIAL EYE as they contain related information.

The style manuals in RESOURCES offer some advice on type and fonts. Additional suggestions are found in the books specifically about type.

Checklist of typesetting terms

- ☑ Classification (serif, sans serif, decorative)
- ☑ Typeface (Times Roman, Arial)
- ☑ Variant (condensed, light)
- ☑ Style (upright, italic)
- ☑ Weight/style (medium, bold)
- ☑ Point size
- ☑ Special characters
- ☑ Letterspacing
- ☑ Word spacing
- ☑ Line spacing (leading)

Book Design

Designing your family history is a simple matter. Books have a number of parts, but there are simple standards to guide you in location, content, and format.

Parts of a book

The parts of a book described here are those most likely to be used by genealogists. The parts, except as noted, appear in the order in which they are listed. Everything before the main text is referred to as *front matter*. Everything after the main text is *back matter*.

As you review the material that follows, remember to record your choices in your style guide.

Front matter

Much of the front matter requires special formatting. The title page and copyright page do not display a page number, header, or footer but the other pages usually do. (Page numbering, headers, and footers are covered later in this chapter.)

Roman numerals are used for the page numbers in the front matter, beginning with the title page as page i. (Some software lets you specify the page number as a roman numeral.)

As an alternative, it is acceptable to begin the numbering with the title page as arabic page 1. This method does not look as professional, but if it is less confusing for you, it isn't wrong.

Front matter appears in the following order:

➤ *Title page.* The title page is the first page of the book (a *recto* or right-hand page) and contains the title of the book, the subtitle, the name of the author, and the name of the publishing company (and sometimes the city where it is located). The type should be large and attractively displayed. Usually it is centered. Use smaller type for the subtitle. Choose a title that accurately describes your book.

You can really dress up the title page. Try a decorative font. Clip-art graphics and borders can be simple or ornate.

➤ *Copyright page.* Located on the back of the title page, the copyright page is a *verso* (left-hand) page and contains the publishing information about the book: publication information (publisher, place, date, previous printings or editions), copyright notice, Library of Congress cataloging number (LCN) and Cataloging in Publication (CIP) information, and International Standard Book Number (ISBN). (See SELF-PUBLISHING for information on copyright, CIP, and ISBN.)

Include your address on the copyright page so that researchers or family members who see your book can order it from you. The copyright page may also include any credits for maps, illustrations, and lengthy quotations that you are reproducing with permission.

Text on the copyright page is often of a smaller point size than that of the body of the book. The page does not have a printed header, footer, or page number.

➤ *Dedication.* This page is optional. The dedication is usually placed about two or three inches from the top of a right-hand page. The page does not have a printed header, footer, or page number. You may use a decorative font here, such as a script font. If you have a dedication page, the back of the page is blank.

➤ *Acknowledgments.* The acknowledgments page is a right-hand page; it is blank on the back. Acknowledgments may be included in the preface, instead.

> *Table of Contents.* This section should begin on a right-hand page. The Table of Contents can be placed after the forward, acknowledgment, and other front matter, but this increases the likelihood that the reader may overlook the material. Treat the first page of the Table of Contents like the first page of a chapter. The chapter title may be "Table of Contents" or preferably "Contents."

There are several options for placement of page numbers in a table of contents. Placing the numbers flush right, without *leader dots* is preferred. *Leader dots* are a series of fixed-pitch dots leading from the chapter titles to the page numbers. They are unnecessary clutter, and some software does not generate them correctly.

Depending on the length of the chapter titles, you may need to indent the chapter titles to keep the page numbers from being too far away. Conversely, you may have to *stack* the titles (use two or more lines per title) if they are quite long.

Many word processors can automatically generate the Table of Contents if certain conditions are met. Refer to the user's guide for details *before you begin creating the book.*

> *Lists of Charts, Illustrations, Maps or Photographs.* These helpful aids immediately follow the Table of Contents. They may occur on either a left or right page, so it is not necessary to treat them as chapter title pages, but they should have a prominent heading, such as "Illustrations" or "List of Illustrations" and should be listed in the Table of Contents.

If the illustration or photograph is on a regular page, the page number is given even if the page itself does not show the number (as for a large illustration).

If your book has photographs printed on special paper on unnumbered pages, the page number is given as "facing page 34" if it is a single sheet or "following page 34" if there are many. (You may put "following page 34" preceding the list of photographs instead of repeating it for each one.)

> *Foreword.* (Not *forward*!) Most genealogy books do not have forewords. This section is written by someone other than the author. It begins on a right-hand page and may be more than one page long.

> *Preface.* Written by the author, the preface is often about how or why the book was written. The preface may also contain the acknowledgments. The preface begins on a right-hand page and is blank on the back if it has an odd number of pages.

> *Special sections.* Genealogical publications frequently have appropriate and useful special sections. The use of abbreviations in family histories is discouraged, but if you use abbreviations and acronyms, a "List of Abbreviations" should be part of the front matter.

Genealogical charts, maps, chronologies, and special illustrations may appear as part of the front matter or back matter, as appropriate.

> *Introduction.* The introduction is an integral part of the content of the book. If it is very closely tied to the text, it should be paginated with the main text and presented in the same manner as chapters.

An example of material that could be presented as an introduction in a family history is a discussion of the European origins of the family. Any such discussion should clearly indicate the likelihood of the connection (see HOW DO YOU KNOW?). Generalizations about "the family name" and coats of arms are discouraged.

Main text

The main text is made up of *chapters*. Chapters may be grouped together in *parts*.

Information about organization and presentation of the main text is discussed in ORGANIZING AND PRESENTING FAMILY INFORMATION.

Detailed information for formatting considerations for chapter text is discussed in PAGE LAYOUT AND FORMATTING.

Back matter

Appendices. Genealogists find a variety of uses for appendices: individuals who could not be placed in the family, transcripts of documents, research information such as census abstracts, and more. Appendices are "numbered" alphabetically (Appendix A, Appendix B), treated as separate chapters, and paginated as part of the main page sequence.

Notes. You may choose to put endnotes in one section at the back. See the discussion on notes in HOW DO YOU KNOW?

Glossary. There are several applications for glossaries in family histories. The language of our ancestors differed from our own. Terms for their diseases, tools, occupations, and food have disappeared from our everyday language.

If you encounter many such terms, you may want to include a glossary (but don't neglect an explanation of the term in the text also). If your family history includes non-English research, a glossary of foreign terms helps both you and your reader.

Bibliography, Resource List, Reading List, or *Reference List.* This is not a substitute for documentation. However, we often use books and articles for background reading that we don't have reason to cite in the text or notes. If you want to direct your reader to these resources, you may do so. This section begins on a right-hand page and is paginated with the main text.

You can group the resources into categories with headings ("Puritan New England," "Frontier Life," "Women"). Usually the items are then arranged alphabetically by last name of the author. Consult a style manual for proper bibliographic format.

Index. There should be only one index in a genealogy book. See OPENING THE DOOR TO YOUR BOOK for a complete discussion of indexes. The index begins on a right-hand (chapter) page and is paginated with the main text.

Page size

There are several factors to consider in choosing the *page size* that is right for your book.

➤ *Content.* If you have many illustrations or charts, a larger *format* (size) is better. If your book is text intensive, a smaller format with fewer words on each page appears more inviting to the reader.

➤ *Amount of material.* A voluminous family history with many family sketches and photographs may require a large two-column format such as 8½"×11".

➤ *Typography.* The type size and page size are closely interrelated. If you choose a large page size and single columns, a small type size puts too many letters on a line and makes it difficult to read. You may have to compensate with a larger type size and wider margins. Conversely, a smaller page size (hence shorter line length) allows a smaller point size (see PAGE LAYOUT AND FORMATTING).

➤ *Economics.* The cost of printing a book is based in part on the printer's equipment and the size of paper it uses. Check with the printer for suggestions.

➤ *Number of copies.* If you are producing only a few copies for your family and a few libraries, a standard paper size that can be accommodated at a local copy shop or offset printer is a good choice.

Common page sizes

A printer can accommodate any page size you select—at a price. Depending on the type of printer you have chosen, a less-common page size may not require any special handling, but always inquire first.

In practice, there are only a few commonly used page sizes in genealogy. (The actual page size—especially the width—may be slightly less than defined below due to trimming.)

➤ 8½"×11". This is the most efficient size because of the ease with which initial or subsequent production can be done through photocopying. It is convenient, allows minimal *run sizes* (the number of copies printed at once), and is easy to reprint.

This size accommodates two columns of smaller type, so for very large books it is more economical.

If you are printing many books, consider paper cost, storage space, and mailing expense. A smaller page size with smaller type and narrower margins may be more economical and convenient.

8½"×11" pages can be printed on 11"×17" paper and then *saddle-stitched* (stapled in the center), offering an economical alternative for booklets of 64 or fewer pages (depending on the paper weight).

You can have 8½"×11" pages bound with a soft cover or a hard cover, even in small volume. Ask the copy shop or offset printer about *perfect binding* (see Turning Final Copy into Books). Most small offset printers send pages to an outside vendor to be perfect bound. For hard cover, ask your local librarian where they send books for rebinding and contact the company yourself. See Printing in Resources for information on locating binderies.

➤ 6"×9". This is probably the most popular size for bound books produced by printing houses. It is used for thick books, thin books, hard-bound books, and perfect-bound books. If your family history includes photographs, you can often get two photographs on a page without crowding or making them too small.

➤ 5½"×8½". This size is used by some publishing companies, but the page is somewhat crowded and cramped. Consider 6"×9" instead.

Because 5½"×8½" is half of an 8½"×11" page, it offers a nice alternative for small booklets printed by local offset printers or copy shops. Two pages can be printed (or photocopied) on each side of an 8½"×11" sheet of paper, the pages are *collated* (stacked in order) with a cover, saddle-stitched, and folded to create a nice booklet. Because of the saddle stitching, however, this method should be used only for books of 64 or fewer pages.

Getting help

The style manuals in Style manuals, grammars, and typesetting guides in Resources provide additional detail about formatting, typesetting and content for front and back matter.

Checklist of sections of a book

- ☑ Title page
- ☑ Copyright page
- ☑ Dedication
- ☑ Acknowledgments
- ☑ Table of Contents
- ☑ List of Illustrations
- ☑ Foreword
- ☑ Preface
- ☑ Special sections
- ☑ Introduction
- ☑ Main text (Chapters)
- ☑ Appendices
- ☑ Notes
- ☑ Glossary
- ☑ Bibliography
- ☑ Index

Page Layout and Formatting

The role of the typesetter has become obsolete in practice, but even more crucial in function with the advent of sophisticated word processors, page layout programs, laser and ink-jet printers, and scalable fonts. We actually have more options—and hence more decisions to make—than did the typesetter of the past.

The key to easy formatting

If you are using your word processor, but not using styles and templates, you're missing out on the most productive feature of your software.

> ➤ A *paragraph style* is a named collection of all formatting attributes that can be applied to a paragraph, including default text attributes.

> ➤ A *text style* is a named collection of all formatting attributes that can be applied to a piece of text.

> ➤ A *template* is a named collection of all page attributes, paragraph styles, and text styles.

Why use styles and templates?

The most worthwhile investment you can make to produce an attractive book is to spend time learning to use styles and templates—before you start typing. This means reading the user's guide (groan!) and experimenting.

Why would you want to go to all the trouble to set up styles and a template when you can achieve the same appearance manually? Using styles and templates reduces considerably the number of keystrokes and mouse clicks required to format your book. Manual formatting is just that—manual. Every format must be applied by hand.

Styles allow you to define the appearance of your book globally and enter formatting commands only in special cases. They also allow considerable flexibility. If you have used paragraph styles when typesetting your book, you can make changes to font size, paragraph spacing, or headings in a matter of minutes—not days.

You can use macros to save keystrokes in applying formats manually, but macros do not allow flexibility.

What is a paragraph style?

First let's talk about what a paragraph is. Word processors consider every bit of text to be within a paragraph. A typical family history will contain—at the minimum—the following types of paragraphs:

➢ Running header (probably different for left, right, first page)
➢ Chapter title
➢ Heading
➢ Subheading (if not done as part of the paragraph)
➢ Narrative (the normal, basic paragraph)
➢ Child-information
➢ Quotation/transcript
➢ Note
➢ Caption
➢ Table of contents (possibly more than one level)
➢ Index letter heading
➢ Index main heading
➢ Index subheading

You also might have:

➢ Running footer (probably different for left, right, first page)
➢ Illustration
➢ Section divider
➢ Glossary
➢ Bibliography
➢ Census abstracts
➢ Other special formats

Elements of paragraph style

Any paragraph has a number of attributes that define its appearance (the *paragraph style*). These elements relate to the position of the paragraph, its lines, and its tabs. The default text attributes are also part of the paragraph style.

Paragraph attributes
 Left indent/offset
 Special treatment of left edge of first line (hanging, tab)
 Right indent/offset
 Justification
 Space before
 Space after
 Line spacing/height/leading
 Border(s)
 Tab stops (position and type)
 Word spacing, letterspacing (may be text attribute)
Text attributes
 Font (typeface)
 Point size
 Weight (bold)
 Style and effects (italic, underline, small caps)
 Color

Text styles

In addition to styles for paragraphs, some software lets you create styles for text also. This lets you mark a piece of text within a paragraph as having a style different from the rest of the text in the paragraph. It's easy to set the text, and it's easy to change it.

Text styles are a boon to genealogists, who often give the names of individuals a specific treatment, such as bold, small caps. In this book when the title of another chapter is referenced, it is typographically different. On the screen it's even a different color to make it easy to spot. This was done with a text style.

Whether or not your word processor has text styles, think in those terms. Create a macro (short-cut key) that accomplishes the formatting changes.

Templates

Programs that use styles have a default *template* (or *style sheet*, the terminology varies by software), usually called "Normal." What you type is based on that default.

Each paragraph type (chapter title, heading, note and so on) needs a separate style to define its attributes. Styles are stored in one of two places (or both). When you change or create a style within a document, the style is stored with the document file. You also can store it in the template.

Create a template for your family history

Store the styles for your family history in a template. But instead of cluttering the Normal template with them, create a new template, "FamilyHistory." As you define each new paragraph style for your book, store it in the FamilyHistory template.

There's a big difference between using a word processor to write a letter and using it to produce a book. The operative word here is "big." A book is big. Don't do the entire book as one giant file. Create a document file for each chapter. Each time you create a new chapter, base it on the FamilyHistory template.

When it's time to type a child information paragraph, for example, a few keystrokes or mouse clicks say, "I want Child style." The software automatically changes to the new point size, paragraph spacing, hanging indent, and tabs. You just type.

Making decisions

Don't try to tackle all the formatting decisions at once—but don't start the second chapter until you are pleased with the appearance of the first chapter. Making the right decisions is a combination of personal preference, experience, some rules of thumb, and the tools you have available. The best guideline is:

Is it easy to read?

It can be difficult for us to make judgments about formatting text that we see all the time, because it looks normal to us. Show your sample chapter to someone elderly. Ask an honest friend. Try reading it in a dim light and at a slight angle.

Most of the decisions are part of a highly integrated balancing act. The best point size for the type is dependent on the line length, line spacing (leading), and whether or not the text is justified. And vice-versa. If you use paragraph styles, adjustments can be made easily. If you use manual formatting, they can't.

As you make the specific decisions discussed below, keep track of them in your style guide.

Margins

Margins are the amount of space between the edge of the paper and the print area. They serve two purposes:

➢ Margins keep the text from being too close to the edge of the paper, which is distracting to the eye.

➢ Margins control the length of the printed line, which is a critical factor in how readable text is.

Software provides a default margin setting. The default setting is probably inappropriate for book printing. There is no single correct margin setting for books. In general, margins should be between .5" and 1". As a starting point, you might begin with .75" for top, bottom, left, and right margins. For one-column 8½"×11", left and right margins of at least 1" are better. For two-column 8½"×11", try .5" for the margins.

Depending on the software, *margin* may mean the space between the edge of the paper and any printed text (including the header and footer). Or it may mean the space between the edge and the main text. Or it may mean the space between the edge of the paper and the left and right edge of each individual paragraph (top and bottom don't change).

Measure the margins on your printed pages. (For pages less than 8½"×11", trim some of the pages to the final size to be sure your margin settings produce what you expect.)

Two-column layout

Books smaller than 8½"×11" should not be done in two-column format. For voluminous family histories, a two-column format on 8½"×11" pages is an economical choice. Because the *line length* is short (see below), the point size of the type can be smaller, the margins can be smaller, and even the photographs tend to be smaller.

Margins on two-column books can be as small as .5". Try several settings between .5" and .75" until you find the right balance.

The space between columns should be no larger than .5". If the text is nonjustified, you may be able to reduce the space between columns to as little as .25". Print samples at both sizes and several settings in between. (It's amazing what a difference .1" can make in a page layout.)

Gutters

If a book is thick, you must make adjustments for the gutter. The *gutter* is where the left and right facing pages are joined together. (*Gutter* has been used in some software to mean the space between columns, but this is incorrect.)

If a book is very thick, the text may be too close to the binding, making the book difficult to read or photocopy. When this is a problem, you must increase the size of the gutter margin.

If your book has fewer than 200 pages, the paper is not extra thick, and the margins are at least .75", you probably do not need to worry about this, but ask your printer. Most printers have internal standards for proper gutter margins.

Some software lets you adjust the gutter margin automatically. (Check the user's guide under *gutter*, *facing pages*, *inside margins*, or *offset*). If your software does not allow you to make the adjustment, the printer can do it when they make the film negative if the margins are ample enough to allow the adjustment.

Printing smaller than 8½"×11" pages

There is a difference between the *page size* and the *paper size*. The *paper size* is the size of paper that goes into your printer (probably 8½"×11"). The *page size* (*trim size*) is the size of the page in the bound book. How do you handle this?

Suppose you want a 6"×9" book. You have several options, depending on the software.

➢ Set the *page size* to 6"×9" and the margins to .75". Leave the *paper size* at 8½"×11". The software probably will print the page in the upper left corner of the paper. If the software prints crop marks, it makes the appropriate calculations and may center the page.

➤ If the software does not let you define a 6"×9" page, set the right margin as 3.25" (8.5 – 6 + .75) and the bottom margin as 2.75" (11 – 9 + .75). You'll get a 6"×9" page printed in the upper left corner of the paper.

➤ Print the page as 8½"×11" and have the printer reduce it to 6"×9". This method was used often before scalable fonts became so accessible, but is uncommon now. If you plan to do this, discuss it with the printer, who can supply you with guidelines suggesting what margins to use.

Registration and crop marks

Crops marks are two short marks that indicate where the printer should crop (cut) the paper to make the page. The marks stop short of the trim edge, so there is no chance that any mark will end up as part of the printed page. They are used to ensure that the pages are *registered* (aligned) correctly when the negatives are made (see TURNING CAMERA-READY ART INTO BOOKS).

| # | Book Title |

Years ago, when pages were laid out on boards, the layout person drew the crop marks on by hand. Page-layout typesetting equipment and page-layout computer software usually create crop marks automatically. Most word-processing software does not.

Do you need crop marks?

No. Most printers are quite accustomed to receiving camera-ready art without crop marks. As long as the pages are printed consistently, the printer should have no problem with placement, especially if there is a running header. Only on pages where the printer does not have sufficient information about placement would there be a problem.

Page headers and footers

The place at the top and bottom of the page where information such as the book title, chapter title, and page number appears are referred to as the *page header* and *footer*. Because the same information appears from page to page, they are also referred to as *running headers and footers*. You must decide what goes into them, how to format them, and their position on the page.

Most genealogical material does not require a footer. Many graphic designers put the page number in the footer. This puts additional white space on the page, and makes a short book longer. Genealogists rarely need to pad their material and are usually trying to reduce the page count, so we would rather have that space for an additional line or two of text. Therefore we usually put the page number in the header.

The page header and footer are important *indexing devices*. They help the reader find the correct chapter and page quickly.

Record all decisions about headers and footers in your style guide as you make them.

Page numbers

In books the left page number is always even and the right page number is always odd. Thus, page 1 is always a right-hand page. Most software handles page numbering automatically.

# *(even)*	*(odd)* #

In a header, the page number is positioned on the *outside* edge of the page so that you can find the page without opening the book completely. Therefore, you need to define a *left header* with the page number at the left end of the line and a *right header* with the page number at the right end of the line. Consult the user's guide.

Headers: content

The header should also tell the reader what book this is and what chapter it is. (Don't you just hate it when you find a photocopy in your files that has become separated from the title page, and you don't even know what book it is from?)

The more-general information (such as book title) goes in the left header; the more-specific information (such as chapter name) goes in the right. This information can be either centered or placed approximately ¼" from the page number. The page number goes on the outside.

#	*The Jones Family*	*The First Generation*	#

Headers: appearance

Separate the header from the text in some way so that when the reader begins a new page, his or her eye goes to the text instead of the header. You can accomplish this visual separation by putting space between the header and the text, by differentiating the header typographically, by putting a *rule* (line) under the header, or by any combination thereof.

To differentiate typographically, you can use a sans serif font (presuming you used the recommended serif font for the text), use an italic version of the same font (this is commonly done and looks very nice), use bold, and/or use a different point size (try both larger and smaller to see if it makes the page look too busy).

Some pages don't have headers

Now that you've figured out how to do headers, here's the kicker: sometimes you are supposed to leave them off. In particular, the title page, the copyright page, and *the first page of every chapter* do not have page numbers or headers.

Most software can handle this by either *suppressing* the header on specific pages or printing a different (blank) header on the first page of the document. Consult the user's guide.

Sometimes a page-number-only footer is printed on the first page of a chapter in order to put a page number on every page, but this really isn't necessary and may not be all that helpful, because it is inconsistent with the rest of the book.

Pages in the front matter such as the table of contents often look unattractive with a full header. Try using only the page number, but no title or section information.

Using cover pages

A *cover page* makes a nice touch in a multipart family history. For example, if your book includes several surnames, you can use a cover page to introduce each new family. The title of the part ("The Brown Family of Boston") goes on a right-hand page (use a decorative font and lots of white space); the back of that page is blank. Then the chapter actually begins on the next right-hand page. You might choose to put a chart or illustration related to the family on the back of the cover page, instead of leaving it blank.

This provides a nice break in a text-intensive book, but it does increase the page count. Count these pages in the page numbering, but do not print headers or page numbers on them.

The first page of a chapter requires special treatment

We give the first page of a chapter a special appearance in order to help the reader find the beginning of a chapter easily. This visual treatment is an *indexing device* that helps the reader turn quickly to the chapter. As mentioned above, the title page of a chapter does not have a header.

The *chapter title* is normally given special typographical treatment. Some of these treatments include flush left, flush right, or centering the text; putting rules above and/or below the title; using a different font; and emphasizing with bold, italics, small caps, or a larger point size.

There should be extra space above and below the title. Place the title a third of the way down the page (or about 1-2" from the top of the page). Because there is also no header, this white space visually emphasizes a new chapter. Record all these decisions in your style guide.

The first pages of the chapters in a book are always either left pages or right pages, never a mixture. The consistency helps the reader locate information. The right page is favored as the opening page in nonfiction books.

You might take advantage of the left-hand page facing a chapter-title page and use it for an illustration, a map, or a genealogical chart relating to the new chapter.

Headings and subheadings

No one wants to sit down and read page after page of your research. Sorry, that's the way it is. No matter how much they love you and how hard you worked on it, your family won't want to read your book if it is page after page of monotonous text.

To help make text less intimidating—and more inviting—divide it up. (*Chunking* is the technical term for this.) Chunking mechanisms such as *headings* and *subheadings* also serve as *indexing devices* to help the reader find information.

The good (and easy) way to choose headings and subheadings is to sit down and create an outline for the book. I, II, and III levels probably are the chapter divisions; A, B, and C levels probably are main headings; i, ii, and iii levels are candidates for subheadings.

You may want headings to appear in the table of contents. Most software can generate table of contents headings automatically. Consult the user's guide for instructions.

Headings should appear on a line by themselves. They are sometimes centered rather than flush left, have extra space above and below them, and receive special typographical treatment. Traditionally, the space above and below has been equal, but because the heading is actually associated with the following text, some people prefer less space after the heading.

Headings may be *hanging*, as in this book, and project to the left of the text. This is a good option for 8½"×11" pages, as it lets you reduce the line length in the body text without making the margins overly wide.

A heading should always be nonjustified, even when body text is justified.

The typographical options for headings are similar to those discussed under chapter title, but should be less striking than the chapter title.

Subheadings can appear on a line by themselves or as part of the paragraph but set apart typographically. The second alternative provides an index to the information, without making a page too busy.

. . . buried in the family cemetery.

The Family of John Jones and Martha (Miller) Jones

The early years in Georgia. When John and Martha moved their growing family to Oglethorpe County, there were only a few other families in the area . . .

Capitalization

Book title. Capitalize the first and last word. Capitalize everything *except* prepositions (*of, for, with*), articles (*a, an, the*), conjunctions (*and, but*), and the infinitive *to.*

Chapter title. Chapter titles generally follow the capitalization rules for book titles.

Headings. Traditionally, writers capitalized headings and subheadings in the same way in which they capitalized the titles of books and chapters. In recent years, however, there has been a trend toward treating headings more informally like body text and capitalizing only the first word as is done in this book.

Look at the type of headings and subheadings you plan. If they are more like titles, use the traditional approach; if they are more like phrases, use the informal approach. You can choose a traditional style for headings and an informal style for subheadings, but be consistent within type. Record your choices in your style guide.

Paragraph spacing

Typographical treatment of paragraphs serves two purposes— uniting the text within one paragraph and separating the text in two different paragraphs.

In typing class we learned there are exactly two ways to identify a paragraph: an opening tab of ½" or five spaces (informal style) *or* a blank line (business style), but not both. That's still true. Almost. The size of the tab is not necessarily ½" (see below) and the height of the blank line can be less than one line (try ½ to ¾ of a line).

You may choose either method. Generally, tabs work well in flowing narrative (like a novel or a magazine article), but adding extra space above and below the paragraph is preferred for structured information. For a family history, which uses indentation to display family group information and to set apart quoted material, paragraph spacing is preferred.

Other paragraph attributes

The software may have options related to keeping the paragraph together, preventing widows and orphans, keeping the paragraph with the next paragraph, and forcing a page break before the paragraph.

In this book, paragraphs are never broken between two pages. This works well in guidebooks and textbooks, but not for fiction as it results in irregular white space at the bottom of the page. Whether or not it is appropriate for your family history depends largely on the format you have chosen and the type of text.

Widows and orphans (single lines at the bottom or top of a page) are discussed in DEVELOPING AN EDITORIAL EYE. With widow and orphan control, the white space at the bottom of a page may be uneven by one line.

You should always select the keep-this-paragraph-with-the-next option for headings. There's nothing tackier than a lonely heading at the bottom of a page separated from its text. In addition, we often set this option manually for any paragraph that introduces the paragraph that follows (like a transcript or illustration). Be aware that this may make the bottom margin uneven.

There are other options available. If you want every family to start on a new page, for example, you can usually set an automatic option in the style.

Indents and offsets

Indented or *offset text* is text in which the entire paragraph is set away from the left margin. Genealogists use indented paragraphs for lengthy quotations of documents such as obituaries or wills. In addition to the offset, such text also often receives special typographical treatment such as a 1-point reduction in size, italics, or even a change in font (see YOU MUST HAVE STYLE).

For guidance on the width of the indentation, see the discussion on tabs later in this chapter. Traditionally the indentation occurs only on the left. However, many people like the balance of indenting an equal amount on the right.

If you have used a tab rather than paragraph spacing to identify the beginning of a paragraph, the beginning of indented text is sometimes difficult to recognize. You may find it necessary to add paragraph spacing above and below the indented text, even though you don't use it elsewhere.

A *hanging indent* is a paragraph in which the first line begins at the left margin and all subsequent lines are indented. Genealogists most frequently encounter this format in bibliographies, glossaries, and the child information section.

The child information paragraphs require special treatment (see ORGANIZING AND PRESENTING FAMILY INFORMATION). They have a deep indent (about 1") with tab settings for the individual number (right tab), child number (right or decimal tab), *and* the text (left tab), as shown below.

R   R L

+ 555   i. JOHN[5] JONES, born 1 Jan. 1818 in Greene Co., Penn.; died 22 Mar. 1867 in . . .

Line spacing, line height, and leading

As we read a paragraph, each time we reach the end of one line our eyes automatically move to the beginning of the next line. If the next line is too far from—or too close to—the current line, we might return to the beginning of the current line or skip the next line entirely. Each time we back up to correct for this, it has interfered a little with our comprehension.

Line spacing, line height, and *leading* are used to control the amount of space between two lines of text. When metal type was set by hand, leading referred to the strip of lead that was placed between each row of type. It was measured in points, so typesetting instructions might refer to "9 on 10" or 9-point type on a 10-point line, which required a lead strip 1 point high.

In general, you need one or two points of leading in text-sized fonts. (In other words, the line spacing should be one to two points greater than the font size.) The terminology used varies between software, but adjusting line spacing, line height, or leading all accomplish the same thing.

Begin with the default settings of the software and adjust as necessary. Large type or long lines require extra space between the lines. You can usually adjust both font size and line spacing in increments of less than one point, so try something like a 10.5-point font on a 12-point line. Once you've found the right combination, make a note in your style guide.

The automatic (or single) line spacing option does not always work well for family histories. In some software, this setting allows extra line spacing to be added for a line with superscripts or special characters in it. This uneven spacing is undesirable. If this happens to text in your book, set the line spacing explicitly. (You may need to change other software settings also.)

Line length

The *line length* of the *body text* is part of the balancing act with margins, point size and leading. Watch for line lengths that are too wide. What's too wide? There are several rules of thumb. A popular measure is that lines should not average more than 80 characters per line. Less is better.

This book averages fewer than 65 characters per line. Notice that to achieve this character-per-line count, the left side of the paragraph is indented by .5". If this were not done, the count would have been about six more characters per line.

If you must have a long line length (as with 8½"×11" pages, for example), use a full two points of leading.

Nonjustified text is easier to read

When word-processing software became available for personal computers, it was the neatest thing since sliced bread. Word processors allowed us to revise text without retyping, save our work for later, spell-check, and justify text. And justify text we did. No matter how inappropriate, how ugly, or how difficult to read the results were.

Justification gets in the way of comprehension if the amount of space between words is too great. This is especially a problem for fixed pitch fonts, large type sizes, narrow line lengths (as in two-column formats and around illustrations), and in text with longer than average word length (a characteristic of genealogical publications).

The trend in many professional writing groups is toward nonjustified text, also called *ragged right* or *left justified.*

If you want to justify the text in your family history, be aware it requires careful copy editing to assure that the word spacing isn't a problem. Schedule extra time for it.

Avoid hyphenation

"But the columns look prettier if I hyphenate" is the response often given to this advice. Remember what your mother said about "Pretty is as pretty does"? That's exactly the point here. The primary purpose of typesetting is *to help convey information to the reader.* It is *not* to look pretty. When the two are in conflict, conveying information should always win.

As our eyes complete the sweep to the end of a line, our brain processes the letters and words. If one of the words is incomplete (i.e., hyphenated) our brain tries to fill in the blank. For example, we see "He was in-" and dozens of ideas for the incomplete word come to mind, most of them negative (inept, incompetent, inaccurate, and so on). If the sentence were actually "He was indeed a wonderful person," we must stop reading and rethink things—not very efficient.

So, when should you hyphenate? In nonjustified text if a grossly large blank space is created at the end of a line because of a long word at the beginning of the next, you might hyphenate the long word. Professionals often *recast* (reword) a sentence instead of hyphenating.

If you are using justified text, it is indeed a balancing act. Hyphenate when the spread between words becomes so large that it interferes with comprehension more than hyphenation does.

Initial caps

This paragraph begins with a *drop cap*. When properly sized, the base of the drop cap is flush with the base of the lower line. The software may let you create drop caps easily. Do not overdo their use. One per chapter is enough.

Another way to dress up the opening paragraph is with a *raised initial cap*. Here we simply chose a letter from a decorative font and set it in a larger point size.

Letterspacing and word spacing

Depending on the software, you may be able to control letterspacing and word spacing easily, only for justified text, or only for individual words and letters. Fortunately, it is usually fine without any adjustments.

Only one space between sentences

Yes, I know your high-school typing teacher taught you that every sentence was followed by two spaces—taught you so well, in fact, that period-space-space became a reflex action. That was appropriate for fixed-pitch type such as that used on a typewriter, but it is inappropriate for proportional fonts.

Proportionally-spaced type is designed to facilitate the eye seeing—and the brain absorbing—as much information as possible at one time. This occurs more efficiently if there is only one space between sentences. To make your book look professional—use only one space between sentences.

Tabs

Remember high-school typing class and how you hit tab-tab-tab to move text away from the left margin? Forget it. The same is true of hitting space-space-space to align information in a table. One of the most useful things you can do when you first acquire a word processor is to learn to set and use tabs—left tabs, right tabs, center tabs, decimal tabs. If you have not done so, read the documentation and practice a bit.

The opening tab in professionally typeset paragraphs is not necessarily (in fact, rarely) ½". That is, however, usually the software default. What size should the tab be? It's (surprise!) a matter of balance, dependent on point size and line length. Small type and double-column text looks best with an tab near .2", while an 8½"×11" page with 11-point type suggests something around .4". As a starter, try a tab equal in width to the word "And" or "The" (not including the space after).

If you use a tab to begin a paragraph, use the same setting for the offset amount for indented paragraphs to avoid a drunken look to the left edge of the text.

White space is a most valuable asset

White space refers to the places on a page where there is no printing. It serves as the balance to the text and, quite frankly, keeps a page from looking too boring. We've already considered several locations for white space: margins, below the header, around the chapter title, around headings, between paragraphs, and to the left of quotations and transcripts.

The trick isn't *how much* white space is on a page, but rather *where it is.* To be effective, white space should occur throughout the page *in a meaningful way.* For example, very wide margins with concentrated text in the center of the page is an ineffective use of white space. Narrower margins with headings to break up the text and greater paragraph spacing is a more effective use.

Section dividers

Family histories divide logically into sections. In addition to using headings and subheadings to divide the text and serve as indexing devices, you can use a graphic device at the end of the text. This indicates "done" or "end" to the reader.

The graphic device is generally a rule, a graphic, or *dingbat* characters centered below the last line of text, and surrounded with extra white space. *Dingbat* characters look like graphics, but are treated as text by the software (✍ ❦ ✂ ☞ 📖 ✖ ✒ ➳).

John Jones died 27 August 1897 and is buried in the Mount Hope Cemetery.

John Jones died 27 August 1897 and is buried in the Mount Hope Cemetery.

John Jones died 27 August 1897 and is buried in the Mount Hope Cemetery.

In publications in which space is at a premium, place a dingbat character at the end of the last paragraph, either flushright or separated a bit from the text.

John Jones died 27 August 1897 and is buried in the Mount Hope Cemetery. 📖

Special paragraph styles

The formatting options for some paragraph types are discussed in other chapters. Formatting the table of contents is in BOOK DESIGN. Formatting notes is in HOW DO YOU KNOW? Formatting illustrations and their captions is in ILLUSTRATIONS, CHARTS, AND PHOTOGRAPHS. Formatting the index is in OPENING THE DOOR TO YOUR BOOK.

As you include information from your research in the book, you may find a need for some special formats. If you use any format more than once, create a style for it. Census abstracts or military roles with lots of tab settings are an example of a special format you may want to create.

What if my word processor doesn't use styles?

Think in styles. Create macros that set the options or use copy-and-paste to copy the format settings to where you need them.

What is a macro?

A *macro* is a string of commands that you can access with one or two keystrokes. Don't be intimidated when you look it up in the user's guide and it has all this stuff about programming. In most word processors, you can create simple *keystroke macros* by typing the series of keystrokes that accomplish a task and assigning a name to the sequence.

Details vary considerably among different software programs. Look for instructions in the user's guide.

Tips

Learn to work with the typesetting codes and nonprinting characters displayed (revealed). You don't have to do this all of the time, but there are instances in which it will save many headaches.

Learn how to enter nonprinting and special characters. Learn what they look like and when to use them. Consult the user's guide.

Paragraph mark
Line break
Tab
Space (hard or nonbreaking)
Space (normal)
Hyphen (hard or nonbreaking)
Hyphen (soft or optional)
Em dashes
En dashes
Page break (hard or manual)
Page break (soft or automatic)
Column break (hard or manual)
Column break (soft or automatic)

Terminology

Much of the terminology of style varies considerably between and even within programs. The means of implementing particular features varies even more. This is an unavoidable result of the evolution from hand typesetting through photocomposition to page-layout software to sophisticated word processors. Just be flexible and check both the index *and* the table of contents in the user's guide to find the appropriate sections.

Master documents

Master documents are supposed to help with managing multidocument publications such as books in which each chapter is in a different file. Many word processors have a master-document feature. Investigate it. Some things are more difficult with the master document and others are easier, depending on the software and the particulars of your publication.

Master documents are used for generating a master table of contents, generating the index, and providing continuous page numbering.

To create the index, you probably need to combine the files in some way. There are several techniques you can use. You can use a master document, copy each file into one large file, or link the files to a master file. The best suggestion is to ask around and find someone who has successfully merged files and generated an index with the *same version* of the software that you are using.

Generating a family history from a database

Many lineage-linked database programs and several auxiliary programs can create formatted text directly from a database or from a GEDCOM (Genealogical Data Communication) file.

They are not magic wands. The text will not look like what we have discussed in this chapter. Many of the dates will not be in the proper form, and the documentation likely will not be associated properly with each fact and relationship.

However, such tools can provide a head start *if* you work intensively with a sample chapter *before* entering the data into the database. In this way you can determine how to enter information into the database in order to generate text that is closest to what you want for the final product.

Getting help

This chapter should be read in conjunction with BOOK DESIGN, UNDERSTANDING TYPE AND FONTS, and DEVELOPING AN EDITORIAL EYE, as they all contain related information.

Your best resource is software documentation. Read it. Practice. Read it. Practice. Play with one new feature every day. In a short time you'll be comfortable and proficient with formatting, styles, and templates.

Checklist of paragraph styles

☑ Table of contents

☑ Running header (left, right, first page)

☑ Running footer (left, right, first page)

☑ Chapter title

☑ Heading

☑ Subheading

☑ Narrative (normal)

☑ Child-information

☑ Quotation/transcript

☑ Note

☑ End-of-section

☑ Illustration

☑ Caption

☑ Glossary

☑ Bibliography

☑ Index letter separator

☑ Index main heading

☑ Index subheading

☑ Census abstracts

Organizing and Presenting Family Information

Genealogical numbering systems have been around for a long time, about a century and a half. Along the way many new ideas have been presented. The good ones were accepted; the poor ones were discarded. We can—and should—look to existing models for how to organize and present our family information.

A genealogical numbering system is more than numbers

A *genealogical numbering system* is not merely how you number individuals in a genealogy. It has many more functions than that.

➢ It identifies an individual unambiguously.

➢ It presents information on an individual in a structured manner.

➢ It places an individual in context with his or her ancestors.

➢ It places an individual in context with his or her descendants.

➢ It places an individual in context with his or her siblings.

➢ It facilitates finding fuller information on the ancestors.

➢ It facilitates finding fuller information on the descendants.

This chapter does not explain numbering systems. "Numbering Your Genealogy" by Joan Curran, a *National Genealogical Society Quarterly* article (or NGS special publication), should be read by anyone who is not completely familiar with numbering systems before proceeding with this chapter (see NUMBERING SYSTEMS in RESOURCES).

Accepted numbering systems

Two almost-identical numbering systems fulfill these goals: the *Register system* (used by the *New England Historical and Genealogical Register*) and the *NGSQ system* (used by the *National Genealogical Society Quarterly*). The NGSQ system has also been called the *Modified Register system* and the *Record system* (for the *New York Genealogical and Biographical Record*, which has reverted to the Register system).

Certainly many other numbering systems have been invented (and reinvented). But because most merely number individuals and do not place the individual in the context of his or her family gracefully, they have failed to gain acceptance.

Additionally, some other systems are awkward typographically because the individual numbers are lengthy and difficult to remember (as in the *Henry system*) or because the presentation is difficult to follow and an inefficient use of space (as in the indented format of the *outline system*).

Elements of the accepted descendants-of numbering systems

Virtually all elements of the Register and NGSQ systems are the same. The only difference is in the arabic number and carry-forward indicator for individuals.

The elements can be grouped into three sections for each primary individual: individual information, parent-child transition, and children information. The minimum information required is:

Individual information
➤ Arabic number of individual
➤ Name of individual
➤ Generation number of individual
➤ Linear ancestry of individual, with generation numbers
➤ Narrative about individual

Parent-child transition
➤ Name of individual
➤ Name of spouse

Children information
➤ Roman-numerals indicating order of birth
➤ Name of child
➤ Generation number for first child
➤ Vital information and narrative for children
➤ Individual arabic number for child (systems differ)
➤ Carry-forward indication (systems differ)

Presentation of research results

Some facets of presenting your research are determined by the nature of a genealogical numbering system. However, in writing and typesetting you'll quickly discover that the general stuff is a piece of cake—it's the details that are hard to pin down. We're going to focus on these details.

The two most-widely accepted genealogical numbering systems, as currently presented in the *New England Historical and Genealogical Register* and the *National Genealogical Society Quarterly*, have numerous stylistic differences. The style is the choice of the publication. It is not a part of the numbering system.

However, it is precisely those style decisions that you as writer-editor-typesetter-layout person-publisher are responsible for making. Therefore, in the discussion below, particular attention is paid to describing style alternatives, and making some recommendations.

Example

This example is presented only to help the reader follow the discussion. It is not necessarily presented as a model.

167. DEBORAH[4] DAVIS (Christian[3], Benjamin[2], Andrew[1]) was born in 1834 in Barren County, Kentucky. She married EDWARD EDWARDS there on 15 May 1853. She died 19 September 1902 in Barren County and is buried beside her husband in Mount Hope Cemetery.

Children of Deborah (Davis) and Edward Edwards include:

345	i.	FRANKLIN[5] EDWARDS, born 20 June 1855, Barren Co.; died 22 June 1855.
+ 346	ii.	FRANKLIN EDWARDS, born 5 March 1857, Barren Co.; married ANN ADAMS 1 April 1880, Barren Co.; died November 1905, Gibson Co., Ind.

Individual information

Narrative paragraph. The information for the individual being discussed is in a paragraph in the general style of the publication. For example, if your chosen style (see PAGE LAYOUT AND FORMATTING) is not to tab at the beginning of a paragraph, the individual information should begin with the arabic number of the individual at the left margin.

Individual (arabic) number. We are now at the first of our many typographical quandaries. Should the individual (arabic) number be bold, italic, or unemphasized? Should it be followed by a period or not? The choice is yours. Look at some examples, try some samples with your software and printer, decide what you like, record it in your style guide (see You Must Have Style)—and stick with it throughout the book.

Put a tab (not spaces) after the number to begin the paragraph. If you use spaces and have justified text, the gap between the number and name can change annoyingly from one sketch to the next.

Name. The name of the individual immediately follows the number (and tab). While it would be possible to incorporate the name into a sentence (such as "The immigrant was John Jones . . ."), typically this is not done. The full name is used. Women are listed by their maiden name only.

You want the name to stand out so that your reader can easily find the sketch he or she is seeking. There are several typographical options. Some are shown below. *Print* several samples before deciding. (You'll note, for example, that in the font use here, bold isn't much heavier than normal weight; it shows as much heavier on-screen.) Make your choice and record it in your style guide.

no emphasis (not recommended)	John Jesse Jones
bold	**John Jesse Jones**
all caps (not recommended)	JOHN JESSE JONES
small caps	John Jesse Jones
bold small caps	**John Jesse Jones**
italic (not recommended)	*John Jesse Jones*

The option of special typographical treatment only for the surname, which is often seen in published abstracts, is less helpful in family histories.

Generation number. The superscript number following the given name tells how many generations this individual is from the progenitor. Some editors italicize all generation numbers to help differentiate them from note numbers. Note your preference in your style guide.

Lineage. Placed in parentheses, these names (beginning with the father of the individual) trace the lineage back to the progenitor. They are one of the most useful features of the Register and NGSQ numbering systems because they uniquely—and meaningfully—place the individual within the family and in relationship to other family members.

If the ascent is within the surname, it is only necessary to list the given names (with their appropriate generation numbers). If, however, women are named in the list (or other surname changes such as patronymics are involved), surnames are also listed, as shown in the following example.

99. DAVID^4 DAVIS (*Connie^3 Cotton, Benjamin^2 Adams, Andrew^1*)

You may choose to put the lineage names in italics (or not—it's your choice). Sometimes the generation numbers are combined if the given name is repeated in adjoining generations (Benjamin$^{1-3}$), but this may be distracting to the nongenealogist and doesn't save significant space.

Individual narrative. Finally! It's time to write words. But should those words be in sentences? It is (naturally!) your choice. You could follow the lineage with something like ", born 1834 in Hopkins County, Kentucky; died 19 September 1902 in Hopkins County." But it seems much friendlier to your reader (and more in keeping with the trend towards writing family history rather than genealogy) to use complete sentences.

In fact, if you can vary the form of the sentences (without sacrificing any information), it makes more interesting reading for your audience. "Although a poorly mended broken leg suffered when he was forty caused him to limp, he actively farmed his land on Goose Creek up until a few days before his death. He caught influenza in a local epidemic and died 19 September 1902 in Hopkins County, Kentucky, after only a few days illness."

It is suggested that you spell out the names of the months, the names of states, the words "County" and "Township," and most other words you might be tempted to abbreviate. The overall effect on the page count is minimal (or nonexistent), but the increase in readability is considerable.

Does marriage information go before or after death information?

There's no right or wrong answer. Some people prefer to get the end posts (birth and death) out of the way first (possibly because everyone has exactly one of each), and then deal with marriages and the awkward phrasing of multiple spouses or unidentified wives, simply because it's neater and more organized.

Other people seem to find neatness in a chronological presentation of facts. For them, marriage always comes in the middle.

Distinguish the name of each spouse typographically in the same manner as that of the individual. Use the special treatment the first time a name is mentioned, but not thereafter.

Look at family histories and journals that publish compiled genealogies (see EXAMPLES in RESOURCES). Make careful notes about what you think is awkward and which approaches you like.

What goes in the individual narrative?

In several journals listed in RESOURCES, family information is often in a section at the end of the article entitled something like "Genealogical Summary." It may have been preceded by many pages of discussion of the problem and expanded information about the progenitor and early generations.

In these, the individual narrative is generally a single paragraph, containing basic information such as birth, death, marriage, occupation, and residence. But for a family history we often have much more to tell. There are several possibilities.

➢ Place the expanded information at the beginning of the sketch, as the journals do, and then precede the individual sketch with "Genealogical Summary."

➢ Expand the individual narrative to include everything related to that individual. This might include a detailed analysis of the research, all of the facts that you have uncovered about the ancestor's life, and contextual information about the time and place.

➢ Write a single obituary-style paragraph about the individual, with vital information and highlights. Follow it immediately with the parent-child transition and children information. Place the analysis, life details and context information *after* the children information.

Whatever choice you make, be consistent throughout your book.

Parent-child transition

In a genealogy most individuals are identified as children of a parent (in the lineage section of the individual information), as a spouse (in the individual narrative), and as a parent.

Parent-child information is transitional. It identifies the other parent and introduces the children. The death of a spouse and remarriage were frequent occurrences in earlier times, and the ancestor may have had children by more than one spouse, requiring more than one parent-child transition.

Sometimes the transitional sentence is placed at the end of the individual paragraph. However, this is not especially helpful in the instance of multiple marriages. Furthermore, creating a separate paragraph for the parent-child transition helps set off and structure the presentation of the children better.

The transition should include the father's full name and the mother's full name. The names do not receive special typographical treatment. Style decisions that you must make include which name comes first, whether the mother's maiden name should be in parentheses, and whether the transition should be a full sentence, a phrase, or an introductory phrase. The following examples illustrate only a few of the many options.

Children; surname Smith:

Children (Smith) of John[2] and Mary Miles:

The children of Mary (Miles) and John Smith were:

John Smith and Mary (Miles) had children, including:

The last example points out the importance of words. In the first three examples the implication is that the children who follow are *all* of the children of John and Mary. The last example clearly indicates that the author is not confident that the names that follow include all of the children.

Additionally, the parent-child transition may contain information that applies globally to the children information that follows. For example:

Children of Mary Miles and John Smith, all born in Middletown:

John Smith had children, possibly by wife Mary Miles, listed in the order given in his will:

Note that in no instance does this type of wording substitute for proper and complete documentation.

Children information

Carry-forward indicator. The Register system does not assign an arabic number to children who are not carried forward. The NGSQ system assigns an arabic number to all and uses a + to indicate that additional information can be found about a child in the next generation. The journal *NGSQ* indents this + from the left margin a bit to emphasize that it is part of the children information, but on a narrow page, you may prefer to put it at the left margin.

Individual number (arabic numeral). In the NGSQ system this number is assigned for all individuals. In the Register system it is assigned only to those covered more fully in the next generation. Much time, breath, ink, and passion has been spent debating the relative merits of the two systems, but let's get down to the really important stuff: should there or should there not be a period following the individual number? As with the choice of numbering system, it is a matter of personal taste. Just make the decision and stick with it.

We should mention an important concept in typesetting— numbers frequently should be right-justified. (Think for a moment how difficult it would be to add a column of numbers if they were left-justified.) This is one of those instances.

To accomplish this, you need to set a right tab (right-justified tab stop). If you don't know how to do this, go get the user's guide right now and look it up. You'll be using right tabs frequently.

R	R	L (same as indent)
345	i.	FRANKLIN[5] EDWARDS, born 20 June 1855, Barren Co.; died 22 June 1855.
+ 346	ii.	FRANKLIN EDWARDS, born 5 March 1857, Barren Co.; married ANN ADAMS 1 April 1880, Barren Co.; died November 1905, Gibson Co., Ind.

Child number (roman numeral). The children are listed in order of birth. The roman numeral indicates the birth position of a child within the family. If the birth position is not known for certain, the roman numerals are still used. If your choice of order is based on particular criteria (such as dates of the children's marriages or order in a will), you may wish to indicate this in the parent-child transition, in the child descriptions, or in a note.

What should you do about the roman numerals when there are children by more than one spouse? You may either continue the roman numeral numbering (the theory being that these are all the children of the individual of interest) or begin the numbering over with "i" for each new spouse (the theory being that you are presenting family units). Either choice is acceptable, just remember to use the same style throughout your family history.

The roman numeral is right justified (use that right tab we mentioned above). It is a lowercase roman numeral (i, ii, iii, not I, II, III). You may omit the period following the child number, but it looks better and helps separate it from the paragraph if you use a period. If you use periods after the arabic or roman numerals, decimal tabs work the same as right tabs.

Narrative paragraph. The carry-forward indicator, the individual number, and the child number all appear in the white space to the left of the paragraph. This means that the paragraph itself is indented. The paragraph style is a *hanging indent.* (Some software accomplishes this by specifying a negative indent for the first line.)

Make the narrative portion of the paragraph a solid block. Put a left tab at the same position where the hanging indent begins (at about 1"). This aligns the text in an orderly paragraph style.

Some publications do not do this, putting a few letters of the child's name in the white space also, presumably for ease in finding the name. The child's name is distinguished typographically, so this is unnecessarily confusing. A block-indented paragraph is easier for readers to follow.

Usually the children information section is in a smaller point size. This, along with the indent, distinguishes it visually from the rest of the text. Because of the indent, the line length is shorter than that of the general narrative. This means that the smaller type is still readable unless your normal type size is small.

Child's name. Although many publications use only the given names in this section, be kind to your reader and put both given names and surname for every child. It doesn't take much extra room and saves much confusion for nongenealogists (and genealogists, too).

The typographical options for highlighting the name of the child and spouse(s) are the same as those described above for the individual. Some publications use an entirely different typographical method to highlight the children than they do to highlight the individual, but this is distracting and unnecessary (the indent and smaller point size are sufficient to separate children from individuals).

Generation number. The first child should have a generation number, as described above for the individual. Optionally, you may wish to include the generation number for every child. Try a sample and decide if this is helpful to the reader or distracting given the typographical options you have chosen (it is extra work, too).

Do not include the lineage information for the children, as it is easily obtained from the parent.

Vital information and narrative. For children who are carried forward and treated more fully in the next generation, this section generally is brief. It probably includes only birth, death, and marriage information. The style favored by many in the past that gave only the birth information for children carried forward should not be used—this is insufficient.

If a child is not carried forward, include all information that you have on that child. Thus, some paragraphs may be much longer than others. This is OK. If a paragraph seems to be getting unwieldy but you do not want to carry the child forward, consider moving some of the information to notes, rather than leaving it out.

For example, you might say, "He farmed the same piece of land for 50 years.[27]" in the paragraph and put information in the note about his homestead application, location of the farm, taxes paid, crops grown, and ear marks registered.

The date and place of baptism or christening often must be substituted for birth information. Likewise, the date of a burial or the making or probating of a will may substitute for death information. Indicate clearly what event you are citing. See You Must Have Style for suggestions on how to present nonstandard vital information.

When approximating a marriage date, be gracious and suggest the marriage occurred at least nine months before the birth of the first child.

Although it is not done traditionally, you can choose to include the name of the cemetery as basic vital data. This information is often very meaningful to descendants.

Most journals separate vital dates with semicolons rather than use full sentences because they must conserve space. This is much less readable to nongenealogists. Likewise, most journals use abbreviations. Avoid abbreviations in family histories. They are unfriendly to the reader and typographically ugly.

Which children should I carry forward?

The decision on whether or not to *carry forward* a child and present information about them in the next generation (chapter) of the book must be based on the type of family history you are preparing and the volume of information you have collected.

➤ If you are preparing an all-my-ancestors book, carry forward only the individual in your direct line.

➤ You may choose to carry forward only those individuals for whom you wish to document children.

➤ You may choose to carry forward all individuals through a certain generation.

➤ You may choose to carry forward individuals based on the amount of information beyond vital facts that you have to present.

If you have identified children for an individual whom you are not going to carry forward, include that information, either in the child information or a note, "They had children, including John J. (died 1878, aged one month, buried next to his parents)."

Getting help

In RESOURCES, the section STANDARDS FOR GENEALOGICAL PUBLISHING lists several helpful information sources for organization, presentation, and numbering. The section NUMBERING SYSTEMS directs you to the most current articles on the subject. One article treats special circumstances, such as adoptions and step-families.

The EXAMPLES: JOURNALS sections in RESOURCES lists the most reputable journals publishing compiled genealogies. EXAMPLES: BOOKS lists several well-received books that use recognized numbering systems.

Checklist for presenting family information

Individual information

☑ Arabic number of individual

☑ Name of individual

☑ Generation of individual

☑ Linear ancestry of individual, with generation numbers

☑ Narrative about individual

Parent-child transition

☑ Name of individual

☑ Name of spouse

Children information

☑ Roman-numeral numbers for children

☑ Name of child

☑ Generation number for first child

☑ Vital information and narrative for children

☑ Individual arabic number for child [systems differ]

☑ Carry-forward indication [systems differ]

How Do You Know?

Genealogical research does not consist merely of pulling books from shelves and blithely writing down what we find. The most important part of genealogical research takes place in our minds. Therefore, it is often inadequate to cite the book and be done with it. Our publications must document the pertinent portion of that analysis—it must tell why we believe the information is correct.

The three rules of genealogy

These three rules have been arrived at independently by a number of genealogical lecturers and writers:

Rule 1   Document your sources!

Rule 2   Document your sources!

Rule 3   Document your sources!

But just what does that mean? It means that for *every* statement of fact—a date, a place, a name, or a relationship—you *must* provide a *citation*. A *citation* states where you found that piece of information.

Proper documentation ties each fact to its source

A list of sources is not a citation. A citation ties the exact source to *each* specific piece of information. Even a brief sketch can have a dozen or more sources, and the number of sources for an interesting ancestor may approach 100. Don't make your reader wade through them all (some of which may not be readily available) to find out where you got that marriage date.

Don't forget that a *relationship* is a fact. You must document how you know that John is the son of William *and* how you know that John is the son of Margaret.

Basic citations

Do not work on your family history without a reference book on citations at your fingertips (literally—if you must get out of your chair, it's too far away). This chapter is in no way a replacement for such a reference. Elizabeth Shown Mills' *Evidence: Citation & Analysis for the Family Historian* (see DOCUMENTATION AND EVIDENCE in RESOURCES) is a mandatory accompaniment to this chapter.

The examples that follow show basic, minimal citations for some types of records commonly used by genealogists. A basic citation merely states the source of the information and is generally inadequate for family histories, as will be seen.

1. Effie M. Smith, *A Genealogy of the Van Pelt Family* (n.p.: the author, 1913?), 200–205.

2. Patricia Law Hatcher, "Problem-Solving by Hypothesis: Two McAllister Examples," *The Maine Genealogist* 16 (August 1994): 62–66.

3. Will of Elijah Sansom. Montgomery County, Kentucky, Will Book A:1.

4. 1810 US Census, Hopkins County, Kentucky, page 378. NARA M252, roll 6.

5. Oral interview with Hattie (Smith) Jones.

Documentation is more than citing sources

Good documentation includes much more information than mere citations, however. This information may range from additional information about the source itself to additional details for locating the source.

"How Do You Know?" encompasses not just citing where you found it—but also why you believe it to be both correct and applicable to your ancestor.

Furthermore, "documentation" isn't confined to the citations. Some documentation is found within the text.

Why do you believe it is correct?

Good genealogy and family history is not collecting information and repackaging it in a slightly revised manner.

Good genealogy and family history is the analysis that we as researchers apply to that collection of information in order to arrive at our conclusions. If we don't include the key parts of that analysis in our documentation—text or notes—then we aren't sharing our most important work with our readers.

For each fact we present in the genealogy, we should indicate why we included it. This may sound somewhat daunting, but it really isn't. If you do as suggested in WHAT TO WRITE; WHEN TO WRITE IT and write as you go, it's easy and a great research tool.

Probably, possibly, likely, maybe

Our evaluation of the records with which we work is crucial. Good genealogists know that just because it is in print, doesn't make it true. They also know that handwritten documents aren't always completely accurate, either, and may be difficult to read.

We must analyze each source in its context—everything we know about the source and everything we know about the specifics of the problem, along with a broader knowledge of the background—and then decide why we do or do not believe it. And we need to say so.

Genealogies often say, "Mary was the daughter of William Smith." So where does all this analysis fit in? Try "Mary was *probably* the daughter of William Smith," or maybe "*It is unlikely that* Mary was the daughter of William Smith." State the reasons for your conclusions in the text or note.

Choosing the words

For convenience, I use a ranking I call "Pat's Personal Comfort Factor." I simply assign a number from 0 to 5 that rates how good I feel about a fact or a relationship. This table shows the comfort rating, the evaluation of the evidence, and words I could use to describe my analysis succinctly.

Notice that the most words are provided for comfort factor 4. This is because in genealogy we often find ourselves having to present information where we'd like to have something a little more definite, but we simply couldn't find it. I steer away from using "proved" or "proof" anywhere, because these terms are used loosely by some genealogists.

	Evaluation	Words to use
0	"This is just plain wrong."	false, not true, impossible, conflicting.
1	"I have serious doubts."	not reasonable, improbable, difficult to accept, illogical.
2	"I'm uncomfortable about this."	probably not, inadequate, unlikely, not likely.
3	"This might be correct."	reasonable, possible, might be, could be, possibly, more likely than not, maybe.
4	"This looks pretty good."	probable, apparent, logical, convincing, consistent, apparently, probably, clearly, likely, most likely, fairly likely, highly likely, logically.
5	"I believe this is correct."	definitely, surely, positively. (none required)

About the format

When it comes to matters of punctuation, typography, and formatting for notes, there is often disagreement among authorities. This is because punctuation, typography, and format are matters of style, and style is determined by the editor, publisher, or writer of a specific publication.

Look at several guides and choose the format with which you are most comfortable. The formats used in this chapter are based primarily on *Chicago*, Turabian, and Lackey.

The traditional format for notes is to put a tab at the beginning of the paragraph, indent, and then superscript the number of the note. It is difficult and tedious to find the correct note number.

[1]Photograph of Fredrik Christian Jensen (1835–after 1917) and Ane Magreta Christiandatter (1832–1917), parents of Christina (Fredericksen) Madsen.

The hanging-indent style is more reader friendly. It lets the note number be the convenient *indexing device* that it is supposed to be. (An *indexing device* is something that lets you find what you are looking for quickly and easily.) It also lets you break a note into more than one paragraph for readability.

1. Photograph of Fredrik Christian Jensen (1835–after 1917) and Ane Magreta Christiandatter (1832–1917), parents of Christina (Fredericksen) Madsen.

Unfortunately, the automated note features of some software has severe limitations in formatting and other options. Experiment with it before committing to using it.

Footnotes

Footnotes are used in scholarly publications, but are rarely used elsewhere because they are intrusive. They are useful when they contain material that must be referred to frequently.

Footnotes are printed at the bottom of the page on which the note reference occurs. Extremely long notes may be continued onto the next page. Footnotes are usually set two points smaller than body text. Separate them visually with white space. Or you may use a thin *rule* (line) against the left margin, about an inch wide (rather than the full width of the line).

Several methods have been used for numbering and format. If you wish to use footnotes, find an example you like, record it in your style guide, and follow it.

Endnotes

Endnotes are the documentation method favored by family historians. The question is where to place them. Often they are located at the back of the book with other back matter (see BOOK DESIGN). However, you may find it more useful (and easier to manage) to place endnotes as a section at the end of each chapter (or as a chapter at the end of each part in a multipart book).

When placed at the end of a chapter, the beginning of the notes section should be given special treatment to separate it visually from the narrative. A decorative graphic or a centered rule helps indicate the end of the narrative section. The title of the notes section should be at least as prominent as the section headings within the narrative.

No matter where you place endnotes, add helpful headers if possible so the reader can correlate the notes with the text easily ("Notes on the Adams Family," "Notes for the First Generation of the Brown Family," "Notes for pages 1–38").

Documentation formats not to use

There are three types of documentation that are inappropriate for a family history.

> *Bibliographies.* A bibliography is a list of books (and other publications). It does not contain specific references, such as the page number or the date of a document. The items in the list aren't tied to specific facts, which is absolutely essential in a family history. A bibliography should never be used in place of notes.

Bibliographies *can* be used to list books that provide background reading on ethnic groups, religious history, or social customs, for example. Depending on your publication, it may be preferable to mention such books in notes at the appropriate places. The style manuals and documentation guides in RESOURCES give the proper formats to use if you choose to include a bibliography for background reading.

➤ *In-text citations.* Many New England genealogies have used this format, which is rapidly falling into disfavor. Embedding the documentation in parentheses within the text was accepted for scholarly articles, especially when the document explicitly states the fact, but if a detailed explanation is required, it either must be included in the text or omitted entirely. Some information, such as the name of the publisher, is often omitted from in-text citations.

Narrative is extremely difficult to follow when interrupted constantly by in-text citations. When the venerable *New England Historical and Genealogical Register* switched to footnotes in 1994, the primary reason was to make the articles easier to read.

➤ *Parenthetical reference or author-date systems.* These are kind of a cross between a bibliography and in-text citations. The full publication information is contained in a "Works Cited" list, which is similar to a bibliography. Within the text, the author's surname (or a code tied to the Works Cited list), year of publication (sometimes omitted), volume, and page number are placed in parentheses. This is generally undesirable for the reasons given above.

Recommended documentation format

Because of their flexibility, notes (footnotes and endnotes) are the format of choice for family historians. They can accommodate text that is brief *or* extensive.

Footnotes and endnotes are identical in content, only their location in the book differs. Which you choose is largely a matter of personal preference, although someone whose primary focus is a family publication should probably use endnotes, as they make the narrative pages friendlier looking.

Note numbering

The note number may occur in any of three places: immediately after each fact, at the end of the sentence, or at the end of the paragraph. If you have chosen to put the note at the end of the sentence or paragraph to make the narrative read more smoothly, you will probably be documenting more than one fact or relationship per note. Use wording in the note to differentiate which fact goes with which source. ("The full birth and death dates are on John Smith's tombstone in Zion Cemetery. The marriage . . .")

There should be no space before the note number, which is superscripted and several points smaller than the text. (Some journals place the note number in square brackets to help distinguish it from the generation number.) The note number *follows* any punctuation.

Format details

Capitalization. Capitalization of book titles in citations is something with which genealogists must deal constantly. Three rules cover most situations.

➤ Capitalize it correctly, no matter how it was printed.
➤ Capitalize the first and last word.
➤ Capitalize everything *except* the following:

> prepositions: *of, for, with,* etc.
> articles: *a, an, the*
> conjunctions: *and, but,* etc.
> the infinitive *to*

Titles. The titles of published items such as books, periodicals, and newspapers belong in italics. The edition of a book follows the title, preceded by a comma, but not italicized. The titles of microfilm or CD-ROM publications are generally italicized.

The titles of portions of published works (such as articles or chapters) are placed in quotation marks. Unpublished sources are trickier. If it has something resembling a real title, put that in quotation marks, "A List of Debts due Saml Calland for Dealing at his store on Tomahawk taken 15th Nov 1784," but if it is a single item or a loose collection, don't use italics or quotations (and use your common sense for capitalization).

There is a seeming exception to these general guidelines. Genealogists typically do not give any special treatment to the names of censuses or county records such as will books.

To reduce punctuation clutter, you may find parentheses useful when a citation requires several similar pieces of information (such as the various dates associated with a deed).

Publication information. For books, the publication information is placed in parentheses: (Salt Lake City: Ancestry Incorporated, 1996). It includes these elements:

➤ *Place of publication,* followed by a colon. Include the state if it is not obvious. Use "n.p." (no place) if it isn't given.

➤ *Publisher,* followed by a comma. Use "the author" if it is self-published, as many genealogy books are, or n.p. (no publisher) if you prefer. (You don't have to put n.p.: n.p.—once is sufficient.)

➤ *Date of publication.* Use "n.d." (no date) if it isn't given.

For periodicals the date of publication (month or quarter and year) is placed in parentheses before the page number.

Page numbers. You don't have to use "page," or "p." or "pp." However, if you have further identification, such as a newspaper column number or a census line number, use "page." (Spelling it out is nicer.)

Shortened references. If you refer to something frequently (such as a particular periodical, archives, or set of records), you may find it helpful to use a shortened form or an acronym. Introduce the form in the first reference (preferably for each series of notes), "National Archives Records Administration (hereafter NARA)" or "Transcript of *Acworth Town Records* at the State Capitol, Concord, New Hampshire, FHL#15,053 items 1 & 2. (Hereafter *Acworth Town Records.*)" Alternately, you can include the shortened form in a table in the front matter, but this is often overlooked.

Manuscripts. When citing a manuscript, be very specific about the location. If it is in a collection (at a university, for example), include the document description, box number, collection name, library name (many universities have more than one library), university name—and anything else that might apply.

What to include

Authorities don't agree on exactly *what* is required for a complete citation. Genealogists should take the conservative approach. Include any specific information that you have.

Your citation should be completely unambiguous.

A good rule of thumb is that anyone wanting to look for your source should be able to get to it *immediately*, with only a detour to the catalog for the call number if necessary.

The best way to test the completeness of a citation is to find the source again yourself (preferably in an unfamiliar library) using *only* your own documentation.

Fuller citations

There are a variety of additional facts about a source that you might use for a complete, meaningful citation.

➤ *Where you found it*
➤ *Condition of the record*
➤ *Legibility of the record*
➤ *Supplier of the information*
➤ *His or her reliability*
➤ *Recorder of the information*
➤ *His or her reliability*
➤ *All dates in the record*
➤ *All places in the record*
➤ *All names in the record*
➤ *Your interpretation of the record*
➤ *Anything significant in the record*

Put yourself in your readers' shoes. Do not omit any information unless you are certain that no one would ever be interested in it.

What can be included in a note?

Include any part of your research that you don't want lost. Publishing your family history is your one shot at preserving the records you've located—and the analysis you've done. No one is going to go back later and publish all the stuff you left out. If you think something is important—or interesting—notes are a good place to stash it.

➤ Include *everything* that is required (or important) to someone trying to locate that record.

➤ Include anything that is pertinent to understanding the cited record.

➤ Include anything that is pertinent to understanding something you said in the text.

> Include anything that is pertinent, but would interrupt the smooth flow of the narrative.

> Include anything extra you think might be interesting to the reader, such as additional information on a collateral line or a recommendation for background reading.

How many things could there possibly be to document?

To get a better grasp of what documentation should be about, let's look at an example—a typical family photograph that you are putting in your family history. (Oh! You didn't know you should document the photos? Read on!)

There are four categories of information about a photograph that might be identified as "documentation."

> *The photograph itself.* Is it an original, a copy, or a photocopy? Is it a black and white photograph, a tintype, or a daguerreotype? Is it a studio portrait? If so, is the name of the photographer shown? Is there writing on the back, and if so, what does it say and whose handwriting is it? (Sometimes the name on the back of a snapshot is the person to whom it was to be sent, not the subject.) In whose possession is/was the original?

> *The contents of the photograph.* Who are the people in the photograph? How old are they? How are they dressed? When was it taken? Was it a special occasion? Where was it taken? What is the building in the background?

> *The information source.* Who identified the contents for you? When? How reliable is that person for this information? Was it Uncle George, who went fishing with his grandfather every summer and was 12 when his grandfather died; or was it Uncle Thomas, who was born 3 months before the death?

> *Your analysis of the photograph and information.* Were the alleged subjects still alive at the date the photograph was taken? Had they been born yet? In family groupings, match up each individual with his or her age according to your family group sheet. You may prevent an erroneous caption or even help your research.

No, you don't have to include all that information for every photograph—but where it's appropriate, don't leave it out. Let's look at an example.

Documenting a family photo

This is a personal example. My aunt has a photograph that the family thought was of my immigrant great-grandparents, Hans Madsen and Christina Fredericksen. They were from opposite ends of Denmark and married after each was widowed in Iowa. If I used the photograph in a family history, this would be the caption. Notice the correct identification of the subjects.

Fredrik Christian Jensen and Ane Magreta Christiandatter[1]

This would be the note:

1. Photograph of Fredrik Christian Jensen (1835–after 1917) and Ane Magreta Christiandatter (1832–1917), parents of Christina (Fredericksen) Madsen.

   This photograph is mounted on a stiff backing. The name of the photographer "L. Daugaard, Brovst St." appears to the right of the photo. Margaret (Gregg) Law said the man in the photograph looked like her grandfather Hans, but Hans Madsen and his wife Christina never returned to Denmark. Hans was never in Brovst. Christina's parents moved to Brovst by 1890, and Magreta died in 1917.

   Quite possibly this photograph was taken for their 50th wedding anniversary in 1908 to send to their four daughters in America. Fredrik would have been 73 and Magreta would have been 76.

   In 1994, this photograph was in the possession of their great-granddaughter, Norma (Gregg) Wassung (Mrs. Kent Wassung) of 123 Main Street, Lincoln, Nebraska. The author has made a photographic copy of it.

We had something to say about each of the four categories. We used the note to build a case for our interpretation of who the couple in the photograph is. For photographs, readers especially appreciate full names of the individuals (including maiden names), ages, and relationships.

In the informal note style used above, the format isn't critical, but the information is. It is often helpful if you begin a note with something that assures the reader he or she is reading the correct note (in this case, that it was a photograph and the names of the individuals).

Documentation isn't only in notes

Let's look at another example. Here some of the information (documentation) about the photograph is part of the caption. Documentation can be in a note, in text, or even in a caption.

> *John J. Smith and Emily (Jones) Smith in the living room of their home in Middletown, Kansas, at their 50th wedding anniversary celebration in 1942.*[2]

2. Black and white snapshot of John J. Smith and Emily (Jones) Smith in the possession of their grandson John W. Smith of Sunnyville, Missouri. The anniversary celebration was attended by 17 grandchildren and 5 great-grandchildren, including Mr. Smith. *Middletown Messenger*, 17 May 1942, page 8, column 1.

Documenting documents

Let's look again at the four categories of information we identified when documenting the photograph and apply them to a document such as a will.

➤ The will itself
➤ The contents of the will
➤ The information source
➤ Your analysis of the will and information

With documents such as wills, we also need to be very cognizant of the fact that there are commonly three possible "sources" for "the will," each a different generation of evidence.

➤ A published abstract of the will book
➤ The will book
➤ The original ("loose") will

We must be clear about which versions of the will we consulted. Each version has a different informant and recorder, whose reliability we need to consider and comment on. Also, we might have "seen" the will book or will in person, on microfilm, or as a photocopy from the clerk.

If you used more than one version, say so, because the will book generally has one type of additional information associated with it (dates of court actions, for example); the original has a different type (the original signature, for example).

Documenting a will

Let's compare the minimal citation for a will seen earlier with a more complete one.

> In his will, Elijah Sansom names his wife Elizabeth, daughter Mary Almon, and grandson Samuel Almon.[3]

> 3. Will of Elijah Sansom. Montgomery County, Kentucky, Will Book A:1.

Now let's see what we really know about the will and the sources we used.

> 3. Will of Elijah Sansom; written 6 October 1796 in Clark County, Kentucky; probated 4 July 1797 in Montgomery County, Kentucky. Montgomery was formed from Clark in 1797. This is the first will in Will Book A, recorded on pages 1–2; the inventory follows on page 3. Photocopy from the county clerk in possession of the author. The handwriting is easy to read. Thomas Almond [Elijah's son-in-law] proved the signature on 2 May 1797. It was two months later before the other witness, Robert Wood, appeared to prove the signature so that Elizabeth could request probate.

> The probate packets do not survive.

> N.B.: This will is abstracted, with a number of errors, in Elizabeth Prather Ellsberry's *Will Records of Montgomery County, Kentucky, 1796–1821* (Chillicothe, Mo.: the author, n.d.), 3. It has *Elias Lansom* for Elijah Sansom, Mary *Allison* for Mary Almon, Samuel *Allison* for Samuel Almon, and has a number of omissions. The probate date of 3 May 1797 is incorrect; this date does not even appear. Valuable information is omitted.

In this example, we discussed all three "generations" of the will, provided detail about the will and probate that were not necessary to the narrative, and clearly indicated that we were aware of the numerous errors in the published abstracts.

"N.B." (nota bene) means "mark well" and is used to call attention to something important (in this case a large pitfall). The square brackets (which mean "the editor said this") make it clear that Thomas Almond was not called Elijah's son-in-law anywhere in the document.

Subsequent citations

If a subsequent citation is the following note, you may use "Ibid." (for the Latin *ibidem*, in the same place) or "Ibid., B:10." You also may use an abbreviated form of the title or author. For example:

> Elijah gave one gray mare to Mary.[4] The most valuable item on the inventory, which totaled £39.14.9, is "one old mare & colt, £12." It took only fifteen lines to record everything Elijah owned. The word "old" occurs five times.[5]

> 4. Ibid.

> 5. Elijah Sansom inventory, 3. The inventory (not dated) was taken by Thomas Jameson, James Jameson, D. Wilcox, and Thomas Almon and recorded 1 August 1797.

If a subsequent note occurs many notes later, you may want to consider using the complete citation in the subsequent note as a kindness to your readers.

Evaluating a published source

When we use a published source, whether an abstract, a county history, or a genealogy, we must look beyond the statements about our ancestor and evaluate the book as a whole.

Although our research certainly can't rely entirely upon secondary sources such as compiled genealogies, we do refer to them, and sometimes we use them as sources. For compiled genealogies more than for any other source, we must tell our reader about our evaluation.

Information in genealogies compiled in the nineteenth or early twentieth century was often obtained through correspondence with family members across the country. These family members may have had personal memory of people and events of the nineteenth century. They may have heard family stories (in those pre-television days) that went back for several additional generations. They may have seen family records that are no longer available to us and read tombstones that are now illegible.

Or the genealogies could have been based on inadequate records or wishful thinking. You decide which—and then say so.

> ➤ Look for documentation (there probably won't be much). Even the most respected of genealogists of the past did not document at the level required by today's standards.

> *"The book is not documented."*

➢ Look for "implied" documentation such as "In his will . . ." (And then check the will.)

"The book is not documented, but all of the details that this author has attempted to verify have been correct."

➢ Determine how well the genealogical community respects this particular publication and researcher.

"Walter Goodwin Davis was a highly respected genealogist. This was one of his maternal lines."

➢ Look for wacky conclusions or extremely detailed narratives of events that the author almost surely couldn't have known.

"This book is highly suspect, as it is filled with daughters of lords fleeing to America and other similar tales."

➢ Check for inconsistencies such as children born six months apart or conflicts with facts that you have determined.

"Although some of the information in this book may be correct, a number of errors were noted."

➢ If there are lots of details on the family groups of interest and no conflicts—and they are relatively close in time to the publication date—then the data was probably supplied by that family.

"The level of detail provided on this family indicates that the information was apparently provided by a member of the immediate family."

Documenting a compiled genealogy

When using information from a compiled genealogy, you may have to comment on both the overall book and the specific section you are using. For example:

The wife of Aaron VanPelt was a Gilliland.[6]

6. Effie M. Smith, *A Genealogy of the Van Pelt Family* (n.p.: the author, 1913?), 200–205; copy at FHL. The book is not documented and is primarily a listing of names, dates, and places.

The information about the descendants of Aaron VanPelt is in an appendix on unconnected families. It appears to be provided by Iona or Jesse D. Van Pelt, as there is complete information on their family groups. They were children of Jefferson DeWitt Van Pelt, who moved to Merrick County, Nebraska, in 1879. He was the grandson of Aaron VanPelt. Details are given for the Merrick County families, but only names and a few dates are provided for the Ohio families.

Documenting a census record

Census records are the backbone of much of our genealogical research. Citations should provide sufficient information to allow another researcher to get to the entry as quickly as we did—or even more quickly.

Think about how frustrating it is when your ancestor isn't on the page listed in a published index. You may want to consider using editorial modifiers in your citation: [stamped], [written], [left], [page number in AIS index is incorrect].

Include the dwelling number and family number, along with the township name in the years when they were used, as this is often the most specific way to locate a family. The line number is also helpful, especially for difficult-to-read entries. For later censuses, include the appropriate Enumeration District (ED). Always cite the NARA series and roll number for US census, if that is what you examined.

> 7. 1860 US Census, Posey County, Indiana, Robb Township, page 40 [written], 566 [stamped], dwelling 349, family 291. NARA T7, roll 60.

There were several different census schedules. The primary one genealogists use is referred to as the Population Schedule or Free Schedule. You may omit this term. For other schedules, such as the Slave Schedule, put the schedule name in parentheses after the word "Census." If an early census is alphabetized, say so.

You may want to add an identifying phrase to the beginning of the note or add comments. For example:

> 7. Jno. Almond family. 1860 US Census, Posey County, Indiana, Robb Township, page 40 [written], 566 [stamped], dwelling 349, family 291. NARA T7, roll 60. John Almond 46 ($800, $200), Rebecca 42, Robert D. 16, Joseph 11, Eliza Hill 12. This is apparently the same family as the one reported on page 5 [written], 531 [stamped], dwelling 40, family 35: John Almon 49 ($1500, $400), Rebecca 45, Robert 16, Joseph 13, Rebecca Hill 10. Note the similarities and differences in the two family groups.

Documenting an oral interview

An oral interview isn't necessarily a formal event. Whether it's the stories Grandpa told about his childhood when you were a child or the gossip served up by Aunt Tillie along with the Thanksgiving turkey, you still need to document these sources.

To document information obtained verbally, list the interviewer (if other than the yourself), interviewee, date, place, and whether there are notes or a tape.

Describe the relationship of the person to the information, and possibly an evaluation of his or her reliability. Was it great-aunt Hattie, who meticulously sent an annual birthday card to every niece and nephew? Or great-aunt Hallie, who thought Tennessee was pretty near Pennsylvania? (Be polite!) For example:

John Smith moved to Missouri in 1878 when he was five. They came by train.[8]

8. Notes from an interview with John Smith's granddaughter Hattie Smith at the Smith family reunion 11 August 1995 in Middletown, Kansas. Hattie cared for John until his death in 1945. The entire family appears on the 1880 census in Middletown. The train line had come to Middletown in 1875.

With a bit of overkill, we've included three reasons we believe Aunt Hattie's statements are true (and we didn't even have to mention the birthday cards).

Documenting nontypical information

Sometimes we find ourselves in the position of including information in our publications, both vital dates and relationships, that we have not personally verified. This is often true for an extensive descendants-of genealogy listing hundreds or thousands of individuals.

How do you document such information from a family group sheet, a GEDCOM file, the International Genealogical Index® (IGI), Ancestral File™, a file from someone's Web page, or other nontypical sources?

➤ Describe the source, for example, "GEDCOM file from . . ."

➤ State the creator of the information. Include address or residence, if known. Give the on-line address for an on-line source. If an IGI entry is patron-submitted, get the submitter's name from the batch film.

➤ State any sources indicated by the creator. "Source given as . . ." You *cannot* use this source as your source for the information because you haven't seen it.

> State all dates that apply. This may be the date on the document, the date of the computer file, or the date you received the information. Indicate which date it is: "Family narrative dated 5 January 1994, in text file date-stamped 7 July 1995, received 9 August 1995."

> The IGI and Ancestral File are publications and have typical publication information, including date of publication.

> State any pertinent information about the source. This may include such things as the medium, other "owners" of the document, or any changes made to the information: "Family Group Sheet created by Ann Adams dated 17 February 1968, photocopy received from Barb Brown December 1990. Ink and handwriting indicates that additions probably were made after the 1968 date."

The best rule of thumb is that you should include *everything* that you know about the source.

Documenting problem situations

What should you do if there is information in print that conflicts with your publication? Whether it is a bad abstract, an incorrect page number in an index, a different interpretation of a name, or a different conclusion on a descent, acknowledge that the other publication exists and that you have seen it.

> Acknowledge the other publication.
> Pinpoint the specific differences.
> Provide explicit reasons why your conclusion is correct (or preferred).

You do not have to restate all of the incorrect information. (In fact, often this can confuse the reader.) Identify the crux of the problem and focus on that. And you'd better have good, solid reasons for your case. Be nice, but firm. For example:

Records are more accessible today than when these lineage applications were made. Although information about later generations was personal knowledge of applicants, they apparently based the earlier generations on only a few sources, and therefore fell prey to the same-name, not-the-same-man trap. A 1787 deed makes it clear that the Edward who was claimed as the father of William was already dead by 1787 and could not have been the father of William born in 1790. The deed states . . .

What if someone else has published on some of your lines? Always acknowledge that the other publication exists and that you have looked at it. You may want to add some additional comments. For example:

He married Sarah Williams, daughter of William Williams and Sarah Steel.[9]

9. The Steel family is treated more fully in *Lives of Steel* by Sally Steel (Boston: the author, 1990); copy at NEHGS. This author agrees/disagrees with her conclusion that Sarah was the daughter of . . .

What you don't have to document

The general advice is that you do not have to document commonly known facts. Problems sometimes arise because what one person considers commonly known, another person never heard of.

If a fact seems commonly known to those familiar with the subject, but not to others, try a compromise. You probably found out the fact by reading about the subject. Provide a note mentioning the one or two sources on the subject that you found most helpful or interesting.

You do not have to document *where* you saw a source *if* it is widely available (such as the federal census microfilm, for example). Family histories (both typescript and bound) have limited distribution. Do other researchers a favor and always state where you found the family histories that you reference.

Getting help

See the section DOCUMENTATION AND EVIDENCE in RESOURCES for publications presenting guidelines and formats for genealogical documentation, particularly Mills.

Any good style guide (see the section STYLE MANUALS, GRAMMARS, AND TYPESETTING GUIDES) should contain guidelines and examples for documentation. Turabian seems especially helpful because of the thoroughness of the examples. MLA contains guidelines for the content (but not format) for citing electronic media.

Examine articles in the journals listed in the section EXAMPLES: JOURNALS. Those using endnotes and footnotes provide useful models for you to study. In all of them, examine how evaluation of evidence is presented within the text and in the notes.

Checklist for elements in notes

*Individual notes vary widely. If any of these elements apply,
include them. Arrangement and punctuation vary also.*

☑ Author's name (and editor or compiler, if appropriate)

☑ Type of record

☑ Institution authoring, collecting, compiling, publishing, or
holding the original

☑ Article title (or other portions of published works)

☑ Title of book, journal, microfilm, or CD-ROM

☑ Volume and number for a journal

Publication information

☑ City of publication, plus state if not obvious

☑ Name of publisher

☑ Year of publication

☑ Month and year for a journal

Specific information

☑ Page number. Frame number on microfilm of loose papers.
Column number on newspapers.

☑ Microfilm institution, series number or name, roll number,
item number

☑ For census: state, county, township, PO, ED, SD, all page
numbers, dwelling and family numbers, line number

☑ Dates of record

☑ Condition of record

☑ Recorder of record

☑ Location of record if not widely available

Turning Paper into
People

Why do you research? A sense of family, a sense of history, the thrill of solving a puzzle? Share that with your readers. Help them understand why your hobby has become an obsession. Help them understand that these aren't names on paper, they are your family, they are real people. By learning about the context of our ancestors' lives, we can turn those scraps of paper in our files into people—and share that magic with others.

Is this context stuff necessary?

Nope. But it makes your book more readable, more enjoyable, more valuable. The idea of putting our ancestors in context has grown in popularity recently. We are coming to understand that some research problems can be solved (or solved *correctly*) only if we place the individuals in context. And it's always been fairly obvious that no one is thrilled about reading lists of names and dates.

What should you write about?

Write about what interests you. As an avid researcher, you may want to share the research process. What did it feel like the first time you stood in front of that ancestor's grave? How long had the search taken? Describe the contrast between the dark, dusty courthouse basements where the search took place and this bright sunny spot with the smell of new mown hay from the surrounding field (or how it took four-wheel drive and crawling up a steep muddy hill to get here).

Write about the records. Why were they created, and how did your ancestor feel about them? The census taker was often resented (and the tax assessor wasn't real popular either), but the deed for 160 acres of land may have been the most meaningful piece of paper your ancestor possessed. Point out to your readers that the decennial census and annual taxes are not a recent innovation.

Write about the people. Help your readers see their world.

Getting ideas

Close your eyes and try to think about your ancestors' lives. What do you need to know in order to bring the details into sharp focus? Picture your ancestor standing in his or her kitchen. Now try to zoom in on the clothing, the utensils, the furnishings, on what the person is doing. Chances are that the best you can get is a fuzzy picture. Research the answers and write about them.

To help get your thinking in gear, the next several sections list dozens and dozens of questions about a few of the contexts of your ancestors' lives. Just glance at them quickly now to see what's there.

When you are ready to sit down and write, read through all of the questions. If one of these questions prompts another one in your mind (and if this is your book), write it down in the margin. Underline any questions you think sound interesting.

And remember—there are many additional questions to ask, many additional contexts to explore.

The context of everyday life

What kind of clothing did each family member wear? How about shoes? Did the women and children go barefoot? Did they spin or weave? Did they buy clothing, shoes, cloth? If so, where?

What kind of food did they eat? What was breakfast, lunch, dinner like? How many plates, spoons, knives, forks, bowls did they have? Is this number fewer than the number of family members? How do you think they managed?

How was the food prepared? How many pots and skillets did they use? Did they cook on a fireplace or a stove? Was the kitchen part of the main room, a lean-to, a separate building? What did it smell like? Was it smoky?

Where did they get their food? Which items did they buy, grow, raise, slaughter? What kinds of animals did they own?

Who were their nearest neighbors? How far away did they live? Did they travel by road or water to visit? How many other young people lived within, say, a two-mile radius?

Was there a school? How far away? Did all the children go to school? At what age did their education end? What topics were taught? Who was the teacher? What books were used?

What diseases were prevalent? What names were used to describe them? How were they treated? By whom?

The context of housing

Was the house built of boards, stripped logs, sod? How did they seal out the weather? What was the roof made of? What was the foundation made of? How many rooms were there? How big were they? What was each room used for?

Was there a porch, a lean-to? What about out-buildings? How was the chimney constructed? Did the farm animals stay in a building that was attached or detached?

What material was the floor made of? Was it raised? How about the walls? Were they finished, wallpapered, newspapered? Were there any decorations? Were there windows? How many? What shape and size? Did they have glass? Did they open? How?

What was the finest possession in the home?

The context of work

Was your ancestor a farmer? What crops did he grow? How big were his fields? How large were the crop yields? What farm implements did he use? Did he plow with a horse, a mule, an ox—or was the plow man-powered? Was it good farm land or bad? Were the fields fenced?

What types of farm animals did they raise? Did they have a cow for milk, chickens for eggs? Did they raise hogs? Was butchering a community affair? Were the animals fenced or free range? What was his brand or mark?

Did the head of household have a secondary occupation or craft? Why do you think he was most often listed as a farmer? Was it preference or necessity? What tools did he own?

How did the wife and children contribute to the family economy? Was there a spinning wheel or loom that created goods that might be bartered or sold?

Were there hired hands or slaves in the household? Where did they live? What were their lives like?

What were the daily, weekly, and annual tasks and chores performed by the wife and children?

What were the daily, weekly, and annual tasks and chores performed by the father and older sons?

The context of environment

What is the geography or topography of the land? Is it hilly, flat, wooded? Are there many waterways or few? What is the soil type? What kinds of trees are native to the area? What kinds of birds and wildlife?

What is the average weather like in the area? When does the first frost occur? How did the climate affect the way the homes were built? How did it affect the crops they grew?

Were there major environmental events during your ancestor's life—the year with no summer, the blizzard of '88, hordes of grasshoppers, a prairie fire? How was the family affected?

How did your ancestor get around? Was it by road or water, on horse or on foot? How far was the family from "civilization" such as courthouse, store, church, school?

The context of land and migration

Was your ancestor one of the first into an area, or did he come only after the area was settled? Did he move with a group?

What route did he follow to make the move? What were the roads like—or did the family use trains, canals, or river barges? Were many other people following the route at the same time?

Did he patent land? If he homesteaded, which law was it under, and what were the requirements? Was he able to fulfill the requirements?

Where was the land? Can you locate it exactly? How big was it? What shape was it? Was it surveyed in metes and bounds or the rectangular survey system? How and why do you think he chose this particular piece of land? Did it have a creek running through it? If not, where do you think they got their water?

The context of military duties

Was your ancestor in a militia? What did that mean? How was the group organized? How often did he have to drill? Did they wear uniforms? What kind of gun did he have? Did he even have a gun?

If your ancestor saw service, what campaigns did he participate in? What was life like between battles? How far did they have to march? Were any of his friends, neighbors, relatives in his unit? Was it a mounted or a foot unit? What kind of weapons did they use? Was he wounded or ill? What was the medical care like? What kind of hats did they wear?

How did your ancestor's family survive while he was gone?

Did your ancestor (or his widow) get a pension? What were the requirements? Did they have to be destitute? How did they apply? Did your ancestor have to go into court to give a deposition? Are there stories buried in the pension files? How much was the payment? Did he have to go somewhere to pick it up?

The context of religion

What local church did your ancestors attend? How many members did it have? Who was the minister? Was he educated as a minister, or was he a farmer called to preach? How important was the church in the social life of the community? Did the church have assigned pews? Where was the pulpit? Did they sing in church? What hymns?

What denomination were they? What did it mean to be a Quaker, a Freewill Baptist, a Cumberland Presbyterian, a Puritan? How did the religion affect family life, their clothing, marriage customs, burial customs, their outlook on life and the afterlife?

Does your ancestor have a gravestone? How is the theology of the times represented by the gravestones? Does it have a symbol on it? What does that symbol signify? What does the epitaph say? Who carved the stone? What material is it made of? What shape is it? Who is buried nearby?

The context of family

What was the average size of a family in this time and place? How far apart were the children spaced? What was the usual age at first marriage for a man, a woman? What was the child mortality rate? What was the average life span? How did your ancestor's family compare to the norm?

Were the elderly typically a part of the family? What roles did they play? What were the procedures involved in getting married? Did the couple live with the parents at first?

Why did the mother and father choose the names for the children that they did? Were they family names or names that were popular at the time? Were they Biblical names? Did they give middle names? Were nicknames routinely used?

The context of history and politics

Did any of the events of history and politics affect your ancestor and his family significantly, or were they distant? What party did he belong to?

Was there a newspaper through which your ancestor could learn of the events? Did he subscribe? Could he read?

Were the battles of war fought nearby—or far away? Did any historical people or places touch the life of your ancestor?

The context of community

Was your ancestor living in a settled community or on the frontier? How were the relations with the Indians? Was there a nearby fort or town in case of trouble?

Was the community governed by a town meeting? Who attended? Where was the court held? How often?

Where did your ancestor fit economically within the community? Was he a large landowner—or does his name appear in the warnings out?

The context of ethnicity

How did your ancestor's ethnic background affect his life? Did it influence his food preferences, economic goals, farming methods, favorite songs, church affiliation, holiday celebrations, even the structure of the family?

The context of society

How did the social structure affect your ancestor? Your ancestress? Were their roles strictly defined? How did society view children? Were they the center of attention, or were they ignored until they grew older? What was courtship like?

Were your ancestors slaves? Slave owners? Or one of the many non-slave-owning families in slavery areas? How did slavery affect your ancestors' lives? Was your ancestor an indentured servant? How was this condition different from/the same as slavery?

The context of law

At what age could a boy marry? A girl? What were the minimum and maximum ages for poll taxes? Through what age could a child be indentured? At what age could a child choose his or her own guardian?

What happened procedurally when someone died without a will? Who inherited the land? Who inherited the personal property? Did the widow have dower rights? What were they?

When land was sold, did a woman have to release dower? What was required to get a divorce? Who could run a tavern? Could your ancestor vote?

The context of records

Was any kind of official record created when your ancestor died? Why or why not? Had some doctor gotten interested in causes of mortality and gotten a law passed? How many people complied?

What types of questions were asked on the census—and why? How did your ancestor's answers compare with other residents of the area?

Could your ancestor write? If not, who put those entries in the Family Bible? Did the entries appear to be written by a man or a woman, young or old, well or poorly educated?

Did your ancestor's church keep records? What kind? How were the records they kept related to their beliefs?

Is your ancestor listed in a city directory or a business directory? How big was the directory? How often was it published? How many others shared his occupation? What are the advertisements like?

How much should you write?

You needn't (and probably shouldn't) answer each and every question. Choose those that interest you or are part of your life.

> ➤ Are you a teacher? Investigate and write about the schooling.

> ➤ Were you raised on a farm, with a feel for the rhythm of crop cycles? Describe the seasons and the tools for planting, tending, and harvesting your ancestor's crop.

> ➤ Is your hobby needlework, woodwork, or music? There's much written that you can explore in these areas.

> ➤ Who do you empathize with? The father hunting for food? The mother keeping house in a dirt-floored cabin? The youngest child, getting the most worn hand-me-downs—or the oldest daughter, mothering her own siblings? Write about it.

If you are focusing on one family's life, you may answer many of these questions. If you are creating a compiled genealogy, perhaps you might choose one or two questions that are pertinent to the records you located about that particular family.

What to write

As you write, keep the following in mind:

> ➤ If your family history is primarily stories and narratives, you must provide the context of reality and history. If a Civil-War letter mentions participation in a battle, provide the historical, geographical, and political context for that battle.

> ➤ Imagining isn't enough. You must have sound reasons for what you write. You can't say, "They probably had cornbread for dinner every night," if corn wasn't a basic crop of their locality. Maybe rice was their starchy staple. Find out.

> ➤ Annual tax roles generally list the number of certain livestock owned. Look at estate inventories and mortgages to obtain detailed lists of almost everything your ancestor owned, from tools to animals to stored grain to "one olde pott." Try to imagine a life based on these possessions—and no others.

> ➤ If you find only a few details about your ancestor, look for a diary kept by a neighbor, letters written by the minister, ledgers from a nearby store, or local newspapers.

> ➤ The topics you write about belong in the index. See OPENING THE DOOR TO YOUR BOOK.

How to write

Research in three different sources, put them aside, and write. Don't copy. Paraphrase. Go back and skim the sources to see if there is something additional you want to say.

When you cannot find direct evidence about your ancestor, don't pretend that you did. Interweave facts about your ancestors with the contextual information. For example:

> . . . Childbirth in New England in the late eighteenth century was generally attended by a midwife.[1] Seven of Polly's eight children were born during the winter. Perhaps there were anxious moments before the midwife arrived in the ice and snow.

> . . . A typical frontier cabin was a single room. Only after the farm was established would there be time to add a second. It must have seemed crowded for the family comprised of John and Martha, her mother, and their seven children, the oldest only thirteen. Probably they spent much of their time out of doors, with the children running to explore the creek with its minnows and frogs as soon as their chores were done.

> . . . Mary's daily routine was probably very much like that of her neighbor, Barbra Brown, who recorded the many dawn-to-dusk tasks of her life in a diary.[2] Once a week, she boiled water to begin the laundry. . .

Notice that we used a note reference in the first example. We did this for two reasons. It is a fairly specific fact, and we also wanted to point our reader to a source that they might find interesting to read on their own. In the third example, we used a note reference because we are referring to a very specific document, one which readers might also be interested in investigating on their own. See How Do You Know? for information on notes.

Using quotations

Use quotations when their use adds to the text. You may incorporate quotes within paragraphs using quotation marks if they are brief or set them apart as block quotes (indented paragraphs) if they are longer. See You Must Have Style for guidelines on using quotations.

Do not copy someone else's words as your own. That's plagiarism. You can, however, read the words and ideas of others (preferably more than one) and express them in your own way. That's scholarship. If you are using facts or ideas that are not common knowledge, give a citation.

Where can you find stuff to use for context?

The same place you do research. No, not the genealogy section—the rest of the library. You know, those rows and rows of books you hurriedly bypass each time you go digging for ancestors.

Ask your librarian for guidance. Librarians are usually happy to point you toward their favorite sources.

And you know what? Unlike genealogy books, you can check out many of these books. Curl up in front of the fireplace with the book, a cup of cocoa, and a notepad. Some are so interesting, you'll read every word. Others may be dull but full of good information. Almost all have extensive notes and bibliographies leading you to additional sources.

Use technological tools

Locating a variety of sources for contextual information is becoming faster and simpler thanks to technology. If your library has an on-line catalog, learn to use it effectively.

Better yet, browse the catalogs of libraries around the country—from the comfort of your own home through a computer modem. Many institutions, particularly university libraries, have on-line catalogs available through Telnet. Often the catalog is regional, allowing you to search several collections at once. Best of all, many of them can be accessed by nonstudents.

You can identify books, articles, and dissertations that address your topic, and then ask the Interlibrary Loan department of your public library about borrowing the material.

Electronic bibliographic databases on CD-ROM or on-line are becoming increasingly available at libraries and through on-line services. They can lead to citations for books, articles, dissertations, book reviews, newspaper articles, special publications, and a variety of other resources (some of which may never have appeared in paper form). Additionally, you may be able to access, print, or download abstracts—or even complete text—of the items. Costs and conditions vary widely.

Genealogists should look for *America: History and Life,* an annual publication of abstracts of articles and listings of book reviews from a variety of publications, including journals of state historical societies. An electronic version combining previous annual volumes is now available.

Some source material is in nonpaper format. Many libraries have microfiche or high-density microfiche collections of publications, both new and out-of-print. Full-text-search capabilities for similar collections on CD-ROM or on-line let you quickly scan for words or combinations of words within numerous topics.

Encyclopedias on CD-ROM provide fairly superficial information, but most list their sources, which can lead you quickly to more detailed information.

Books, articles, dissertations, and documents on CD-ROM can be a gold mine of contextual information. The number is growing, fueled by the educational market. Ask a librarian, "What's new?"

Be a detective

To find contextual material successfully, you often must be a detective. Some of the best material isn't widely available, and it may be cataloged under a variety of subject terms in indexes and catalogs. Esoteric topics may be especially difficult to track down because they are cataloged under a much broader topic. Try these tips when searching:

➤ Keep three running lists for each topic you are researching, adding to them as you find new information: a bibliography of *all* books or articles that might pertain, a list of subject headings (and which cataloging systems use them), and a list of Dewey decimal and/or Library of Congress classification numbers.

➤ In a catalog or index, search for a title or author you already know about. Write down *all* subject headings listed for the item (be exact), and then use those search terms as seeds for a search.

➤ Scan library shelves for all books using the Dewey decimal or Library of Congress numbers you've identified. You may find additional books on the topic of interest.

➤ Identify a periodical, journal, or publication series that has titles of interest, and then browse the tables of contents for every issue to identify other items.

➤ Don't ignore the book reviews in pertinent journals or listed in electronic databases, which can lead to excellent publications, especially those published recently but not yet widely available.

➤ When you visit a new library, ask about their electronic reference tools and search again. Do not assume there is nothing new for you to find.

> Be flexible. You may not be able to find a resource on your exact topic. Look for resources on similar topics. For example, if you can't find an article on the diet of poor farmers in eighteenth-century Virginia, investigate an article on slave diet at Monticello. It may address your question as part of its context, and it should contain references that lead to other sources.

What types of sources provide contextual information?

You can find information in a variety of places. The CONTEXT section in RESOURCES suggests additional resources.

> *Documents you have found in your research.* Reread the wills, deeds, obituaries, and other records in your files, searching for details that you may have overlooked in your enthusiastic search for names and dates.

> *Documents created by others in the same community or undergoing similar experiences.* In particular, look for diaries, letters, store ledgers, and account books. Sometimes these have been published. In other instances, you'll be looking in manuscript collections.

> *Publications of the times.* Newspapers in particular may offer great detail related to your ancestors' lives. Read the national news to learn about "history" as it was being made. Read the local news to learn about their daily lives. Read the ads to find out what products were popular—and what promises they made.

For late nineteenth-century ancestors, look for a reprint of the *Sears and Roebuck Catalog.* You'll find hundreds and hundreds of illustrations for the items your ancestors wanted to own.

In mug books and county histories, read the general sections that tell about the county, its geography, and its settlers.

> *Scholarly works.* Scholars, from students writing dissertations to professors working in a publish-or-perish world, often study cultural or historical topics. It may be mortality rate, songs, food, crops—or hundreds of other topics. These works are published in both books and periodicals.

> *Statistics and demographics.* Many of the questions that government officials asked our ancestors were posed solely to gather statistics. Seek out the statistical compilation or an analysis to determine, for example, how many people of the same country of origin immigrated in the same year as your ancestor (and what percentage they were of the total) or whether your ancestor's farm was larger or smaller than average for the locality.

Atlases, which we often think of only as containing maps, also have statistical information. Use a modern atlas to contrast the demographics of your ancestor's time to the demographics of today.

➤ *Exhibit catalogs.* Special exhibits at museums often have well-researched catalogs created just for the exhibit. These catalogs provide good background information about the items shown in the exhibit, whether needlework or tools.

➤ *Archeological investigations.* Some American sites are now old enough to be of interest to archeologists (Martin's Hundred and the slave quarters at Monticello, for example). Books and articles based on the findings have much to tell us about the daily life of the inhabitants.

➤ *Books for kids.* Try the youth section of your public library. You'll often find easy-to-read survey books on the topics that interest you.

➤ *College and university libraries.* A college library may have more books and periodicals on the topics you are researching than a public library.

➤ *Used-book stores.* Look especially at large stores and those near a college or university. Also watch for library deaccessioning sales.

➤ *Book vendors.* Some genealogical book vendors are starting to carry more and more titles on social history of interest to genealogists.

Bookstores attached to museums, national parks, and historical sites have excellent books. Any bookstore that carries titles from university presses is a good place to look.

➤ *Map and tourist publications.* Use these to create a mental picture of the area, the landscape, and special features. Tourist publications are helpful for providing local color when you cannot visit the area yourself.

Use USGS topographic maps to learn the "lay of the land."

Getting help

CONTEXT in RESOURCES is an integral part of this chapter. It suggests many books that help you find other books and also many books that are typical of the sources you are seeking. Almost all of the items listed have extensive documentation and bibliographies that can point you toward other sources that might be a better fit for your ancestors' lives.

Checklist for context ideas

- ☑ Cities
- ☑ Clothing
- ☑ Communication
- ☑ Crops
- ☑ Customs
- ☑ Environment
- ☑ Ethnic
- ☑ Everyday life
- ☑ Factories
- ☑ Food
- ☑ Furniture
- ☑ Geography
- ☑ Government
- ☑ Housing
- ☑ Law
- ☑ Medicine
- ☑ Military
- ☑ Music
- ☑ Needlework
- ☑ Occupation
- ☑ Religion
- ☑ Schooling
- ☑ Social
- ☑ Trades
- ☑ Transportation
- ☑ Work

Illustrations, Charts, and Photographs

A picture is worth a thousand words. Don't forget that time-worn bromide when preparing your family history. Graphic devices such as illustrations, charts, and photographs can dress up your family history, add interest, and convey information quickly and easily.

Do I really need to include graphics?

Only a genealogist could love a book without pictures! Family members *and* genealogists will appreciate your family history more if it is illustrated.

➤ When illustrations are sprinkled throughout the book, they serve to break up the monotony of the text.

➤ Information is better understood when it is presented in graphic format. Maps, pedigree charts, descendant charts, and drop-line charts in family histories are an enormous help to the reader in keeping information organized.

Using maps effectively

Most genealogists love maps. We collect them by the dozens. So it's surprising how few family histories include them. You may know quite well where Oglethorpe County is, but many of your readers don't have a clue. As your readers use your book, the maps help them organize information about location. Maps also help place the ancestor in context.

Before using a printed map, check on its copyright status. If it is protected by copyright, get permission to use it (see YOU MUST HAVE STYLE). Most maps published by the federal government and many maps from state and local governments are public domain.

When you include a copy of a map, annotate it. Show *which* counties your ancestors lived in and *which* trails they followed when migrating. Circle the location, add labels, add symbols, or add shading. (You can buy press-on film with a variety of shading patterns at graphics supply or drafting supply stores.)

Consider creating your own map. You needn't be a great artist, but neatness helps. Experiment with tracing paper or transparency film to trace the routes of roads and waterways. USGS quadrangle maps and county highway maps are most likely to be of an appropriate scale and level of detail.

Next add symbols for the homes of your ancestor's family and neighbors, the church, the school, the cemetery where the family is buried—all the places that were part of their lives. Print labels last, after the geographic elements are in place. If you are all thumbs, hire a drafting student to draw the final version.

Creating genealogical charts

There are three popular and useful genealogical charts: pedigree, descendant, and drop-line. In addition, it is often useful to create special charts to illustrate in-law relationships.

You can draw the chart by hand. You can create it in a drawing program. You can create it entirely as text. Several lineage-linked database programs have good charting capabilities. You may be able to export the chart to a file, or you may have to print it and possibly reduce it in size.

Names can be simple text or enclosed in a graphic box. The tools you have, the format of your book, and your patience in creating the charts determine the format. There are a few conventions, which are demonstrated in the examples below.

A word of warning—don't pack everything into one chart. Avoid too many people or too much detail in one chart. Large charts are more difficult too create, harder to read because of the small type, and confusing to the nongenealogist. Create several smaller, simpler charts instead and use them throughout the book.

A wide chart or illustration may require that you place it *broadside* (sideways). If so, the top belongs at the left. Try to avoid this as much as possible.

Pedigree charts

Most genealogists are familiar with *pedigree charts*, and the form is well-established. The male is always an even number, and the paternal line is always above the maternal line. Aside from that, you have many options. You can use graphic boxes, you can use fancy fonts, you can include dates and places, you can add icons for military service or immigrant ancestor. It's up to you.

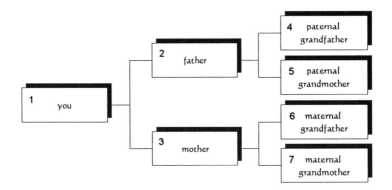

Descendant charts

A chart showing the children of a couple can get crowded for large families. Instead of a horizontal chart, try a vertical *descendant chart.*

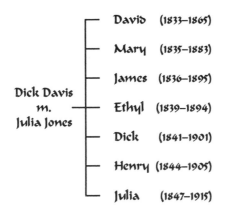

Relationship charts

You can use variations of a descendants chart to show extended relationships. The family line is highlighted here.

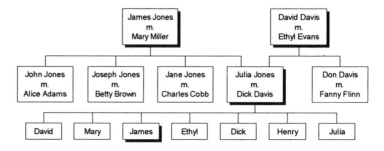

Drop-line charts

Drop line charts are used to show a single line of descent—from an immigrant ancestor to you, for example. Drop-line charts are helpful in multifamily descendants-of genealogies at the beginning of each surname section to orient the reader.

Put the husband on the left. An equal sign indicates a marriage. You may include dates and places below the names. Center-tab settings were used in this example to center names and dates.

Hutchinson to Steel

Richard Hutchinson	=	Alice Bosworth
1603 Eng– Mass	1627	Eng–1688 Mass

Thomas Hale	=	Mary Hutchinson
1633 Eng–1688 Mass	1657	1630 Eng– Mass

Edward Putnam	=	Mary Hale
1654 Mass–1747 Mass	1681	1660 Mass–aft 1747 Mass

Edward Putnam	=	Sarah Miles
1682 Mass–1755 Mass	1705	1686 Mass– Mass

Joseph Steel	=	Sarah Putnam
ca 1706 Ire?–1788 NH	1731	1708 Mass– ?

Ananias McAllister	=	Jane Steel
ca 1743 Ire–aft 1813 Maine	ca 1760	1742 Mass–by 1797 Maine

Land plats

Many genealogists are interested in platting metes-and-bounds descriptions from deeds. Whether done by hand or using computer software, these plats make interesting additions to a family history, especially when annotated with the names of neighbors and significant geographic features.

Copyright-free art and clip art

Clip art is available as books of drawings, on diskettes, and with some software. *Copyright-free art* is often called *clip art*, but not all clip art is copyright free. (Most is, but read the notes in the book or software to be sure.)

Do not use clip art unless it is appropriate for your family history. There is clip art available of nineteenth-century (Victorian) clothing, transportation, military, and patriotic subjects.

When using computer clip art, print a sample to be certain that the resolution of the drawing and the resolution of your printer result in an image of publishable quality. If you can see the jagged edges on curves, it may not be a good idea.

Sketches

In the nineteenth century many books, newspapers, and magazines were illustrated with *line art* such as sketches. All of these are now in the public domain. You may be able to find a town history with a sketch of your ancestor's church that would make a wonderful addition to your family history.

Early mail-order catalogues are out of copyright and many of them have been reprinted. They are rich in drawings of the items of everyday life.

Halftones and photographs

A *halftone* is a graphic that is not entirely black and white, but also includes shades of gray. Halftones are the opposite of line art.

Photographs and documents are common types of halftones. Halftones present a problem at printing time, because ink is black, not gray. Grays reproduce with a muddy effect.

This problem is avoided with *screening*. Screening is the process of turning solid areas of gray and black into discrete black dots by photographing them through a white screen.

Screens come in various densities from coarse (65 lines per inch) to fine (300 lines per inch). Look at a photograph in your local newspaper. You can see the dots because newspaper photographs use a coarse screen.

If the book printer you select is inserting the photographs, they probably will take care of the screening. If you are using an offset printer, the printer can take care of this step if you ask for it. If you are using a local copy shop, you are responsible for getting the photographs screened.

A reprographics company can make screened copies of photographs. The photographs can be resized at the same time. Shop around (this isn't cheap). If you put several photographs on a larger sheet, you usually can save money. Then you cut out the screened photograph and place it on the final copy (see PREPARING CAMERA-READY ART).

If your book will be photocopied, you might consider Copyscreen, a 10"×13" acetate sheet with white screening dots that comes in three densities, available from graphics supply stores (under $4). Cut a piece slightly larger than each photograph and tape it over the photograph. This is not a wonderful solution, but it is better than nothing.

Scanning a photograph creates the effect of a screen. The quality varies depending on the scanning resolution. If you are incorporating scanned halftones in your book, you do not need to do any further screening.

Using photographs

The original photographs can be black and white or color. If they are color, make a photocopy to check that there is sufficient contrast. For example, green letters on a red background may be one solid gray blob in black and white.

Don't be limited by assuming that people are the only photographic subjects appropriate for you book. (For one thing, prior to the mid-nineteenth century, there weren't photographs.) There are additional photographic options.

➤ Buildings such as homes, barns, churches, courthouses, stores, railroad stations, taverns, and schools
➤ Cemeteries, tombstones, and cemetery gates
➤ Signs such as historical markers, town signs, cemetery signs, and anything with the name and "established" thus-and-so year on it

Taking quality snapshots

A bit of planning before you click the shutter can greatly improve the quality of the snapshots for your book.

➢ Fill the frame. Whether you are photographing people or tombstones, get as close as your camera permits.

➢ Faces should not be in deep shadow or in bright sunlight.

➢ Look for contrast in light and dark, not color. On a tombstone you want dark letters on a light background, or vice versa.

➢ Look for—and avoid—intrusive items such as telephone poles, power lines, and automobiles.

Most camera shops and bookstores stock simple guidebooks on taking quality pictures that are a worthwhile investment.

Does it need to be cropped?

You don't need to include everything in the book that is in the original photograph. This is especially true of snapshots. You can *crop* (cut off) unwanted and distracting portions.

Decide what is really important in the picture. If the snapshot is of grandma and grandpa, crop the picture so that they fill the frame. Get rid of the picnic table, those two unidentifiable people in the background, and the corner of the family reunion sign.

Cropping accomplishes two things. It focuses attention on what is important. And for the same size illustration in the book, you can include a larger image of the subject.

In addition to snapshots of people, snapshots of tombstones and buildings are good candidates for cropping.

If the photograph is scanned, crop the picture in an image editor.

What if the printer is handling the photos?

You can indicate to the printer that you want cropping by using a tissue overlay. Cut a piece of tracing paper or tissue paper ½" taller than the photograph. Fold over the ½" and tape it to the back of the photograph with Scotch™ 811 Removable Magic™ Tape. Gently draw a rectangle on the tissue showing where you want the photograph cropped.

If you prefer, you can mount the photograph to a larger sheet and tape the tissue to that sheet instead.

A third alternative is to buy glassine envelopes at photographic or stamp supply stores and put the photograph in the envelope. This protects the photograph and also provides a place for you to identify the location in the book where the photograph belongs.

Discuss options about handling photographs with your printer before you begin the preparation.

Electronic images

When using electronic images, do not insert them into the document until near the end of the project. They increase file size considerably. This increases the time required to load, save, display, and print. However, you may want to create empty place-holders for them by inserting a single blank line of the required height, a frame, or a box.

The quality of any electronic image, whether a scanned file or clip art, is affected by the printing resolution of your printer in addition to the quality of the original. Print a properly-sized sample of any electronic image and examine it critically before deciding to include it in your family history.

The Library of Congress has begun two projects to digitize its collection of historical maps and photographs (including the Mathew Brady Civil War photographs) and to make the images available on the World Wide Web. Not all images are in the public domain, so investigate before downloading and using them in your family history (see the ILLUSTRATIONS AND ARTWORK section of RESOURCES).

At present over 200,000 items have been digitized and many more will be done before the end of this decade. The map project has just begun.

Some federal and state agencies are beginning to make present-day digital maps available to the public. Generally, you can include these in your documents (but check to be certain).

Images of documents

In YOU MUST HAVE STYLE we discussed ways of setting off transcripts of documents typographically. For a few very special documents, you may want to include an image of the document. You might get the image by scanning, taking a photograph, or a making a photocopy.

Old handwriting is difficult to read for those who haven't spent hours in front of a microfilm reader. Provide a transcript to help your readers appreciate the wording of the document.

Scanned images

If you plan on including scanned images in your family history, whether of photographs, signatures, or entire documents, learn to use image-editing software. (Some probably came with the scanner.) There are five basic tasks that you should learn (if they are available in your software). You can accomplish some of these tasks with drawing programs.

➤ *Rotation.* You may need to *rotate* an image because it was not properly aligned on the scanner.

➤ *Cropping.* You can *crop* (cut off) unwanted portions. This reduces the size of the computer file and makes it simpler to handle the image in the word processor.

➤ *Resizing.* You can *resize* the image to the production size in the image editor rather than the word processor. This makes the image simpler to handle. Calculating the proper size is explained below.

➤ *Adding borders.* The edge of a gray-scale image (which is what a scanned image is) looks slightly jagged on white paper. A one-pixel black border around the edge, especially for photographs, gives the illustration a nice, clean edge. (A *pixel* is one dot in the image.)

➤ *Adjusting contrast.* The scanned image may be too light or too dark to reproduce well. You cannot judge by its appearance on a lighted screen. Always print a sample before adjusting contrast.

Editing images

You may want to experiment with repairing or improving scanned images of damaged photographs, lichen-encrusted tombstones, mildewed documents, or power-line-draped buildings.

Be extremely judicious. Do *not* add anything to nor remove anything from any portion that provides genealogical information. You may, however, very carefully adjust contrast or blur the image in noncritical areas to focus attention on the important part.

In the following image, the mildew, paper rules, and unrelated text reduce the impact of the signatures.

Unedited—distracting background

If we completely remove these items, we risk changing the original, as in this case, where the dot over the i on the first line was lost.

Over-edited—reader can't see original

The proper method is to *push* these items to the background in order to focus on the signatures. This technique is also useful to highlight a key paragraph, sentence, or phrase when an entire page is reproduced.

About right—focus is on signatures

Consult the user's guide for instructions on masking, adjusting contrast, blurring, and other techniques.

Captions

All photographs, illustrations, and documents must have a caption explaining who, what, and when. Extra information can be provided as a note, in a special appendix, or as part of the caption (the main caption can be done in bold or italic.)

> **Will of John Jones.** The will was made on 17 May 1813 and probated 30 September 1813 in Greene County, Pennsylvania.

Captions generally go below illustrations, either centered or left justified. Centered looks better for photographs; left justified is preferred if the illustration has a number. Captions may be a single line or an entire paragraph.

Most illustrations should be documented. See HOW DO YOU KNOW? for a detailed example of why and how to document a photograph. If you don't like the idea of footnote numbers in captions, create an appendix "Notes on Illustrations." Identify each illustration (photograph, map, and so on) with the page number and the caption.

> Page 67. *Fredrik Christian Jensen and Ane Magreta Christiandatter.* They are the parents of Christina (Fredericksen) Madsen. This photograph is mounted on a stiff backing. The name . . .

Borders and frames

You can use borders, frames, and white space to set off both images and text. This extra touch can do a lot to dress up a book. Consider putting text-intensive items such as obituaries, funeral cards, and wedding announcements in some type of frame.

Simple borders such as lines of varying widths or drop shadows can be created in most word processors. Fancy borders for photographs are available as clip art. Simple white space surrounding a photograph or a document transcript also creates a framing effect (use at least ¼" of white space).

Calculating size for illustrations

The original photographs for your family history probably come in a variety of sizes and shapes. They need to be *scaled* (resized) for consistency and balance. Calculate the production size of illustrations and photographs based on the *width of the text area.* Height is the variable. The formula is:

> *book height = book width × photo height ÷ photo width*

Suppose your grandparents' wedding photograph is 8"×10". Your book has two-column 8½"×11" pages. Each column is 3½" wide, so the width of the photo in the book will be 3½".

book height = 3.5 [book width] × 10 [photo height] ÷ 8 [photo width]
book height = 3.5 × 10 ÷ 8 = 4.375"

If you are putting a border, frame, or white space around the photograph, *book width* should be the size *within* the frame.

You may need to calculate the percentage of original size also. *Ask the printer for instructions.* If you state the percentage, also include the final size to avoid any chance of misinterpretation.

percentage of original size = book width ÷ photo width

The percentage of original size for the example above is 28%.

percentage of original size = 3.5 [book width] ÷ 8 [photo width]
percentage of original size = 3.5 ÷ 8 = 28%

The same principle applies when the photograph is to be enlarged. There are wheels, scales, and charts for calculating size and reduction factors if you prefer.

If the printer is inserting the photographs, ask how the area for the photograph should be treated on the page. See Preparing Camera-Ready Art for more information on handling illustrations.

Wrapping text around an illustration

Most software has a feature that lets you flow text around an illustration. Don't use this feature on anything narrower than one-column 8½"×11" pages. Coordinating the size of the illustration, the size of the white space around it, and the spacing of the text on layouts with shorter line lengths is a balancing act requiring the skilled eye of a professional.

Wrapping text should be avoided with justified text. The white space created between words and between letters in words is simply too much.

Other graphical elements

In addition to illustrations, you can use minor graphical elements. Special characters (called *dingbats*) and clip art design elements are both decorative and useful at the end of a section or chapter or to dress up the dedication page.

See PAGE LAYOUT AND FORMATTING for additional examples.

Using the Clipboard

You can copy clip art and some drawings you create in other programs into a word processor via the Windows or Macintosh Clipboard. (In other words, you can cut, copy, and paste between documents and programs, in addition to within a program.) Sometimes this is a better alternative than saving the artwork as a separate file.

If both pieces of software support OLE (Object Linking and Embedding), you can copy more complex items and even keep them linked to the original program for future editing. Consult the user's guide.

Getting help

There are many books available on graphic design. Check libraries, book stores, and art, drafting, graphics, and photographic supply stores. Consult ILLUSTRATIONS AND ARTWORK in RESOURCES.

Checklist of illustration and graphics ideas

Photographs

☑ People (holidays and special events)

☑ Cemeteries and tombstones

☑ Houses, churches, schools, courthouses, stores, taverns

☑ Signs and markers

Maps

☑ Migration

☑ Neighborhood

Drawings

☑ Sketches from old histories

☑ Clip art

Miscellaneous

☑ Scrapbook items (announcements, invitations, clippings)

☑ Documents (wills, marriage registrations, Bible pages)

☑ Signatures

☑ Land plats

Opening the Door
to Your Book

*Genealogists enter family histories through the back door, through the
index. If a book has no index, that door is closed. If it has a poor index,
the door is open only to a selected few. If it has a thoughtful and
thorough index, the research presented in the book is available to all.*

Using an index

Think about it. What do you do when you pull a new book from
the shelf? Your thumb automatically goes to a spot about 20
pages from the back, and you flip the book open. If there is an
index, you immediately look for your ancestor's name. If the
book did not open to an index, your heart sinks a bit, but you
flip the pages, hoping you just missed it. If the index is only a
surname index, you sigh.

Suppose the index has both surnames and given names—and
there are 45 page numbers after "Jones, John." Do you check
them all? Or what if your ancestor's name isn't there, but you
suspect this might be the correct line? You might begin looking
for collateral names, locations, or activities such as Revolutionary
War Service as alternate methods to locate information.

What if your efforts draw a blank? You may flip around a bit, but
you'll soon reshelve the book—and your hand will reach
hopefully for the next volume.

Here's the bad news. Your ancestral line was in that book. It
went all the way back to the immigrant, even made an overseas
connection—and it was well-researched and well-documented.
"That's never happened to me," you're thinking, right? Well,
how do you know? We never know about what we've missed.

The greatest crime of nonexistent, poor, or inadequate indexes is that they can hide good research. Quality research is not accessible unless the book has a quality index.

Constructing an index

Informational material must be written and constructed in a way that facilitates *access* rather than reading. Most people don't *read* family histories—they *look up* things in them. But you can't be sure exactly what they'll be seeking.

The trick to facilitating access is to design not from the inside out, but from the outside in. Put yourself in the readers' shoes—and construct an index that meets their needs.

Genealogists are familiar with those needs, but all too often we forget them as we produce our own family histories. If you skipped the first section of this chapter because you already knew how to use an index, read it now. We're going to discuss facilitating that process *from the reader's perspective.*

Location and size

Indexes are located at the back of the book. That's fairly standard. If you print small booklets for each of your surnames during the research phase and generate an index for each (an excellent idea), generate *one merged* index for the final book combining all the families.

Which brings up the topic of creating separate indexes, such as different indexes for names and places, or for descendants and collateral names, or for the families of each son of the immigrant. Don't. Create one index. Otherwise the danger of the correct index being overlooked is great.

We expect genealogical publications to have fairly substantial indexes. Many variables determine the number of pages in an index—type of family history, size of pages, size of font. As an estimate, though, plan on the index being 10% of the pages in your book (slightly fewer for a three-column index).

The first page

The first page of the index is treated as a chapter title page (see Book Design). Some publishers do not keep the full amount of white space before the title because the columnar format of the index is typographically distinctive enough to set it apart from the rest of the book.

Immediately after the chapter title ("Index") comes a very important element—the *introduction* to the index. You will make many decisions while constructing your index. Some affect individual entries. Others affect a broad class of entries. You tell your reader about the broader decisions in this introduction. The text of the introduction is discussed in more detail below.

Most readers won't turn immediately to the introduction, but some do if they don't find the entry they seek. In any case, it is important that you make the introduction *very* noticeable. You can use several devices to make the introduction *pop* (grab the readers' attention).

Use typographic devices such as a different font, italics, bold, or a larger point size. Use layout devices such as white space, rules above and below or on the sides, or place the index in a box. Experiment to find a combination that works in your book.

Body of the index

Indexes are set in columns—two columns for a small-format page (5½"×8½" or 6"×9") and two or three columns for a large-format page (8½"×11"). The lines should be nonjustified, and the numbers should immediately follow the index entry (not flushright). The space between the columns can be fairly narrow, often .25".

The index should look like a part of the book. Use the same font and the same style of page headers. If the index is generated in a different font, change it before printing.

The point size for the index is always one to two points less than that of the text. For example, if your text is 11 points, try 9 points for the index; if your text is 9 points, try 8 points for the index. There should be no paragraph spacing between lines and no extra leading.

We do not worry about creating inviting white space in indexes, because people look things up in indexes, rather than reading them. The typesetting guidelines are that words and numbers should be readable, that lines and words should not blur together, and that columns should be clearly delineated.

You set some of these options in the software during the index setup or index generation process, and then the software automatically takes care of them. You may specify some of the format options as styles or manually, just as you do for regular text. Consult the user's guide.

Index

This index lists all people and all places mentioned in this book. Variant spellings for names have been conflated into single entries for the reader's convenience. Page numbers in bold are to the primary sketch on an individual. Page numbers in italics are to photographs or illustrations.

Women are listed under their maiden name and all married names. Individuals with unknown surnames are at the beginning of the index, except for individuals identified as slaves, who are listed under Slaves.

Churches, cemeteries, waterways, towns, and counties are listed under the state or country in which they are presently located.

Many additional topics are indexed. Major categories include Family, Revolutionary War, War of 1812, Civil War, and Immigrant Ancestors. Specific military battles, prisons, and units are listed under the name of the war.

Organization

A quality family history has a thorough and thoughtful index.

➤ A *thorough* index lists every name and every place. It also lists other items of interest, such as historical events, family stories, and context (see more detailed discussion below).

➤ A *thoughtful* index has a characteristic that surprises some people— it has entries that do not necessarily match the text on the page in the book. In particular, all variant spellings are *conflated* (merged), and sometimes there are entries when the proper name doesn't even appear on the page (stay tuned for more on this topic).

The easiest-to-use index is an *indented, two-level* index with *entries* organized by *main headings* and *subheadings*. An *entry* contains the *main heading* or *subheading*, any *locators* (page numbers), and any *cross-references*. A well-constructed index includes two organizational aids: *letter headings* and *continuation headings*.

The index and its entries are *generated* from *index codes* that you have *inserted* or *marked* throughout the manuscript. (The terminology varies.)

Touring an index

Let's look at an index through the reader's eyes. Along the way we'll discuss why and how the index is the way it is. The line-by-line tour begins at the abridged sample index on page 168. Like the typical reader, we'll skip the introduction and jump right into the index.

Letter heading

The first line (–?–) is a *letter heading*. These lines are typographically distinctive and serve as *indexing devices* to help the reader get quickly to the correct letter. In this sample they are centered, are in bold, have an em dash on each side of the letter, and have extra white space above them. If your software does not automatically create letter headings, add them just before you print the camera-ready art.

Unknown surnames

Entries for unknown surnames belong at the beginning of the index, where the reader is more likely to find them than at the end. Likewise, entries for unknown given names belong at the beginning of the given names. (Usually special characters and numbers sort at the beginning of the alphabet, but occasionally they end up elsewhere, and you must move them.)

You can style the unknown names as "–?–", "——", "Unknown surnames," or other options. The style used in the index need not match the style used in the chapters. For example, you can use "–" in the chapters, but "Surname not known" in the index.

Indexing requirements

As can be seen in the sample, unknown surnames occur most frequently for women. Here we have identified two of the women further with the surnames of their husbands. For the third we didn't have that information. Must you do that in your index?

There are *minimum* requirements for a good, adequate index. But there is much more that *can* be done. The decision about *how much extra* to do is up to you.

Extras are of two major classes: additional entries or something added to entries. We'll look at both minimums and extras on this tour.

In this first section, the minimum is that you must index individuals with unknown surnames. The extra is placing the woman's married name in square brackets. We used square brackets because we have another use for parentheses.

Nicknames

Our ancestors frequently were referred to by nicknames. Often these names and nicknames were quite dissimilar—Polly for Mary or Dick for Richard. The indexer cannot be certain which name a researcher or family member might look under. You have several options: you can ignore the nickname (that's acceptable for a minimal index), add the nickname after the formal name (a good extra), or create a separate entry under the nickname (an excellent extra).

For the second option, you have some style decisions. Do you want to use a "/" to separate the names or perhaps quotation marks around the nickname? (Parentheses don't work well if you are using that technique to indicate a woman's maiden name.)

Format of entries

Look at left edges of the lines the sample index on page 168. A *heading* is flush with the left margin. A *subheading* is indented. The *wrapped* line for an entry that is more than one line is indented even further. This format helps the reader find an item more quickly. The heading is the primary *indexing device* and the subheading is the secondary *indexing device*.

If your software doesn't format entries this way, you probably can change the style or formatting so that it does.

The heading or subheading is followed by a comma in this sample. Some style manuals prefer no comma. It isn't important. Stick with whatever your software generates automatically.

Page numbers

Technically, the page numbers following a heading or subheading is called a *locator*. You've probably used indexes with locators like "125n" if the reference is in a footnote or "123.45" if it is to a section number. Family histories usually don't need this.

Notice that the entry for Anne/Nanney shows page "8-13." The standard for professional indexing is that a page range indicates the topic is covered fairly continuously and "8, 9, 10, 11, 12, 13" indicates discrete, unrelated references on those pages.

Including locators for all pages that mention the person is the minimum. (However, it is acceptable to provide only the opening page number for a sketch or paragraph that continues onto a second page.)

Differentiating between the two types of page ranges is extra and is probably more than is expected by genealogists. Your software may generate discrete page numbers only, it may automatically merge them, or it may allow you to indicate when you want a page range. Using page-range format can sometimes shorten the length of an index.

Page range means "through," so the character in the middle should be an en dash. Unfortunately, some software generates this as a hyphen. It's a nice extra to replace the hyphen with an en dash in the *final* version. (But beware of hyphenated names if you do a global search-and-replace. And remember that any editing to the index itself will be lost if the index is regenerated.)

Whew! An awful lot of thought and decision-making went into those entries for three women without surnames, didn't it? Let's move on.

Style decisions—appearance

In the example, the *main heading* "Allman/Allmon" is in bold. Scanning the rest of the index, we can see that all main headings (except cross-references) are treated this way. This is a style decision related to the format (appearance) of the index. This is an extra.

Note that just the main heading, not the entire entry, is in bold. Your software may allow you to do this easily, or it may require manually formatting after the final index is generated. (This is one of those things that takes a bit of time to do, but you feel good about it afterwards.)

Style decisions—content

There are many, many style decisions to make concerning index entries. In fact, there are probably more style decisions for the content of the index than for the chapters. This is because if you are inconsistent in the style for, say, a name in a chapter, either accidentally or on purpose ("Thos. Almond" in a deed and "Thomas Allmon" in text, for example), nothing awful happens.

If that same inconsistency is between two index codes, it will generate two separate entries in the index, and you'll need to change one so that the entries will be correctly conflated. It's easier to get it right the first time.

Style sheet

During indexing, your style guide is absolutely indispensable for index codes. For the index, you may find it easiest to use a form of style guide called a *style sheet*. This is one or more sheets of paper, divided into a rough grid, with each square identified by a letter of the alphabet. This makes a convenient place for you to keep track of your indexing decisions. Here's a partial sample.

Notice that the style sheet isn't formal, it's just an organized place to jot notes to yourself. By the way, if you are getting ideas for your own index during this tour, don't forget to note them in your style guide or style sheet.

Style Sheet Index Entries for Allmon Family History	
General unknown —?— (married) women duplicate entry use birth year (year) if more that one Spell out states abbr. Co., Mt., Cem.	*See* Battle of Tippecanoe to War of 1812 Aulman to Allmon Altman to Allmon *See also* Arkansas to Missouri Terr.
A Allman/Allmon Allmon for all Anne/Nanney William use wife's name Arnett (2 t's)	*B* Barr Cyntha
C	*D*

Conflating entries

The first main heading beginning with "A" in the sample is "Allman/Allmon." That heading represents a broad range of spellings, including Aldmand, Allman, Allmon, Alman, Almand, Almon, Almond, Altman, Aulman—and a few more. We have *conflated* (merged) them to help the reader. Imagine how confusing it would be if you had to look up names under all of those entries.

We listed the two most common spellings in the heading.

Pronouns and other nameless references

Let's move on to the first subheading, "Anne/Nanney." Again, we've conflated entries for Ann, Anne, and Nanney. But none of those names appears on page 23. So why is there an index entry? On page 23 the reference is to the phrase "my wife" in a statement by Thomas Almand. There is no name on page 11 either. We indexed the pronoun "she." Both statements referred to Anne, so she deserves an index entry.

> *The purpose of an index is to get the reader to the correct page quickly and efficiently, no matter how the name is spelled, and whether or not the name itself actually appears on the page. Indexing is not a mechanical process—it is a thoughtful process.*

Dividing entries

In other words, you create an index entry whenever there is a reference to a person or place—whether that reference is explicit or implicit.

Moving on, we observe that there are two entries for Arnett Allmon. Why? The purpose of an index is to get the reader to the correct page quickly. How long will that take with the entry below? Has this happened to you?

Jones
    John, 13, 15, 16, 17, 18, 19, 29, 42, 43,
       47, 55, 70, 71, 101, 115, 116, 119,
       121, 122, 126

Would you (the reader) prefer the following?

Jones
    John, 101
    John (1708), 13, 15, 16
    John (1733), 15, 16, 17, 43
    John (1780), 47, 55, 70, 71
    John (Boston), 126
    John (minister), 18, 19, 29, 42, 43
    John (Revolutionary War records), 115,
       116, 119, 121, 122

When the number of locators for a particular heading grows to more than about 6 to 10, think about dividing them. If the references belong together, don't divide them. But in family histories we often can identify several individuals in the list and make separate entries for each.

You may select the modifier that seems most helpful. Year of birth, generation number, residence, name of spouse, and occupation are all meaningful modifiers.

You need not add modifiers for every individual. In the example above, there was one entry with no modifier. The entry "(Revolutionary War)" was to names in an appendix listing all Revolutionary War records located for the surname Jones, so further identification was neither possible nor necessary.

Jr. and Sr. are not appropriate modifiers except in the twentieth century. And while the individual numbers (1 for the progenitor and so on) would be unique modifiers, they are not at all informative to the reader using the index.

More page numbers

Look at the page numbers after "Arnett (1803)" in the sample index. Page number 32 is in bold, indicating the primary sketch on the individual. Page number 124 is in italics, indicating an illustration or photograph.

Yes, you have to index photographs. That's a minimum. Putting page numbers in bold or italic is extra. Some software lets you set the bold and italic when you create the index code.

Married women

Note that the page numbers for Allmon, Cyntha (Barr) are the same as those for Barr, Cyntha. Every married woman should have at least two entries, one under her married surname with her maiden name in parentheses, and a second under her maiden name.

There are two appropriate styles for double entries: duplicating all locators or using a *See* reference. You may choose either one.

➢ Duplicate *all* locators in both entries.

    Allman/Allmon
        Susannah (Woods), 29, 47
    Woods
        Susannah, 29, 47

As an extra, you may wish to include the married name with the maiden-name entry.

    Woods
        Susannah [Allmon], 29, 47

> Use a *See* cross-reference for one of them. The *See* reference should go from the married name to the maiden name. Cross-references are described more fully below.

> Allman/Allmon
>> Susannah (Woods). *See* Woods
> Woods
>> Susannah, 29, 47

Cross-references

The remainder of the Allmon entries contain further examples of nicknames, references to married women, and modifiers such as year of birth or the names of the wives (all three Williams were born about the same year).

Then we come to a *cross-reference*. This is an index entry that sends you to another index entry. There are two types of cross-references.

> *See* entries are used for headings that have no associated locators. It usually indicates a synonym or an alternate spelling. Do not create a *See* entry for every spelling variant. However, for any variant that is significantly different or would be removed from the principal heading by more than a few entries or a few inches, it is a service to your reader to create one.

> *See also* entries are used for headings that do have associated locators. It directs the reader to a related topic, usually a broader topic.

The format for *See* and *See also* cross-references is the same. Put a period after the heading and locators (if it is a *See also*), italicize *See* or *See also*, and then set the other heading in normal font (if it is a subheading, put the heading, a comma, and then the subheading).

In our sample index, we've used *See* cross-references for two variant spellings (Altman and Aulman) and a battle (Battle of Tippecanoe). We used a *See also* to point out that some early Arkansas references may be under Missouri Territory. Probably none of these were necessary, but they were nice extras.

Localities

At last we can switch from people to places. Don't over organize the localities. As researchers we focus on jurisdiction, particularly counties, so we usually know what county a place is in. The same isn't true for our families. Put every locality in a state under the name of the state (or country—see the entry under "France").

You may wish to add an extra modifier such as the name of the county, as we did for Mt. Zion Church.

Don't limit locality references to the names of towns and counties. Include geographic features. Include the places of everyday life—churches, schools, cemeteries, and even the family farm.

If a place reference is to a cemetery, farm, or landmark named after a family, include a duplicate entry under the surname, as was done for the Barr farm and the Wilson cemetery. Some indexers add main heading entries for almost all locality subheadings (this can greatly increase the length of an index).

Abbreviations

In this sample index, we chose to use abbreviations for Cem. and Co., but not Church, Territory, or Company. It is appropriate to use abbreviations in an index to control length. Keep careful track on your style sheet of any abbreviations you are using, both for consistency and to avoid generating split entries. If any of the abbreviations might not be familiar to your reader, mention them in the Introduction to the index.

Continuation headings

Look what happened—right in the middle of Arkansas, we ran out of room and had to go to a new column. The sample index shows a *continuation heading*. Continuation headings repeat the current *main heading* at the top of each column. This assures the reader that he or she is in the correct place.

In a family history, the entries for major surnames can easily go on for pages. If the main heading isn't continued at the top of each column, the reader must flip pages to be certain that this entry is for Joshua Jones, not Joshua Johnson.

This is technically an extra, but it should be mandatory. You must add continuation headings manually after you've generated the final index. (Most word processors don't generate them because they don't know where the column is going to end up after any manual editing that you do to the index). It only takes a few minutes and is one of the nicest things you can do.

Topics of interest

We've seen people and places thus far in this tiny sample index. We now encounter several "things"—the Battle of Tippecanoe ("the" is omitted in indexes), the War of 1812, a family reunion, twins, farm crops, and a militia unit.

Our family histories no longer are recitations of names, dates, and places. The index shouldn't be either. Which contextual items you choose to include in the index is dependent on the scope of your book and your preferences.

Introduction to the index

"Things" are the most difficult entries to code. A quick glance at a two-level index tells the reader that people are arranged by surname and that localities are arranged by state. That's fairly straightforward. But it is difficult to determine just what a stranger would look under for information about military experience or land ownership.

What can you do to help the reader? Group many entries together under a broader topic where it might catch a browsing eye. (You can put it under a specific entry, too, if you want.) Then use the introduction to the index to point out some of these major topics.

Read the introduction to our sample index to get some ideas.

The checklist for this chapter gives some ideas for topics of interest and suggests some broader categories.

When to index

It is simplest to create the index entries and generate the index from final page proofs after the writing process is completed. However, this means that you will miss out on the benefits of using the index as a research tool and the ability to test the index by using it (see below).

If you make changes to the text after you create the index, make certain that you add, change, or delete the index entries accordingly.

Testing the index

There are two ways to test an index—review it and use it. Tips for reviewing an index are given in DEVELOPING AN EDITORIAL EYE. If you have the opportunity before the final production, use the index every time you need to find something in the book. In this way, you may become aware of problems you want to correct or improvements you want to make.

The final index

Any manual formatting should be done only to the final, final, final index. (Although you should test any manual formatting on a few pages to see that your index will look like you want it.) Each time you regenerate an index, any manual formatting that you have done will be lost.

Getting help

This chapter is not a thorough guide to indexing a family history. It should be used in conjunction with the *National Genealogical Society Quarterly* article (and NGS special publication), "Indexing Family Histories," by this author and John V. Wylie (see INDEXING in RESOURCES). The article defines some standards, provides examples, and explains the process of indexing with word-processing software.

Checklist of index topics of interest

Family/Family stories/Family memorabilia

- ☑ possessions
- ☑ stories
- ☑ diaries and letters
- ☑ family gatherings

Military/name of war

- ☑ battles
- ☑ units
- ☑ prisons
- ☑ leaders
- ☑ everyday life: uniforms, weapons, disease

Frontier life/Everyday life/Home life

- ☑ food, housing, clothing, family relations
- ☑ church, school, community
- ☑ trades, crops, tools
- ☑ disease, childbirth
- ☑ other topics from the chapter on context

Immigrant experience

- ☑ list of immigrants
- ☑ names of ships
- ☑ foreign origins
- ☑ customs and traditions
- ☑ adjustment

Land

- ☑ grants, purchases
- ☑ surveying, platting, processioning
- ☑ homesteading
- ☑ records

Research

- ☑ what it's like
- ☑ types of records
- ☑ methodology and standards
- ☑ who helped

Developing an Editorial Eye

Editing a manuscript is one of the most important steps in producing a quality family history. Unfortunately, it is also the step most often shortchanged. We rarely allocate enough time for it, and first-time writers generally aren't familiar with the tasks involved.

What does an editor do?

The editor is responsible for quality assurance. In the ideal situation there is more than one editor. Someone reviews the manuscript for content. Someone reviews it for language. Someone reviews it for layout and typography. Someone proofreads the final draft. Someone checks the camera-ready art. There may be several reviewers in any of these tasks. Often the lines between tasks are blurred.

Who should edit your manuscript?

For best results, you should not be your own editor.

It is extremely difficult for even the best professional writers and editors to review their own work. It is almost impossible for the novice. *Enlist some outside help.* It will make a big difference both in the quality of the result and in the state of your sanity.

For a writer to edit his or her own work well, he or she must develop a split personality and divorce the editor from the writer. It isn't easy. But in reality, most genealogists do the majority of the editing on their own family histories, so it's necessary.

When should you edit?

You need to allocate several weeks at the end of the project for editing, production, and proofreading tasks.

You'll find this final stage considerably more efficient and less burdensome if you also have reviewed the material incrementally as you finished each section.

You'll also benefit from an intensive edit by one or more outsiders on an early chapter. Incorporate their suggestions into the remaining chapters as you write.

Getting help

Get help early. The more you expose your writing to others for comments and critiques, the better your final effort will be. Fortunately, there are many opportunities available.

➢ Write an article. Genealogists depend on articles to help us with our research. Periodical editors have a tough time finding enough quality material. What does an editor want? Basically those same standards we've been discussing throughout this book. The material also must be compatible with the types of articles the periodical publishes.

Writing an article is a good exercise in conciseness. Anything you write will be *at least* 20% too long. After you finish writing, focus on reducing the word count by 20% *before* you submit the article.

Most editors are well-qualified genealogists. Getting their comments is like hiring a professional genealogist—for free. Good editors make suggestions and/or changes to improve the article. These changes may be about content, writing style, format, or clarity. Most of them will apply to your book also.

Carefully compare the published version of the article to your first draft in order to understand what types of improvements were made. Incorporate the improvements in your book.

➢ Several societies sponsor writing contests. The discipline of structuring and writing a submission for a contest is an excellent experience that will benefit your future writing. Most contests return the judges' comments to you—another way to get the advice of topnotch genealogists and editors for free.

➢ Pair up with a research buddy and make a joint commitment that this is the year you both finish your family histories. The moral support will be great. And you can trade review time.

➤ Better yet, form a writing group. Make it a team effort. Reserve a block of time at each meeting for a round-robin review of everyone's most recent chapter. You'll develop the editing skills you need to apply to your own book, get some good ideas to incorporate into your family history, and receive helpful suggestions for improvement.

➤ Hire an editor to look at just one chapter. You can set a fixed number of hours not to be exceeded. You can ask for a list of the ten things you need to work on most. If you can't find a professional editor, hire an English teacher.

➤ Hire a professional genealogist to look at one chapter. If you've got a chapter where you are presenting a circumstantial case, find out if you make your case. Ask for overall comments on the research, presentation, documentation, and argument.

➤ Enlist the help of another family member, one who is seriously interested in making your family history a quality publication. If he or she questions something, don't be tempted to explain it—fix it in the book instead. Remember that you cannot answer questions for each and every reader.

➤ Run the grammar checker in strictest mode for at least one chapter. Make a list of ten things you need to watch for as you write future chapters.

Getting the proper attitude

Many novice writers (and a few misguided professionals) see editorial comments as negative criticism or personal attacks. They aren't. The editor is in partnership with the writer to produce a better final product. Yes, often the editor points out flaws. Sometimes these flaws are not the result of the writer's lack of knowledge or ability, but the result of a lack of distance. The editor provides the distance.

You do not have to make every change suggested by the person reviewing your work. Be aware, however, that the suggestion was made *because* there was a problem. Identify the *problem*, and then seek to eliminate it. The solution may be different from the one suggested, but some change is usually in order.

Let it get cold

Let your manuscript sit before reviewing it. One day is not enough. Two days is not enough. One week is not enough. Two weeks is the minimum amount of time that you should let a manuscript sit before reviewing it. This applies to both incremental reviews and final reviews.

As you are writing the book, don't review each chapter as you finish it. Wait until after you finish the *next* chapter. This should help you distance yourself from the people, places, dates, facts, and relationships in the review chapter.

The rule for reviewing is that the text must be completely self-contained and self-explanatory. It cannot rely on any information that resides in your head or your files. When you have just completed a chapter, you have those folks nicely organized in your brain. You won't recognize that you have forgotten to explain who the witness Thomas Taylor was, and why that is so significant. The colder the material you are reviewing, the more likely you are to spot errors and omissions.

Let software help

Actually, you've already got some outside help right at your fingertips. You have several very powerful software tools. Use them. They can help with many of the tasks performed by an editor. They don't replace the person, but do relieve some of the drudgery. Their use is covered more specifically in the steps below.

Use your style guide

Earlier we discussed your style guide as a writing and typesetting tool. It also is a critical editing tool. Refer to it often. Many outside editors ask for the style guide before beginning a review.

Editorial tasks

Editing breaks down into three basic categories.

➢ *Content.* Does this family history meet the standards set forth in the *Characteristics of a Quality Family History* at the beginning of this book? Does it meet them in general—and does it meet them in particular?

➢ *Language.* This category encompasses every boring thing you suffered through in what used to be called "English class"—spelling, grammar, punctuation, and word use.

➢ *Layout and typography.* Unlike the other two categories, this one is highly visual and ignores words. You'll find it a welcome relief after the first two.

Procedure

The best approach is to tackle the items below sequentially. Do every step individually. You will make many *complete, separate* passes through the manuscript looking for just one thing. Sometimes you will make that pass electronically; sometimes you will look at the printout.

Occasionally you'll be able to combine a *few* tasks together in one pass, but it's simply not possible to think of everything at once. By making separate passes looking for particular problems *but not reading the text,* you'll be more likely to find those problems instead of getting caught up in the words.

➢ When marking the manuscript, use a colored pen and don't be hesitant. It's easy to overlook tentative little pencil marks when entering corrections on the computer. Many editors favor red pens and comment to the writer, "Sorry, I bled all over it," when returning a manuscript.

➢ If you make a mark within the body text—adding a comma, for example—write "comma" in the margin to assure that you don't overlook it.

➢ If you mark an edit and then change your mind, don't scribble it out. Write "stet" (let it stand) instead.

Reviewing for content

Put on your genealogist hat. Pretend this family history is about your family—but you have a totally different theory about who is descended from whom. How does it measure up? Is it truly a quality family history?

➢ Are most of the citations to original sources rather than to other compiled genealogies?

➢ Is it easy to follow a line up or down? Begin with the youngest son of the youngest son and follow that line as a test.

➢ Does the book use one of these numbering systems: pedigree, Register, or NGSQ?

➢ Is there a note number following every fact? If there is one per sentence or paragraph, can you tell which source in the note goes with which fact? Is every relationship documented?

➢ Are weak links identified as such?

➢ Does it tell about the people—or is it merely research notes?

Read the book

Read your book as if you'd never seen it before. Ask yourself:

➤ Is this book worth printing?
➤ Would I buy it?
➤ Would I show it to a good genealogist?
➤ Can I wholeheartedly recommend it to someone else?

Tips for reviewing content and organization

➤ Read just the headings. Are they all about the same level of detail? Are they helpful for finding your way around?

➤ Read just the first sentence of each paragraph. Remember topic sentences in English class? Does the sentence introduce the contents of the paragraph?

➤ If your software has an outline feature, use it to get an overview of the organization.

➤ If you are maintaining the individuals in a computer database that has a problem-alert feature, run that option. Carefully review your *research* for any marriage before age 21 or after age 30, every birth less than one year after marriage (or before), every death after age 70, and any births when the mother was under 21 or over 40.

Check the index

As you edit and review your manuscript, always use the index when you need to check another section instead of flipping pages. Usage is the best test for an index. (See OPENING THE DOOR TO YOUR BOOK for guidelines on indexing.)

➤ Does the *introduction to the index* describe all the conventions used in creating the index? Does it point the reader toward the major topics? Is it visually distinctive enough that it catches the attention of the reader?

➤ Check every female name in the index. For every married woman, there should be at least two entries. Use a highlighter to mark them off. If duplicate page entry style is used, does every pair match? Any remaining unhighlighted female name should be for a single woman (or one whose husband is not identified in the book).

It's tempting to save the index-checking for the very end (or, even worse, omit it entirely), but often this step highlights problems with either the research or the text, so it should be done earlier.

➤ Look at any entries with more than, say, 6 to 10 page references. Is there an appropriate way to divide them? (Does a name entry refer to more than one person, for example?)

➤ Look for entries that should be conflated.

➤ Are there additional places where a *See* or *See also* entry would be helpful? Check every existing *See* or *See also* entry to assure that it is not a dead end or an endless loop.

➤ If this is the camera-ready art, check that column continuation headings such as "Smith (continued)" have been added—and that they haven't migrated to the bottom of the previous column or down a line or two.

Reviewing for language

Before beginning an edit for language, review the chapters YOU MUST HAVE STYLE and WRITING.

There are two dangers in being your own editor. One is that you know what the text is *supposed* to say. The second is that if you-the-writer didn't know the correct grammar or punctuation, you-the-editor won't either.

If you force yourself to concentrate on each sentence individually as a structure rather than something with meaning, you can help overcome the first. Also, many errors of grammar and punctuation are actually typos, the result of cut-and-paste commands, rewriting sentences, or fingers typing independently of your brain.

Tips for reviewing for language

Pretend that you've never seen a word of your manuscript before. We speak of "changing to our editor's hat," but changing eyes and brain may be more like it. That's not an easy thing to do. Here are some tricks to detach yourself from the text.

➤ *Use a file card.* Try this trick when editing for content and meaning. Begin at the beginning. Place a blank 5"×7" file card below the first sentence. Read the sentence. If it's OK, move the card to below the second sentence. Do *not* slide the card as you are reading—you'll get caught up in the flow. The point is to consider each sentence alone on its own merits.

➤ *Read backwards.* This is the best way to edit for grammar, punctuation, and typos, especially for the inexperienced editor. Begin at the back of the book. Examine the last sentence. If it's OK, examine the next-to-the-last sentence. And so on. Go through sentence-by-sentence—not paragraph-by-paragraph—so you don't fall into the trap of reading for meaning when you're supposed to be focusing on grammar, punctuation, and typos.

> *Ignore body text.* It's tempting to focus on the text when editing, but mistakes seem to occur disproportionately often in places such as page headers, headings, captions, and front matter. Make one full pass looking at *everything but* the body text for spelling errors, typos, and formatting errors.

> *Print a manuscript draft.* Many people (both professionals and first-time writers) find it difficult to review a copy that is in the final format because it looks "good" or "final." Do you have this problem? If you have used paragraph styles as recommended in PAGE LAYOUT AND FORMATTING, the solution is simple.

Make a duplicate copy of your files in another directory. Change the page size to 8½"×11" with 1.5" margins. Change the font to a fixed pitch font (like Courier New in 8 points) and the line spacing to 1.5 or 2 lines in all styles. Print. You'll have an old-fashioned, "typed" manuscript to edit, with plenty of space for editorial comments.

Software help for language checking

Use your software to help with spelling and grammar.

> Print out your custom dictionary. Look it over (with real dictionary at hand) and make sure that you didn't click Add when you meant Change. If it contains errors, consult the user's guide on editing the dictionary.

> Run the spell checker on every chapter. Don't forget the introduction, acknowledgments, list of illustrations, and *all* other pieces of text you created.

> Run the grammar checker. If you ran a strict edit on one chapter, you have a good idea of which errors it can help you find. Set the appropriate level of difficulty or create a custom level.

Occasionally you'll be offered a bit of humor, as when one grammar checker gently suggested to the genealogist that she find a less gender-specific term for "maiden name."

> When you find an error, use the search feature to locate any other occurrences of the same error. Some word processors or operating systems let you search multiple files for text strings. If so, use it each time you find an error and correct it in all files immediately. (If you cannot search across files, keep a list of errors. When there are half a dozen items on the list, check and correct the other files.)

For example, suppose you have trouble with "which" and "that." Search all documents for "which," assuring yourself that the phrase is indeed optional and that you did put in the commas. Then make a second pass through all documents for "that," which identifies a mandatory phrase with no commas.

Use the search options such as case, font, or style to optimize searching. Suppose you intended each family to begin with a heading "The Family of John Jones and Mary Smith" but you discover that you omitted "The Family of" from some headings. If you search for FamilyHead style or "space-and-space" in bold, you can scan every heading quickly, fixing problems as you go.

Grammar and spelling

Before you begin, make a list of about ten things that you think you should keep your eyes open for, including the following:

➤ Check for people *did* and documents *do*. Here's a shortcut. Search for "marries," "dies," "moves," "buys," "sells," and "signs." These are common people-verbs should be past tense ("married," "died," etc.).

Once you've fixed the people-verbs, search for "said," "noted," "recorded," "described" and "reported." Those often should be present-tense document-verbs.

➤ Read a few passages. Are the sentences too long? Do they contain meaningless phrases or phrases that could be replaced with more concise terminology? Use the grammar checker to find long sentences. Use the search feature to weed out colloquial phrases.

➤ If you have problems with subject-verb agreement, try this trick. Go through the manuscript and underline just the subject (noun or pronoun, no modifiers) and just the verb (no adverbs or modifiers). (Use a different color pen than you are using for editing.) Say each subject-verb pair out loud. You should catch most of the problems this way.

➤ Split infinitives and split verbs are no longer considered incorrect, but the sound of them annoys many traditionalists. If split infinitives drive you nuts, you can search for "space-to-space," but be forewarned, it takes a while.

➤ Eliminate erroneously hyphenated words beginning with *re, non,* or *multi* by searching all documents for "re-," "non-," and "multi-."

➤ Check that relationships are correctly spelled and hyphenated: "great-great-grandmother," "great-aunt," "grandniece," and "brother-in-law."

➤ If you have a grammar guide with a section on common usage errors, review it for any that apply to you. Use the search feature to locate any occurrences.

Punctuation

When you review for punctuation, envision the sentence as parts of speech, not meaningful words.

➤ If a sentence begins with "If" or "When," you almost always need a comma following the clause before the main part of the sentence begins. See this paragraph and the preceding one for examples. Use the search feature to search for "If" and "When."

➤ Keep your eyes open for any series that does not follow your style for using a comma before *and* or *or*. If this is a problem for you, it is worthwhile to do a software search for "space-and-space" and "space-or-space" and really focus on it.

➤ Use the search feature to locate plain hyphens that should be en dashes, em dashes, or nonbreaking hyphens.

➤ Search for ")" and confirm that the punctuation is inside the parentheses if they enclose a complete sentence (with a capital letter at the beginning) and outside otherwise.

➤ Use the software to scan for mismatched pairs: parentheses, square brackets, quotation marks, and em dashes. That's seven searches in all—once each for (,), [,], ", ", and —.

➤ Watch for commas with compound sentences (should be there) and compound verbs (shouldn't be there). Watch for unmatched commas with parenthetical elements. There's no automated way to scan for these.

➤ Commas are often mismatched, but the only pairs you can scan for effectively are before and after the year in formal dates and before and after the name of a state following a town or county.

➤ Search each chapter for your personal most-common-error list.

Style and typos

Review your style guide before beginning this step to refresh your memory as to the numerous style decisions you made. (The first time you produce a family history, you will refer repeatedly to your style guide for spelling, punctuation, typographic, and layout decisions. As you continue writing, many of those decisions will become second nature to you, and you'll need to refer to the style guide less frequently.)

➤ Check the *book title* everywhere it occurs: cover, spine, title page, copyright page, left page headers, and anywhere else you used it. Make certain that all occurrences match, that all the words are there, that they are spelled correctly, and that they are capitalized correctly.

➤ Check the *chapter title* everywhere it occurs: table of contents, first page of the chapter, right page headers, any cross-references, and anywhere else you used it. Make certain that all occurrences match, that all the words are there, that they are spelled correctly, and that they are capitalized correctly.

➤ Scan quickly for dates. They should all be the correct style. Use the search feature to scan for "Dec-space" or "December," whichever is *incorrect*. If the style varies between, say, body text and notes, use search parameters such as style name or point size.

While you're looking at dates, check to see that you've included modifiers such as "circa," "say," and "calculated" where appropriate.

➤ Review your decisions on abbreviations and search for items that don't match your style.

➤ Search for "0's" to assure that you have typed 1860s instead of 1860's.

➤ Search for "centur" (to find both singular and plural) and check that you consistently followed your style for "18th century" versus "eighteenth century." And while you're there, make sure the words are hyphenated when modifying a noun.

➤ Check for more than one space between sentences. Use the search feature to ferret out the pesky things. It's very difficult to see them on the screen, and even if you usually type only one between sentences, they'll sneak in other places during cut-and-paste operations.

➤ Search for the space-period or space-comma that sometimes remains after a cut-and-paste.

➤ Verify that the page numbers run consistently through the entire book.

Reviewing for layout and typography

In the traditional publishing cycle, an editor was responsible for marking all the text for typographic treatment and then checking it. A proofreader often verified the manuscript against the typeset copy. Each change in typeface, point size, and leading had to be entered separately, so it was necessary to review carefully for typesetting errors.

If you have used paragraph and text styles, however, this task is fairly superficial.

Tips for reviewing for layout

To review for layout, you need to ignore the words. You might find this easier to do if you can't read the words.

➤ Use the page view or print preview to flip quickly through pages looking for layout and formatting problems such as widows and orphans, pages too long or too short, and awkward page breaks.

➤ Review the layout with the pages at a distance where the words are out of focus. Try laying the pages on the floor. Back off or squint until you can't see the words.

Check the camera-ready art

Although you can review for problems with layout and format during a preliminary review, you must check every page of the camera-ready art very carefully.

➤ Examine every offset (indented) extract, transcript, or quotation for font, point size, text style, amount of indent, space above and space below. If you have used a style to define these attributes, everything should be fine, but double-check the white space before and after. Depending on the style of preceding or following paragraphs, you may need to adjust this manually.

➤ Look at every heading on every page. White space is most likely to be too much or too little above and below headings and other types of section breaks.

➤ Check the illustrations. Are they located where they'll be useful? Maps and charts should be located before or near the beginning of the related text. Do they have interesting and meaningful captions? Is the heading at the left for any extra-wide illustrations placed *broadside* (sideways)?

➤ How is the overall balance of white and black? With the pages spread out on the floor, you should get an impression of balance. The page heading should not merge into the text, nor float lonesomely far away. Section breaks should be readily apparent from white space, special graphics, or the next heading.

➤ Get a little closer to the pages, but do not read. Look down the *left* edge of every line. The indents should all be even. There should be no sense of jaggedness or waviness. Keep an eye open for oddities such as a special character or punctuation beginning a line.

➤ Now look at the *right* edge of every line. If the text is nonjustified, look for a lot of white at the end of a line (called *deep rag*). You may need to hyphenate a long word or *recast* (reword) the sentence. You might want to watch for odd silhouettes formed by the right edge.

Watch for weird line breaks at special characters like en dashes and em dashes, especially in notes. Look for dangling numbers at the end of a line (between the day and month, for example).

➤ Still at a distance, look for bad flow such as rivers and stacked words. A *river* is white space that creates a flowing pattern within a paragraph. Sometimes the same word or phrase appears in the same position on two or three lines in a row. This is distracting and makes it easy for the reader to get lost.

➤ In justified text look for word spacing and letterspacing too wide or too narrow.

➤ Check for consistency between chapters. Lay the first page of each chapter side-by-side and compare to ensure that they are all formatted identically. Compare the format of the page headers in each chapter.

Widows, orphans, and other bad breaks

Widows and orphans are lonesome lines. This generic phrase covers two potential problem areas. Whether or not you fix them depends on how much they bother you and how much the changes would affect the flow of the text elsewhere.

➤ The last line of a paragraph—especially a short line—that appears by itself at the top of a page looks lonely. Short-line orphans at the top of a page should always be fixed. Some editors say longer-line orphans are acceptable if they do not interfere with readability.

➤ If the last line of any paragraph is very short (only one word), many (but not all) editors fix it also.

Some software lets you set widow and orphan control. In this case the software automatically adjusts the page break, which usually creates an uneven bottom margin. That's OK, the reader doesn't notice.

Professional writers and editors generally prefer to eliminate widows and orphans by rewriting the paragraph (or a previous one) to change the line count.

Professional typesetters minutely adjust paragraph spacing, line spacing, word space, or letterspacing throughout the paragraph or page to make the adjustment.

Watch for other types of bad breaks.

➤ Do not allow headings to be separated from the first line of the associated text. Set the keep-with-next parameter in the paragraph style for headings. Some editors prefer to keep at least two lines of body text with any heading.

➤ Avoid leaving introductory paragraphs (such as the parent-child transition or the introduction to a quotation) at the bottom of a page.

➤ In fact, if only a few lines of the beginning or ending of a section appear on a page, see if a better arrangement is possible.

➤ Closing elements such as the graphic used to separate sketches should not fall at the top of a page.

➤ The last page of a chapter should have at least four or five lines of text on it, preferably more.

Making corrections

A thoroughly edited page can be filled with a jumble of marks. As you edit, you may decide that there are so many marks on a page that you can't follow it. It's time to enter corrections and reprint the pages before continuing. As you enter each correction, check it off. (Use a different color pen than the one you used for editing.)

As you finish the changes to a paragraph, stop and read the paragraph before continuing. It is very easy to introduce new errors into the text when making changes. In particular, look for "leftover" words that don't belong, subject-verb disagreement, and problems with tense.

Reprint the pages and continue your editing.

Revision-tracking

You may prefer to make all of the changes and then review the revised text. Some word processors offer *revision-tracking* features. Revision-tracking can keep track of changes as you make them within a document, using color or markings to highlight added or deleted text.

You can view the differences on-screen or print them. The revision-tracking feature can, instead, compare an old version of a file with the current one and highlight the changes. Consult the user's guide for more information.

Getting help

Once again, we should highly recommend that you not be the only person to review your copy. No matter how hard you try, you cannot completely put yourself in the shoes of your reader.

This chapter is not self-contained. It must be used in conjunction with the other chapters in this book. The style manuals in RESOURCES contain additional information and suggestions on reviewing and editing.

Checklist for reviewing layout

Chapter

- ☑ No page heading on first page
- ☑ Space above and below title is consistent for all chapters
- ☑ Font, point size, style of title is consistent for all chapters
- ☑ Chapter title matches right page headings in chapter/section
- ☑ Chapter title matches Table of Contents
- ☑ Begins on right-hand (odd) page
- ☑ Page number is correct

Headings and subheadings

- ☑ Font/point size
- ☑ Spacing
- ☑ Capitalization
- ☑ Wording

Body text

- ☑ Font/point size
- ☑ Spacing

Quotations

- ☑ Font/point size
- ☑ Spacing
- ☑ Indentation

Child information

- ☑ Font/point size
- ☑ Spacing
- ☑ Indentation
- ☑ Tabs

Illustrations

- ☑ Vertical position
- ☑ Horizontal position
- ☑ Caption: appearance, wording, source

Preparing
Camera-Ready Art

The person who prepares the camera-ready art must be virtuous:
prepared, clean, neat, organized, thorough, and careful. This stage
should not be rushed.

What is camera-ready art?

Camera-ready art (also called *camera-ready copy, final art,* or *final*
copy) is what you deliver to the person who is going to print your
book. Camera-ready art is a clean copy of every page in the book,
just as you expect it to appear in print (with the possible
exception of photographs or special illustrations to be inserted
by the printer).

Steps involved

There are only a few steps in preparing camera-ready art, but they
will take some time. Don't let yourself rush through this stage.

1. Create a clean environment.

2. Print every page of your book.

3. Add sheets for any blank pages or special pages.

4. Prepare a page guide.

5. Check page numbering and count pages.

6. Review every page of your book.

7. Paste up illustrations.

8. Write any special instructions.

9. Package the camera-ready art for delivery.

Step 1: Create a clean environment

Book printing begins with making a photographic negative of your camera-ready art (see Turning Camera-Ready Art into Books). The camera will pick up any stray marks or dirt that is on the paper, so cleanliness is important.

Don't try to assemble camera-ready art on your desk. Use a table. A separate surface is much easier to keep clean and organized.

Clear the table top and thoroughly wash it and your hands with soap. Remove colored fingernail polish, which can leave streaks (the camera sees red as black). Keep food and drink away from the table. Wash any rulers or triangles that you will be using.

Quality printing

The quality of your *printer* and the quality of the *paper* you use will have a significant impact on how good your book looks.

Laser printers

The quality, resolution, and flexibility of scalable fonts and laser printers achieved publishing quality several years ago. They have continued to improve. The *resolution* of a laser printer describes how many dots it is capable of printing in an inch (*dpi*). However, this measurement is not absolute. The quality can vary considerably between printers with the same nominal dpi.

300-dpi laser printers vary from fair to excellent in the quality of the text they produce. For halftones and line art, however, they range only from fair to good. 600 dpi printers provide a significant improvement for artwork. Today, 1800 dpi laser printers are available, but with a substantial price tag. The future will undoubtedly see some of the technology in these production-quality printers appearing in lower-cost personal printers.

To evaluate the quality of a laser printer for text, look at the smoothness of the curve of a 24-point capital C. To evaluate the quality for halftones (if you have scanned photographs for inclusion), print the darkest photograph you will be using. To evaluate for line art, print a sample and look for jagged lines.

If you do not own a good laser printer, you may want to consider using a service bureau or DocuTech to produce the camera-ready art (see Options from Technology).

Paper

You can print drafts on the least expensive paper that your printer accepts, but when it comes to the camera-ready art, you must use a top quality laser paper.

The paper should be 60-pound paper rather than 20-pound paper (the weight is measured according to two different systems) and will cost several dollars more for a package of 500 sheets—a worthwhile expenditure. Hammermill Papers makes two papers (LaserPrint and LaserPlus) that are widely available at present. Check at office supply and computer stores for other brands.

Ink-jet printers

Ink-jet printers allow the same font flexibility as laser printers. However, the text printing quality from an ink-jet printer is considerably lower than that of a laser printer, even when the *dpi* numbers (see above) are the same. (Look at the fuzziness around the edges of individual letters and splattering effects.)

It is therefore especially important that you print the final copy on the highest-quality ink-jet paper you can obtain. This special paper helps minimize spattering or bleeding as the jet of ink sprays onto the paper.

Color ink-jet printing

If you have a color ink-jet printer and you are self-printing just a few copies of your book for your family (see OPTIONS FROM TECHNOLOGY), you may want to use color to dress it up.

Ink-jet colors are subject to serious fading and alteration. The manufacturers are working to improve this situation, and there has been improvement, but it still isn't satisfactory in the long-term.

For most things you print, longevity isn't a concern, but you certainly hope your family history will be around for a while. Follow these suggestions:

➢ The problem is worsened by light, heat, and humidity. Avoid them. Light is the worst offender.

➢ Never leave the pages in direct sunlight. (You may lay them out to dry to avoid smearing, but put them away when they are dry.)

➢ If you are printing a self-cover, don't use color on it. Save the color for the inside title page.

➤ Avoid using color on every page just to use color. For example, don't put the name of every direct ancestor in red. But by all means, use it where appropriate, such as maps and family photographs.

➤ If you are including scanned photographs, you may want to print those pages separately on a high quality clay-coated paper (available at most computer and office stores) to get really sharp images.

Step 2: Print every page of your book

In BOOK DESIGN we discussed the many parts of a book. Review that chapter now to be sure that you have created a document for each part of your book.

Print the pages and stack them in order.

Step 3: Add sheets for any blank or special pages

If you have planned any blank pages in your book such as the back of the dedication or the left-hand page facing a new chapter, put a blank sheet of paper in for that page. Add a blank sheet for any blank pages at the back of the book, too.

We mentioned above that the camera sees red as black. There is a color of blue that it sees as white. You can buy pencils and pens in "nonrepro (nonreproducible) blue" or "nonphoto blue." Write "page iv blank" or "page 84 blank" in *nonrepro blue* on each blank page. Mark the page number of unnumbered pages in nonrepro blue.

You may also have some special pages, such as drop-in pages for photographs, that will be done by the printer. Add sheets for these pages and write the page number and an explanation in nonrepro blue. (Theoretically, you could write these in black, but the printer is more apt to notice the nonrepro blue.)

Step 4: Prepare a page guide

Use a word processor or spreadsheet software to create a page-by-page listing of your book. This serves two purposes.

➤ A page guide helps keep *you* organized. Use it to check that you have prepared all the pages and that they are in order.

➤ A page guide helps avoid any confusion *at the printer*. If the printer makes a mistake but you have given them a good page guide, you are in a much better position to complain.

Look at the sample page guide below for a 160-page book. That's ten 16-page signatures (see TURNING CAMERA-READY ART INTO BOOKS). Notice that there are 160 pages, but the last numbered page is 154. That is because the six pages of front matter are numbered in a separate, roman-numeral sequence (see BOOK DESIGN and PAGE LAYOUT AND FORMATTING).

Parentheses around a page number indicate that the number does not actually appear on the page. Each chapter begins on a right-hand, odd page. There are also notations for photographs to be placed by the printer.

	page number	page count	photographs
title page	(i)	1	
copyright page	(ii)	2	
Table of Contents	iii	3	
List of Illustrations	iv	4	
Acknowledgments	v	5	
blank	(vi)	6	
Introduction	1	7	
	2	8	
	3	9	*Ann Adams*
blank	(4)	10	
Chapter 1: Adams Family	5	11	
	6	12	
	7	13	*Andy Adams*
	8	14	
Chapter 2: Armstrong Family	9	15	
. . .	. . .	. . .	. . .
Index	151	157	
	152	158	
	153	159	
	154	160	

The number of pages printed by the printer is determined by the number of pages in a *signature*, not by the number of pages that you provide (see TURNING CAMERA-READY ART INTO BOOKS). The most common signature size for family histories is 16 pages, but check with your printer.

You pay for all pages, blank or otherwise, so you might as well use them. The page guide will alert you if you are printing on only 1 page of a 16-page signature, for example, in which case you might remove some text to reduce the page count by 1 and reduce printing costs or use the blank pages for additional charts and maps or information on ordering your book.

Step 5: Check page numbering and count pages

After you have printed all pages, turn off the computer and sit down at the work table. Turn every sheet, checking that the page numbers are correct and that everything is in agreement with the page guide.

Step 6: Review every page of your book

In Developing an Editorial Eye we listed a number of things that you should look for in reviewing and editing. Corrections and last minute changes can have unexpected ramifications on later pages. With the computer still off, repeat the review steps from that chapter related to layout and typography.

If you find any corrections that need to be made, do so very carefully. When you print the page, confirm that the correction did not change the pagination (the last word on the page should still be the same). Then carefully *discard* the old page and *replace* it with the new page.

After you have completed all corrections and replaced all pages, repeat the step Check page numbering and page counts above. This is very important. Many of the problems with camera-ready art occur as a result of a little mistake in placing a corrected page.

Step 7: Paste up illustrations

If you have maps, clip art, borders, photographs, or other illustrations that need to be pasted onto the pages, do so after you have reviewed all the printed pages.

Work on one page at a time. Each illustration should be placed squarely. This means that the horizontal and vertical edges must be parallel to the top and sides of the paper. Buy an inexpensive triangle (they are sold with other school supplies at most stores).

Align one edge of the triangle with the side of the paper. Slide it until the other edge is positioned where the base of the illustration should go. Use a well-sharpened nonrepro-blue pencil to draw the line. This makes it easy to keep photographs and other illustrations from looking askew.

If it is necessary to trim the illustration, use a straight edge and blade, not scissors. Trim the illustration squarely, using the triangle for a guide.

If you have pages with many illustrations or photographs, you may want to investigate layout boards or layout paper (available at drafting-supply stores). They look like graph paper with the lines in nonrepro blue.

In the past, many graphics artists mounted illustrations using rubber cement. This is messy and attracts dirt. Next came spray adhesives, which get all over and aren't environmentally friendly.

Then Scotch™ came out with 811 Removable Magic™ Tape, the neatest thing since sliced bread, especially for those of us who didn't have access to a paste-up person and had to place our own illustrations. Like their Post-it™ notes, this tape peels off of paper. So if you don't get the illustration aligned squarely the first time or you discover a typographical error on the page, no problem, just peel up the illustration and start over.

The tape (look for a *blue* box) also peels off the illustration and photographs. However, you should apply it to a minimum amount of the illustration or photograph and be *very* careful when removing it from the artwork.

If the tape is over printing, smooth it firmly. If you must remove it, some of the print will come off on the tape. Discard the tape and reprint the page before reattaching the illustration.

You want to avoid a shadow at the edge where the illustration is attached to the paper. Carefully smooth the tape all the way around the illustration. The edge is more likely to make a shadow on photocopied pages than on printed pages because of the process used to create negatives (see TURNING CAMERA-READY ART INTO BOOKS).

Step 8: Write any special instructions

If the printer is setting the type for the cover, type a page that clearly states the text for the front cover, the spine, and the back cover (see TURNING CAMERA-READY ART INTO BOOKS).

If the printer is *tipping in* (inserting) oversized maps or charts, write an instruction page about the positioning and placement.

Photographs and illustrations handled by the printer

Preparing photographs for publication was discussed in ILLUSTRATIONS, CHARTS, AND PHOTOGRAPHS and TURNING CAMERA-READY ART INTO BOOKS. If the printer is handling the incorporation of the photographs into your book, you need to be very specific in your discussions about how the photographs should be supplied, how they should be labeled, how they should be marked for correlation with the text, and how the text should be marked for correlation with the photographs.

You also should have confirmed how the area for the photograph should be treated on the printed page. Does the printer want it completely blank, a border showing the correct size and location, or a solid black rectangle? (Print the black rectangle only on the camera-ready art, it uses up a cartridge too quickly.)

Step 9: Package the camera-ready art for delivery

Check the pages against the page guide one more time to assure that none have gotten out of order. The pages must be arranged neatly *in order*, and must include *every* page. Check the captions against any illustrations you have placed, to assure that there was no mix up.

Put the pages in a stationery box or put a piece of cardboard before and after the pages and secure with a rubber band. Write your name, address, phone number, book title, and name of the sales representative on the box or cardboard.

What to send with the art

There are two types of aids that you might send to the printer with the camera-ready art.

➤ A page guide as described above (recommended).

➤ A sample of the book (sometimes called a *go-by*), copied double-sided and placed in a three-ring binder. If you are including illustrations or photographs that the printer will place by hand, you can write special instructions on this copy.

Usually a page guide is sufficient. Go-bys aren't usually prepared for the printer, but they can be especially helpful if you have many unnumbered pages, used a nonstandard numbering system, or have many special items to be handled by the printer.

You may feel much safer if you can hand-deliver the camera-ready art to the printer or the printer's representative rather than mailing it, especially if photographs are involved, but follow your printer's suggestions.

Expectations

You don't have to do everything suggested in this chapter. However, most of the suggestions are here because they *weren't* done at some time—and a problem resulted. Printing houses specializing in family histories deal with first-time publishers constantly, with very few problems. But problems do occur, and anything you can do to forestall them is worthwhile.

Getting help

Ask other genealogists who have prepared family histories about their experiences. Ask for any tips they may have. (Don't be dismayed by any horror stories you hear, but use them as lessons on problems to avoid.)

Ask your printer exactly what is expected, especially in regard to photographs. Each printer has a certain way of doing things, and the more you are in sync with that way, the more smoothly things will go.

Checklist of preparing camera-ready art

- ☑ Buy 811 tape, triangle, nonrepro-blue pencil
- ☑ Create a clean environment
- ☑ Print the pages
- ☑ Add and label blank pages
- ☑ Prepare a page guide
- ☑ Check page numbering and count pages
- ☑ Review printed pages
- ☑ Paste in illustrations
- ☑ Label photographs and illustrations
- ☑ Write special instructions
- ☑ Provide text for cover
- ☑ Count pages again
- ☑ Package securely

Turning
Camera-Ready Art
into Books

The printer is responsible for taking the camera-ready art you provide and turning it into books. As a self-publisher, one of your major tasks is to select the printer to print your book. You also must decide the size, paper stock, and binding method to be used.

Who will print your book?

Printing books is a process with many variables—most of which can go wrong. One of the purposes of this book is to help minimize the problems that may be encountered between the genealogical author (especially the first-time author) and the printer.

Two key factors to consider in selecting a printer are access and confidence. You must be comfortable that you have been able to communicate your specifications precisely, and you must be comfortable that the printer can and will deliver quality work. Recommendations from satisfied customers is the best way to ascertain quality.

If you are dealing with a printing house, you will probably meet with a sales representative who can answer many of your questions. If the printing house is in your area, ask for a tour. They can usually arrange it, and you will have a much better idea of why and how the process works. Sections at the end of this chapter discuss getting a cost quote and spending your money where it counts.

Short-run printing

One of the problems we face as genealogical writers and publishers is that we really don't want to print very many books. While 200 books may seem like a lot to you, most printers consider anything under 5,000 or 10,000 books *short-run* printing, and they don't want to do it. They aren't set up to handle short runs, especially those requiring lots of special handling such as that needed for family histories with many photographs.

Types of printers

The need for short-run printing generally leaves you with one of three options: a printing house specializing in small print runs for genealogists, a local offset printer, or a local copy shop.

The printing and binding equipment, processes, and options vary considerably between these three classes of printers, and between individual vendors within each class. (Detailed explanations of printing and binding methods and processes are found later in this chapter.)

➢ A *printing house.* There are several printing houses that specialize in short-run printing for genealogists. These companies often are vendors at larger workshops and conferences and have ads in genealogical publications. (Note: Some printing companies have "publishing" in their name, but they do not market nor distribute books. They only print books.)

If you want a hard-cover, smyth-sewn book, use a printing house. Generally, they print between 250 and 500 copies of a book. Most also do soft-cover, perfect-bound books.

The best way to locate a good printer is to ask genealogists who have published books to give you their personal recommendations. To locate a printer, see PRINTERS in RESOURCES for a source that lists book manufacturers for print runs of at least 250 copies.

➢ A *local offset printer.* Offset-printing shops reproduce pages using offset presses, which produce better quality printing than photocopying. Photographs, especially if *screened*, reproduce better by offset printing than by photocopying.

They can do saddle-stitch (stapled) binding and may be able to offer perfect binding, perhaps by subcontracting to another vendor. They can do short runs, such as 50 to 500 copies.

Major metropolitan areas also have larger offset printing businesses that cater to the business customer. Usually they can provide everything in-house that the printing houses can except hard-cover binding.

Some large printing and reprographics companies are now offering DocuTech printing, which takes advantage of computer files and xerographic processes (see OPTIONS FROM TECHNOLOGY).

➢ *A local copy shop.* Photocopying is the method most often used for very short runs. Through photocopying you can make as few as 2 or 3 copies if you choose. Reprints are easy and relatively inexpensive. Binding methods available may include GBC binding, spiral binding, Velo-Binding, and *saddle stitching* (stapling).

Understanding signatures

Printing houses use large presses that print in signatures. A *signature* is the number of pages of a book that a printing press prints on a large piece of paper at one time. Most books are published in signatures of sixteen pages (eight pages on one side of the paper and eight pages on the other).

To understand signatures, try this:

1. Take a plain sheet of 8½"× 11" paper and fold it in half across, making it 8½"×5½".

2. Fold it again, making it 5½"×4¼".

3. Repeat once more. Your paper should now be 2¾"×4¼".

4. Pretend that your folded paper is a book, and number the front page 1, the second page 2, and so on until you reach page 16. (Don't worry about neatness as you try to number inside the folds.)

5. Unfold the paper. Notice the pattern of the page numbers on both the front and back of the paper. They don't even face the same way.

6. Refold the paper and staple it inside the last fold.

7. Trim off the top, bottom, and side edges.

You have just made one saddle-stitched signature. This exercise helps you understand the printing processes described below.

The printing process at a printing house

The explanation below is generalized. Each printing house, each press within the printing house, and each job has some variations, but this explanation is sufficient for you to understand the printing process in general. Note also that terminology varies within the industry.

The process begins when you deliver the *camera-ready art (final copy)* to the representative of the printer. This may include photographs or special illustrations that are to be inserted by the printer.

There are three stages to the printing process.

➢ Prepress
➢ Printing
➢ Binding

Prepress

Much of the work of the printer takes place before the printing begins and is called *prepress*. The prepress process includes creating a film negative of your camera-ready art, inserting photographs, and then creating a plate from the negative, as described below.

The printing house takes a black-and-white photograph of the pages. Each page is pressed tightly between sheets of glass before the image is snapped. This helps avoid shadows from glued-on artwork.

They then print *film negatives*. Someone carefully examines the film negative on a light table to be certain that no dirt or lint on the original has caused spots or imperfections in the negative. If any are found, they either fix them or reshoot the film.

Next, they take the negatives of eight of the pages, trim them down, and *register* (align) and *imposition* (arrange) them on a large table according to the pattern you observed when you unfolded your sample signature above. They carefully *strip* (tape) the page negatives together.

The large eight-page negative is used to make a *plate*. It is this plate that is mounted on the printing press.

Some vendors use *metal plates*, while others use *paper* or *polyester plates*. Metal plates are durable, crisp, and provide excellent *halftones* (photographs and shading). Paper plates are much less expensive, but do not hold up well under long runs, and produce muddier half-tones. However, for text-only print runs of 250 books or less, they are an economical alternative.

At this stage, most printers make a photographic impression of the large negative. Depending on the process, this may be called a blueline, brownline, or proof. The printer will send this to you for you to look over. Hints on how to review your blueline are given later in this chapter.

Printing

The plate is mounted on the press and printing begins. Depending on the press, printing the back side may require a second pass through the press. One signature is printed at a time. When one signature is finished, the plates are changed and the next signature is printed.

After the sheets of a signature have been printed, they are loaded into a machine that folds each sheet into a signature. What happens next depends on the type of binding.

Binding

Genealogical publications have been bound in almost every way imaginable—from paper clips to beautiful leather covers. The method of binding obviously affects the appearance. It also has a significant impact on the expense and usability of your book.

When we think of binding, we usually think of the cover, but binding is actually what holds the book together. Generally, hard covers are used on books that are smyth sewn, and soft covers are used on books that perfect bound, but the opposite can be done. Hard-cover books are also called *casebound*.

In addition to the traditional book-binding methods, some alternative bindings exist. The type of binding is an important choice.

Smyth-sewn binding

Smyth sewing is the classic, traditional—and most durable—type of binding. It is actually a method of sewing the pages of a book together.

Take a hard-cover book from your bookshelf and look carefully at the top or bottom where the pages meet the spine. Note that the pages seem to be grouped—these are the signatures.

Now open the book to the center. With slight pressure from your hands, the book should open flat. The capability of the book to open flat is an important feature of smyth-sewn bindings for genealogists, who often open books flat to make photocopies. Look carefully at where the pages come together. You should be able to see an indication of where the threads sew the pages together.

Look at the bottom of the spine as the book lays open on the table. Notice that the backs of the signatures are not glued to the spine, but that they pull away from it. This is what provides the flexibility for the book to lay open.

If your book is going to be smyth-sewn, after the signatures are printed, each signature is sewn together, one of each signature is *gathered* (stacked together in order), and then all the signatures are sewn together. There is a black mark on the back of each signature called a *collating mark* that is added to the film negatives during prepress. When the signatures are assembled in proper order, the collating marks form a stair-step pattern. This helps assure correct assembly of the signatures.

Next, the *endpapers* are attached to the first and last page with glue. The pages are squeezed tightly, and the edges are trimmed with a very sharp blade. Glue is applied to the spine, and a strong backing and *headbands* and *footbands* (fabric tape end pieces) are applied.

The title and other text is *stamped* (printed) on the cover as a separate step. Finally, the cover is glued to the endpapers, and your book is finished!

Perfect binding

Adhesive or *soft-cover binding* (usually referred to as *perfect binding*) is less expensive than smyth sewing.

Examine a paperback book from your shelf. Notice that the signatures are not discernible, that the pages are solidly glued to the spine, and that the book does not open flat as easily as a smyth-sewn book.

If your book is to be perfect bound, the signatures are stacked together, and the folded edge (where the spine will go) is abraded until the fold is gone, creating a rough edge for every page. Glue is applied lavishly, and the cover is *wrapped* around the pages. Thus, in perfect binding the cover actually holds the book together. Finally, the edges of the pages and the cover are squeezed and trimmed simultaneously.

Quality-control is important with perfect binding. The glues used in the past tended to become hard and brittle and cracked easily with age or if a book was forced to open flat. The glues today are less brittle, but proper application techniques are still critical or pages can come loose from the book. Ask for samples and recommendations if you are choosing the printer for a perfect-bound book.

A Dallas-based short-run printer has worked with their vendors to develop a more flexible perfect-binding process they call EcoFLEX™. It lets perfect-bound books open flat while meeting or exceeding current strength and longevity.

Saddle stitching and alternative bindings

Saddle stitching is an excellent method to use for books (booklets) with fewer than 64 pages (depending on weight). Although it appears to be simple stapling, saddle stitching is so called because of the saddle over which the book is laid in order to insert the wire staples in the fold. Many genealogical periodicals are saddle stitched.

The binding is durable, although some staples rust over time. It lets the book open flat, an important consideration for genealogists. Most local offset printers and some copy shops offer saddle stitching. Its biggest drawback is the limitation on page count. Depending on the thickness of the paper, books over 64 pages (96 maximum) generally should not be saddle stitched.

Other binding methods that are often available from local printers and copy shops are not as nice for genealogical materials because they do not survive shelf wear at libraries, because they do not allow the book to open flat, or because they are not durable.

➤ *Side stapling.* Books of up to 100 pages can be stapled from the side. A strip of tape is often applied to serve as a spine and cover the staples, or a one-piece cover can be glued on. While generally as durable as the cover material, these books do not open flat.

➤ *Velo-Binding®*. Small holes are drilled near the spine. Plastic tines mounted along a plastic strip are threaded through the holes. A similar strip is placed on the back and heat is used to fuse the tines to the strip. The plastic covers used are durable, but there is no spine for printing, and the book cannot open flat. The tines come loose in books with many pages or books that undergo heavy use.

➤ GBC® *binding* (General Binding Corporation). Rectangular holes are punched along the spine and round plastic combs are inserted. The books lay open, but the pages do not survive heavy use, and there is no spine for printing.

➤ *Wire binding*. There are two types. In spiral binding, holes are drilled along the spine and a spiral wire is threaded through. A wire binding method similar to the GBC method is also available. These bindings allow the book to open flat, but there is no spine for printing, they are not inexpensive, and they do not work well on library shelves.

If you are having a small number of books printed by a local photocopy shop or offset printer, and want something more permanent than the above options, you may need to arrange for the binding yourself.

Ask the printer about vendors for perfect or hard-cover binding or ask your library where they get their rebinding done. The result will not be as durable as smyth-sewn binding, but should be fine for family use. You can even choose to have as few as one or two copies bound for special gifts.

Planning the cover

Consult with your printer on what options he can provide for covers. Because of the special equipment required for printing covers, this is one instance in which it is often easier for the printer to prepare the camera-ready art. You provide the *exact* wording to be used, but the printer does the layout. You should receive a blueline of the cover to approve.

The cover to a book consists of three parts: the front, the back, and the spine.

➤ The title, subtitle, and full name of the author should appear on the front of the cover. In this way, the book is clearly identified when it is lying flat on a table or desk.

➤ The spine of the book should contain at least the main title, but preferably the full title, and the surname of the author.

> On genealogical books, the back cover is generally left blank. You may wish to include the name of your publishing business, the ISBN number, and other information on the cover, but it really isn't necessary for genealogical publications.

Hardback covers

Librarians definitely prefer hardback covers for genealogical books because of their durability. Hardback covers are generally used on smyth-sewn books. They consist of three boards—the front, back, and spine—covered by cloth material. Printers can show you samples of the cover material that they like to use (based on quality, cost, and availability). There are many colors to choose from, and different types and grades.

Once you have chosen the cover material, you can select the color of the lettering. Many genealogists find that gold lettering on a family history really dresses up the appearance, but costs a bit extra. The cover on a hard-cover book is usually stamped rather than printed, so your printer will handle setting the type.

Another possibility is to *screen* (print) a cover, which lets you have drawings or other special treatments on the cover. This adds expense and is not generally done for genealogical books.

Softback covers

There is tremendous variety available in softback covers. You definitely should discuss this with the printer to determine what they offer, what they do not offer, and their preferences.

The cover should always be of heavier paper stock than the pages. Ask to see samples (blank and printed), feel the thickness with your fingers, and make sure that the one you select doesn't bend too easily.

A cover that shows wear easily can make a new book look old very quickly. Uncoated paper covers tend to show scuffing and dirt. A coating—varnish, polyurethane, UV, or film lamination—will protect the lettering and help prevent scuffing. Again, ask your printer what they offer.

A softback cover gives you the option of using one or more colors. (In the printing business, black counts as a color and so does colored background, because the background is printed on the paper, it does not come as part of the paper stock.) A two-color cover can really dress up a book; the extra expense for three or four colors generally isn't justified on a genealogical book.

Choosing paper

Paper is both heavy and voluminous to store, so printers keep on hand only the types of paper that they find to be most popular with their customers. Paper is a commodity, one for which the pricing is quite volatile.

Most printers keep in constant touch with their paper vendors and try to take advantage of "good deals" that come along. This lets them keep the cost to their customers as low as possible. This is one reason that the price quotes you receive from printers are good for a limited amount of time.

Because of this, your first question concerning paper should be, "What do you suggest?" Your printer can order any paper you want, but there will be a time delay, and it will be more expensive.

Three factors that apply to any book-printing paper are color, weight, and opacity.

➢ The color might be anything from bright white to creamy beige. Look at the books on your shelf to determine which color you prefer. Within the white tones, a *brightness* number indicates how white the paper is.

➢ *Weight* describes the thickness of the paper. It affects durability, feel, and how much the printing shows through from the other side. *Basis weight* for book papers is generally measured in pounds (but to confuse matters, these pounds are not comparable to the pounds used to describe cover stock or bond paper). 40-pound paper is not used for genealogical publications. 50-pound paper is popular. 60-pound paper is often used, especially if you are printing photographs on it.

To understand the difference in weights available to you, ask to see samples, both printed and unprinted. Feel the thickness of the paper between your fingers and manipulate it as you would to turn a page.

➢ *Opacity* (a number up to 100) describes how well the paper keeps the printing on the other side from showing through. In the past, weight was the primary factor determining opacity, but in recent years many paper mills have improved the opacity of their stock, and offer 50-pound paper with the opacity of yesteryear's 60-pound paper. Look at a printed sample to judge opacity for yourself.

Acid-free, recycled, and coated papers

There are many kinds of specialty papers available, but three are of particular interest to genealogists.

> ➤ *Acid-free paper.* In the mid-nineteenth century, paper mills began using acid in the paper-making process. Some of the acid remained in the paper and began eating away at the paper itself. This is why we find so many crumbling pages in publications from the latter-nineteenth and early-twentieth centuries. Mills could, and did, make some paper without using acid, but this paper was difficult to obtain and more expensive.
>
> In recent years, however, in response to pressure from both those printing their own books and the librarians and archivists who were attempting to maintain and preserve them (along with some environmental concerns and advances in technology) most mills have converted some, if not all, of their processes. Acid-free paper is now a standard paper, competitively priced.

> ➤ *Recycled paper.* Now our interest has turned to recycled paper. Four types of material may go into recycled paper: virgin wood pulp (this provides strength), preconsumer mill waste (such as trimmings from creating paper rolls), preconsumer processed mill waste (such as trimmings from envelopes; some may have printing), and postconsumer waste (like what you take to your recycling center). Mills have always included some preconsumer waste in their paper. It is on the increased use of postconsumer waste that most interest has focused.
>
> There is no standard for what is required to use the term "recycled." The percentages of preconsumer and postconsumer waste are stated by the mills. Generally, you can find good quality recycled paper that is 40% preconsumer and 10% postconsumer.
>
> All postconsumer waste (and some mill waste) requires special processing to de-ink it. You may recall the gray appearance of early recycled paper—this was residual ink. As demand increased and technology advanced, mills both increased the volume and improved the appearance of recycled papers. Today it is often difficult to tell recycled paper from nonrecycled. Because of the special processing required, recycled paper will always be somewhat more expensive than nonrecycled.
>
> We also might mention that soy-based inks, which are more environmentally friendly, have been developed. You may want to ask your printer about them.

> *Coated paper.* Coated paper has a shiny surface. This makes the edges of printed letters crisper and hence more readable. The most apparent difference between coated and noncoated paper is in the attractiveness of halftones such as photographs. Because coated paper does not allow the dots that comprise the halftone to "bleed" into each other, a muddy appearance is avoided.

Placing the photographs in your family history on a heavier, coated paper stock is often a justifiable expense. Your family is probably more interested in the photographs than they are in your words, so you want the photographs to be as clear and crisp as possible. To use the special paper economically, devote an entire signature (or two or three) to the photographs, rather than interspersing them throughout the book, which requires hand placement of every page.

Books such as two-column county histories that have many photographs are often printed entirely on lighter-weight coated paper to allow photographs to be placed throughout the book.

Cover papers

Some printers offer cover papers for hardback books. These cover papers add considerably to the expense and are not expected on genealogical publications.

Endpapers

Only hardback books have endpapers. The endpapers, which are heavier than the paper used for the pages, are part of the binding structure of the book. They attach the signatures to the cover. *Printed endpapers* offer some interesting possibilities for genealogists.

Look at the front endpaper of a hardback book. It is one continuous sheet, the left side of which is glued to back of the cover, and the right side of which forms a "page." It makes a wonderful place to provide the reader with a map, a pedigree chart, or a descendancy chart. The back endpaper can be printed with the same or a different illustration. Printed endpapers add cost, but they are useful—and popular with readers.

Inserts and foldouts

Printers can *tip in* (place) special items such as oversized maps and charts in the bound pages. However, they require separate printing and hand placing and this adds to the cost. Printed endpapers or reduced-size illustrations are possible alternatives.

Photographs and halftones

It is absolutely imperative that you and your printer communicate about any photographs or halftones that you are using. This is the one item that can have the greatest effect on how satisfied you and your family are with your book.

If the printer is handling the photographs, find out in advance how the photographs should be supplied, how they should be labeled, how they should be marked for correlation with the text, and how the text should be marked for correlation with the photographs.

Fortunately, the printing houses that specialize in genealogies and family histories are quite accustomed to dealing with photographs and have procedures set up to process them safely and efficiently. You want to assure that you understand and cooperate with those procedures.

Special treatment of illustrations

You may want to include an illustration in your book for which you want to keep the reproduction quality high (such as a Bible record, a marriage certificate, a signature, or a map). The illustration may also need resizing. In effect, you treat these illustrations like photographs. Ask about the proper procedure and follow it.

Reviewing bluelines

You will probably receive your bluelines from the printer as stapled signatures. On the day they arrive, *immediately* review them and return them immediately. (Failure of the customer to review bluelines promptly is a common complaint of printers, as it can mess up their schedule severely.)

Bluelines and brownlines are produced on photographic paper. Photographic paper is still light sensitive. If you aren't actually examining the blueline, it should be stored in an envelope. Do not lay the paper in bright light. When exposed to light, the background turns blue, making the bluelines difficult to review.

Reviewing bluelines can be traumatic. Once you've gotten this far, it is too late to be an editor. The *first* thing you will notice when you sit down to review bluelines is something you want to change. *Ignore it!* It is *too late* to create the perfect book. Relax! Remind yourself that overall your book looks pretty darn good, and that it is something you can be really proud of.

So what should you look for?

✓ Check each photograph very carefully. Is the correct caption associated with the photograph? Is the photograph on the correct page? Has it been reduced or enlarged to the proper size? Has it been cropped according to your instructions? Is it left-to-right correct (not flopped)? In general, do the photographs look good?

✓ Check illustrations. Any that required hand placement should be checked for the same things as photographs. Is the appearance of the illustration acceptable? Is the title at the left for any illustrations placed *broadside* (sideways)?

✓ Stack up the signatures like a book and hold them near the "spine." Try fanning the pages (sometimes this is difficult to do because of the special paper), gazing at the page number in the page header as you do so. If the pages have been positioned correctly, the position of the page number should not jump all over.

✓ You should receive bluelines for the cover and printed endpapers, if any. Check the text and spelling very carefully on any type that the printer set for you.

✓ Review the pages in the front and back that do not have running headers. Is each page in the proper sequence? Is the material positioned correctly vertically and horizontally?

✓ Look at every page that does not have a running header or footer (such as the first page of every chapter) to see that the *bottom* line is positioned correctly. For some reason, many printers feel compelled to center text on a page (no matter what instructions you gave about registration and placement), and they move the entire chapter title page up so that the chapter title is near the top.

✓ Finally, look at every page. *Do not read the words.* Sometimes it helps to squint, hold the pages at an out-of-focus distance, or even hold them upside down. Look for any marks or spots on the light background. Look at the text areas for any marks or for any places that the text is missing. Usually these problems occurred when the blueline photograph was made and are not on the negative, but mark them just in case.

Marking bluelines

For any problem you find, circle it on the blueline without obscuring it. Use a ball-point or indelible pen—most felt-tip pens don't write well on blueline paper. Attach a sticky-note to the edge of the page so that it sticks out to flag the location. If necessary, you can write an explanation on the note.

Suppose you discover that you spelled Aunt Hattie's name wrong in a photo caption—and she helped finance the book. Generally, printers are willing to accommodate fixing one or two goofs on your part—but they do have a right to charge for this service.

Once you've reviewed the bluelines and marked and flagged all problems, *immediately* package them up and return them as you were instructed. This may be by meeting with the sales representative, or it may be by mailing them to the plant. If you prepared your material well and have chosen the printer well, there will be few items flagged.

Shrink wrap, boxing, and shipping

Once the printer has received the marked-up bluelines, he schedules your job for the press. After he has printed your books, he may shrink wrap each book (seal it in plastic). This helps significantly to reduce wear and tear on the books before they reach their final audience. There may be an additional charge for this, but many printers include it as part of their basic package.

The books are packed in boxes and shipped to you. Discuss with your printer which carrier they use and about how long it takes for the books to arrive at your door. Shipping may be included in your overall price quote, or it may be stated separately. Because books are heavy, shipping is expensive, so do not be surprised at the cost.

When the boxes arrive, open each box and examine one book from each box. Mistakes do happen, and you want to find them immediately.

Warning: You will probably find a typographical error on the very first page to which you open the book. *Welcome to the world of professional publishing!* You have just experienced Murphy's First Law of Publishing, one with which every professional writer and editor is intimately familiar.

Schedule

Printers are very busy people. They normally have many jobs in-house at any one time. Think of all the separate tasks we have discussed that are involved in producing a book. Each of those tasks involves employees, and each of those employees stays busy all day long. Some jobs take longer at one step than other jobs do. Scheduling is critical, and there is normally another job ready to begin as the current job is completed at each task.

What this means is that when the printer finally gets your camera-ready art, he doesn't run it straight through the system. On the other hand, he doesn't want to keep any more jobs in-house at one time than is necessary because he wants satisfied customers, and because he doesn't want any mistakes on items requiring special handling. Delivery times commonly range from two to twelve weeks.

You can help minimize the time it takes to run your job by asking what are the most and least busy times of year. Genealogical printers are usually swamped in the fall with orders for holidays. Some print school yearbooks also, so they are busy in the spring and early summer, and books for family reunions add to the load. If you schedule your book for a busy season—be patient!

Choosing how many to print

The biggest question of all is, "How many should I print?" Like everything else in publishing, it is a balancing act: getting a good price versus getting stuck with boxes and boxes of books. To establish a reasonable cost for printed books, the minimum print run is generally 200 books, and 300 is much better.

If you are printing a family history, you may be in frequent touch with family members and even have taken advance orders. If so, you also need to print additional books for family members who are late responding or just heard about it. Also, plan on donating books to several major libraries, plus those in areas in which the family lived.

The next biggest factor is how aggressively you intend to market the book, which is itself an added cost. You need to provide a certain number of free copies to reviewers. If you market your books through book dealers, they get a discount.

To understand more of the variables in marketing (and hence how many to print), see Self-Publishing.

Overs and unders

Printers don't print exactly the number of books that you order—the difference is called *overs* and *unders*. At the many quality-control checkpoints, books that do not meet standards are discarded. Therefore, at the end of the process there are almost always an odd number of books.

You need to know how the printer handles overs and unders. Do they guarantee to deliver the number of books you requested, or is it a plus-or-minus percentage. (For example, 300 books plus or minus 5% is actually 285–315 books.)

If they print more than the amount you ordered, will you receive the extras, and if so, will you be billed for them? All of these are reputable ways of handling overs and unders within the industry. You just need to understand what is happening so there are no surprises.

Understanding printing costs

Let's look at a hypothetical example. The printer tells you that 200 copies of your book will cost $1700, or $17 per book. Then he says that 300 copies would cost $3000, or $10 per book. What is happening?

The basic principle of printing books is that the first book is very, very expensive, but subsequent books cost much, much less. No matter how many books you print, there are many fixed costs. Making the negatives, making and inserting the halftones, making the plate, mounting it on the press, plus quality control and management: all of these things take exactly the same amount of time whether you want 1 book, 300 books, or 10,000 books.

Therefore, in effect, that first book may cost $900 to produce. The next 99 books may cost an additional $800—a total of $1700, or $17 per book. From $900 per book to $17 per book is quite a change! And the next 200 books may cost an additional $1300—for a total cost of $10 per book.

The cost for additional books goes down slightly as volume increases because the longer the presses and other mechanical processes can go without stopping, the more efficient it is.

Getting a cost quote

Now that you understand many of the options available to you, you can meet with a representative of the printer to discuss the options, costs, and schedule. (Some printers merely have quote-request forms.) The printer takes many variables into account and bases his pricing estimates on those variables.

Think about all of those variables before meeting with the representative. You don't need to make a final decision before the meeting, but you should have some ideas and questions. Use the checklist at the end of this chapter to review your options. Make a list. Take two copies, one for each of you.

Take samples. If you like the paper or cover on a particular book you have seen, for example, take it with you. It's always easier for the representative if he or she can see what you are talking about.

Remember to ask, "Do you have a less-expensive alternative that you might recommend for any of the requirements?" For example, the printer may have a large stock of a slightly different paper that would cost less, or they may use a type of cover that you had not considered.

Bring a sample of the camera-ready art exactly as you plan to provide it. Confirm that it is acceptable. (Occasionally the representative will want to check with the plant first.) Discuss how you will deliver the camera-ready art and photographs—and how you will get them back. Confirm that you will review bluelines of the body *and* the cover.

Ask about the payment procedure. Often it is a portion on delivery of the camera-ready art, a portion on approval of the bluelines, and the remaining portion when you receive the books. Ask if there is a contract—and read it! Ask what their policy is about overs and unders.

Additionals

Often changes in requirements occur between the first time you meet with the printer's representative and the time the camera-ready art is presented to the printer. These changes are most frequent in three categories: number of copies to be printed, number of pages to be printed, and number of pages of photographs.

So that there will be no surprises, request *additionals* in your quote. For example, if you request a quote for 300 copies of 240 pages with 16 pages of photographs (2 per page), you might also want to request quotes for 50 additional copies or 16 additional text pages or 16 additional pages of photographs. (Note that the additionals quote is for only that item—if you ended requesting all three, the additional charges would be more than the sum of the three.)

Spending your money where it counts

Every single choice that you make, no matter how minor it seems to you, may make a difference in the cost of the book. You want to make choices that improve the quality, appearance, and durability of your book commensurate with the extra expense. Some suggestions follow for the extra-cost items most often selected, but remember that *you* are the customer. Do what *you* prefer.

➢ Special paper for photographs. For audience satisfaction, this is a yes. Often only one copy of a photograph exists, and that copy is in private hands. Thus the only copy that other family members have is the one in your book. It should be good quality.

➢ Special handling for photographs. Printers who specialize in family histories often can do a much better job of resizing and screening photographs than if you do it yourself, but there will be a charge.

➢ Acid-free paper now costs little extra, if any.

➢ Hardback cover and smyth-sewn binding make a family history appear more professional and less amateurish in the eyes of family members, no matter what the content. Compare the price difference—it varies.

Getting help

Review the checklist at the end of this chapter, and then discuss the items with your printer.

Checklist for what to ask the printer

☑ Paper size

☑ Paper weight and color

☑ Signature size

☑ Special paper

☑ Hardback color

☑ Hardback lettering

☑ Binding method

☑ Cover paper

☑ Printed endpapers

☑ Softback stock/coating

☑ Softback colors

☑ Softback artwork

☑ Number of pages

☑ Additional pages

☑ Number of copies

☑ Additional copies

☑ Special paper for photographs

☑ Number of photographs, processing required

☑ Additional photographs (or photograph pages)

☑ Illustrations requiring special handling

☑ Location to ship books to/shipper

☑ Schedule

☑ Bluelines included

☑ Format for camera-ready art

☑ Delivery and return of art and photos

☑ Payment arrangements

☑ Contract

Options from
Technology

Technology has brought about numerous changes in the publishing process for professionals. Some of these changes have, or possibly will, affect genealogists. Technology has also brought about numerous changes in what it means to "publish."

Nontraditional publishing formats

When genealogists think of publishing, they tend to think of the traditional book—hard bound, produced by a printing house using the traditional printing processes. Perhaps they also think of offset-printed or photocopied pages assembled using a less-elegant binding method. Today's publishing world, however, has several interesting alternatives.

Self-printing

You could print all of the copies of your book on your printer. We mentioned in the first chapter that this was the original concept of desktop publishing. If you are doing only a few copies, if there aren't a lot of pages, or if you want to use color, this may be a good option.

There are many specialty papers available for use in laser or ink-jet printers. You might choose a parchment-look paper or maybe a thicker recycled stock. Many word processors allow you to print *duplex* (two-sided) by printing the even pages, reloading the paper, and then printing the odd pages.

Printing your book yourself allows great flexibility in inserting photographs, either black-and-white or color.

➢ You can have color photocopies made of photographs and combine the pages manually with the text pages.

➢ You can print scanned color photographs on a color ink-jet or color laser printer.

➢ Technology to scan photographs and produce high-quality digital color images is available commercially.

➢ Because you are assembling the book yourself, you can even incorporate real snapshots, like in an album.

Binding may be as simple as a report cover or as fancy as hand-bound leather. Any of the binding methods discussed in this book can be obtained separately. It may take several phone calls to locate a vendor, and it will cost more per book than if you are having several done.

You might even create a special binding yourself. Book-binding classes are offered through some community-service, adult-education programs.

Microfiche

Some genealogists who have expensive family histories printed also have copies reproduced on microfiche. In this way they can offer copies of their $45 printed family history to libraries and other researchers for $10 or less, thereby increasing the accessibility of their research.

Microfiche is easy to store (no boxes of books), easy and inexpensive to mail (usually a 6"×9" envelope with 2-ounce first-class postage), and easy to reprint (just pick up the phone). It is durable and holds up well.

To publish on microfiche, you supply the camera-ready pages to the microfiche company. You can locate one through the yellow pages under "microfilming and imaging." The company photographs many pages on each microfiche. They make a master microfiche, which they retain for safe keeping. Then they reproduce copies for you. The minimum order is usually about 10 copies. The overall cost is quite reasonable.

If you need to reprint, just call the vendor. They pull the master fiche from the vault and reproduce the requested copies for you.

The company photographs the paper exactly as you send it, so if your camera-ready art is for a 6"×9" page printed on 8½"×11" paper, you may want to trim the pages to the final size. If you send a bound book, they prefer to cut the pages out of the binding in order to make the best copy.

CD-ROM

A newer method of publishing books is on CD-ROM (Compact Disk—Read-Only Memory). A few firms are currently interested in publishing family histories on CD-ROM and more may become involved. Investigate carefully the charges (if any), the royalties (if any), and the copyright situation. This is still a very new field. We may see it grow and change, or we may see it die out in favor of other options.

There are at least three forms of accessing the information in the family history. Discuss with the vendors what options they offer.

➢ *Images with index.* An electronic image is made of each page of camera-ready art and stored on the CD-ROM. The vendor provides software that lets the user view specific pages based on a table of contents or index entries.

➢ *Full-text-search.* A giant step up in terms of accessibility, this method understands the document as text. The document is usually provided to the vendor as a computer file.

The access software (called a *viewer* or *reader*) lets the user search for any phrase in the document, in addition to table-of-contents and/or index access. Boolean searches, using "and/or" logic let the reader search for words in proximity to each other, such as "Iowa" *and* "corn." A lengthy history could be searched for "wool" *or* "linen" if the user is interested in weavers or for "Wales" *or* "Welsh" if migration clusters are the focus of the search.

The better methods of displaying and printing allow formatting and illustrations.

➢ *Database.* The vendor takes your GEDCOM (Genealogy Data Communications) file and provides an access tool for it. The more focus there is on presenting the notes, documentation, and narrative, the better. This is not a good mechanism for publishing a quality family history as described in this book.

Electronic or on-line publishing

Any time you provide a file or electronic information of any kind to another genealogist, whether on disk, via e-mail, or from a Web page, you *are* publishing. Be certain you have appropriately documented every piece of information that you are sharing.

Within the realm of electronic publishing there is an incredible range and scope of possibilities. At present, there is no clear trend as to what form *quality* electronic or on-line publishing might take, but here's a sampling of the *types* of electronic publication that are being used in some fields. The future for genealogists may include one of these types of publishing—or a concept that hasn't even appeared yet.

➢ *Text and RTF files.* We can (and do) exchange text files and other more-complicated document files on diskette and on-line. This mechanism will undoubtedly continue to be used. There are two significant items to be considered: formatting and copyright.

Text can be plain, unformatted text. However, this does not allow for good presentation. It is difficult to read and understand for more than a few screens. The addition of simple formatting such as bold, italics, tabs and page breaks helps, but it is still difficult to read. RTF (Rich Text Format) files maintain most of the formatting discussed in this book, but must be loaded into a word processor that accepts RTF files in order to be read.

This brings us to copyright. The issue of copyright for electronic publications is a hot topic at present. Technically, once a work is in a fixed media, it has a copyright, whether or not a notice is attached. This means that you cannot share—or change—someone else's work without their express permission.

Many genealogists want to share their work freely. Don't assume that all do. Check with the author before republishing an electronic document.

➢ *Viewers/Readers.* Some software, as mentioned above under CD-ROMs, is designed to allow pages to be read on-screen just as if they were printed—fonts, illustrations, page numbers, and all. Access and search capabilities are part of the software. Software to read the files (called a *viewer* or *reader*) can be distributed with the files, but the expensive software to create it must be purchased.

➢ *Hypertext.* Hypertext refers to the ability to jump between pages of information (topics) by clicking (or double-clicking) on graphics or on terms that are highlighted (usually by underline and/or color). This provides some fascinating options for interactive reading of family histories.

For example, suppose you begin with a pedigree chart. Click on the highlighted name of an individual to jump to his or her sketch. Click on the highlighted spouse's name to jump to that sketch. Suppose they are buried in Pioneer Cemetery. Click on the highlighted phrase "Pioneer Cemetery" to jump to a topic that tells about its founding, provides directions for driving, lists all family members buried there (with hypertext links), and even has a map of the plots.

Windows Help. Some companies have begun using the hypertext features of the Windows on-line Help system, which comes with every Windows operating system, to create interactive documents such as company phone directories and product catalogues. The same possibilities exist for family histories.

Additional software is required to write on-line help, but anyone with Windows can read the file after it is created and compiled.

HTML. Hypertext Mark-up Language is the programming language used to create Web pages on the Internet. This has become so popular recently that several software packages are now available to help you design Web pages without really learning HTML. The World-Wide-Web environment encourages a more graphical and less textual presentation.

➤ *Multimedia.* Depending on which software tools and options you use for electronic publishing, you may be able to jump to and from graphics such as photographs, drawings, and pedigree charts. You also may be able to access brief video clips of a 50th wedding anniversary or the newest great-grandchild.

Nontraditional prepress options

Professional publishing for many businesses has changed drastically in recent years, moving away from the preparation of camera-ready art and directly into the prepress area (see TURNING CAMERA-READY ART INTO BOOKS).

Over the next few years, you may well see some of the options described below coming into use by more printers and more genealogists. All of them illustrate the trend toward a seamless, integrated writing-editing-printing process and respond to a general trend toward faster idea-to-printed-book times and smaller print runs. Undoubtedly the future will bring more interesting and exciting options.

These procedures can be used for books that are *completely* self-contained in the computer file—in other words, there are no photographs or illustrations to be hand placed.

As with any new computer technology, to use them effectively you need to understand computer hardware and software fairly well. If one of these options becomes available to you, discuss it with the vendor in detail.

➢ *DocuTech*®. This may be the wave of the future for genealogical publishing. Xerox® Corporation developed equipment specifically designed to produce short-run publications directly from computer files. Using the photo duplication process, it reproduces the text in signatures of two or four pages at 600 dpi resolution, collates, folds, and trims the pages.

The printing firm then adds the cover using a traditional binding process.

This is not a printing process—each page is an original, the equivalent of printing every page of every book on a 600 dpi laser printer. You can, literally, produce one copy of a book this way, but vendors recommend at least 50–100 copies. For details, check with the vendor.

You create a printer file for each document by printing to a file on disk. This is often as easy as checking a box in the word processor. The pages are previewed on a computer monitor before being printed, so some potential problems can be detected before the pages are produced.

The cost is generally higher than photocopying, but it gives you access to 600-dpi printing even when you don't own a laser printer. In fact, this lets you produce laser camera-ready art (or final book) even if you don't own a laser printer. (You'll have to do the layout and typography review on-screen, but you can proof text for content and grammar by printing on whatever printer you have.)

➢ *From computer file to reproduction-quality paper.* Traditional typesetting actually uses two major pieces of equipment: the composition system and the imagesetter. The resolution quality of the imagesetter, which is used to produce camera-ready art on photographic paper is high (at least 1200 dpi). The photographic process assures sharp, crisp edges to text and smooth, even halftones in screens and graphics.

The composition system is rapidly being replaced by PC-based word processing, page-layout, and composition software. New interfaces have been developed to allow PostScript-based imagesetters to be used on a PC network.

This procedure can be used for books that are completely self-contained in the computer file (in other words, no photographs or illustrations to be hand placed), or it can be used to produce the text where high-resolution is required, but some artwork may need to be placed manually.

At present, this capability is provided by service bureaus to business customers. In the future, we may find it offered by more printers as they acquire new equipment.

➢ *From computer file to film.* Most imagesetters that produce camera-ready art on photographic paper as described above can also print directly to film, which eliminates the manual steps of handling the camera-ready art, photographing it, and reviewing the negatives for dust and dirt.

➢ *From computer file to plate.* There is even equipment that cuts out another step or two and goes directly to the signature film—or to the plate—but it is rare and will probably only be used by business customers.

➢ *Laser plates and films.* It is now possible to produce film or polyester printing plates on specialized high-resolution (1800 dpi) laser printers. Expect some printers and vendors to utilize this relatively inexpensive (as compared to imagesetters) equipment.

Getting help

To keep abreast of the newest options being used by genealogists, don't isolate yourself. The important factor is not what is possible, or even available, but what is being *used*. Join the computer interest group of your local genealogical society. Read computer-genealogy publications. Attend lectures, ask questions, make friends.

When you contact a printer, ask what options they offer. Over time, many printers catering to businesses (who also do short-run printing) will add some of the options described.

Checklist of questions about publishing format

- ☑ How many books do I want to print?
- ☑ How many books can I afford to print?
- ☑ For whom?
- ☑ What kind of binding?
- ☑ Will a photocopy do?
- ☑ Who else do I want to share the information with? How?
- ☑ What options does my printer offer for prepress?
- ☑ Could I publish on microfiche?
- ☑ Would I like to publish electronically?
- ☑ What format: CD-ROM, text file, formatted file?
- ☑ Would I like to publish on-line?

Self-Publishing

The publisher is responsible for management and marketing. A writer who is self-publishing his or her own book is not only a writer (and editor and typesetter and so on), but also the manager of a business, involved in record keeping, promotion, and shipping.

Genealogical publishing is self-publishing

This book is about producing a quality family history. This chapter covers some details about what it means to *produce* a family history. The emphasis of this chapter is less on quality and more on keeping your sanity and controlling expenses.

Almost all family histories are self-published. Most genealogical source material is self-published. So you are not the first genealogist to struggle with self-publishing. This chapter discusses some tasks related to self-publishing, but doesn't go into detail. Ask other self-published genealogists to share their experiences and advice with you.

The role of the publisher

As a self-publisher, you'll find yourself responsible for tasks in three broad areas. These areas are generally sequential, but there is some overlap.

➢ Being a business.
➢ Marketing your books.
➢ Fulfilling orders.

Being a business

Publishing a family of history is often a labor of love done primarily for our family. That does not, however, exempt it from the business tasks of self-publishing. If you can think of yourself as a "business," you'll be more likely to keep on track and less likely to be overwhelmed and frustrated.

As a self-publishing business, there are a number of tasks you'll find yourself performing. (Some of these tasks are optional.) You should begin most of these tasks at least six months before publication.

➢ Choosing and registering a business name.

➢ Opening a checking account and keeping records.

➢ Getting a sales-tax permit.

➢ Registering copyright.

➢ Getting a Library of Congress CIP number.

➢ Getting an ISBN number and *Books in Print* listing.

➢ Contracting with a printer and paying for the printing.

➢ Paying for marketing, fulfillment supplies, and shipping.

➢ Maintaining mailing lists.

Choosing a name

You don't have to have a publishing company name to publish your family history, but it helps. Having a name means that you are serious and that this isn't just playing. A publishing company name will help you think like a business. It will also help you keep track of expenditures.

The name can be simple: Smith Books. It can be your initials: SSS Publishing. Or it can have meaning. This author named her company "Pioneer Heritage Press" in honor of her numerous ancestors who settled on the edge of the newest frontier.

Registering your business name

Once you've chosen a name, you should become a business. Being a business isn't the same as being a corporation. It simply means registering your DBA (Doing Business As) name.

In most states this is done at the county level. Look in the phone book or call the courthouse for information on the requirements. Usually you first check a master list to ensure that no one else has already chosen your name. Then you fill out a form, pay a nominal fee, and receive a certificate stating that you are the only person in the county entitled to do business under that name.

Opening a checking account

Your life will be easier if you set up a separate bank account for the book. Take your DBA certificate with you when applying for the account. Have the account set up and the checks printed with both your name and the business name (Suzy Smith DBA SSS Publishing).

Shop around for the best deal. Don't ask for a business checking account, they are usually too expensive. Begin with your own bank and ask about a personal DBA account. You'll find more flexibility for accounts that require a minimum balance. Inquire about any per-item fees (that's where most business accounts get expensive). You will have (hopefully) many small deposit items as you sell books, so look for an account with a flat fee.

If you plan to sell many books, you may find it easier if you have a rubber stamp made with the name of the company, "for deposit only," and the account number.

Keeping records

You probably won't make a profit publishing your family history. You won't necessarily have to *file* an income tax statement related to the book. But you still must *maintain* certain records. Why? If the IRS should ever question those many small deposits made to your bank account, your life will be much simpler if you can readily identify the deposits as book sales—and show expenses that equal or exceed them.

If you do not set up a separate bank account, you need to keep simple receipt and expense logs. You don't even have to add them up—just faithfully record every deposit and every expense. If you have a separate account, the bank statements and canceled items will be sufficient.

Sales tax

In most states you must collect sales tax on the sale of your book. Generally you must apply for a permit that allows you to collect the tax. Then periodically you must file a tax return, paying to the state the tax you have collected on their behalf.

Certain types of sales such as sales to out-of-state residents and sales to nonprofit institutions may be exempt from sales tax. Learn the guidelines before you begin promoting your book or collecting money.

Copyright page stuff

In BOOK DESIGN we mentioned several items that belong on the back of the title page (usually referred to as the copyright page). We've taken care of one of them, the name of the publishing company. Your address also belongs there. There is no particular reason to get a PO box unless you are uncomfortable about receiving checks at your home mail box.

Three items on the copyright page require some phone calls or correspondence, two of them well in advance of preparing camera-ready art. These items are not mandatory.

➤ Copyright

➤ Library of Congress number (LCN) and Cataloging in Publication (CIP) information

➤ ISBN number (and *Books in Print* listing)

Copyright

Loosely stated, placing a copyright notice on the copyright page and registering your copyright states that you do not want anyone else to reproduce your material, to sell it, or to change it. It does not prohibit someone from photocopying portions of it for research purposes, nor from citing from it and quoting reasonable amounts of text in their own work.

Printing the copyright notice provides a certain amount of protection. The format is "Copyright 1995 Suzy Smith," "Copyright 1995 SSS Publishing," "© 1995 Suzy Smith," or "© 1995 SSS Publishing." © is a special character (see UNDERSTANDING TYPE AND FONTS).

Registering your copyright provides some additional protection. Furthermore, this is how genealogies and family histories get into the genealogy collection of the Library of Congress. At present, in addition to all the paperwork, registering copyright requires $20 and two copies of the book.

Six months before sending your book to the printer, call the Copyright Office (or visit their Web site). Request their booklets on Copyright Basics (circular 1), Copyright Notice (circular 3), and researching the copyright status of a publication (circular 22). Also request several copies of form TX, which is used for registering a copyright.

When the material arrives, read it and follow the directions. (If it doesn't arrive in about a month, request it again.)

Library of Congress Cataloging

While you've got the phone in your hand, call the Library of Congress Cataloging in Publication (CIP) Division at (202) 707-6372 and request form 607-7.

The Cataloging in Publication Division prepares standard card-catalog information for libraries in advance of publication. When you receive the form, complete it as soon as you know all the information and return it.

Based on the title and subtitle, they assign cataloging numbers. This is one good reason to have a meaningful title. You wouldn't want *Roots and Branches* to end up in the horticulture section!

You will receive a preassigned Library of Congress Card Catalog number (LCN), which you should list on the copyright page (for example, "Library of Congress Cataloging-in-Publication Number 95-00000").

After the book is printed, you must send them a copy. That's a total of three copies for the Library of Congress. No comment— except to point out how useful the Library of Congress is to genealogists, so you really should cooperate.

ISBN

R. R. Bowker (see PUBLISHING in RESOURCES) will assign a block of numbers to your publishing company. The International Standard Book Number (ISBN) identifies your book in some book-ordering systems and gets you a listing in *Books in Print*. Assigning the block of numbers was free in the past, but now it costs ($115 at present).

Books that are distributed through normal retail channels need this, but there is little advantage for family histories. We're explaining ISBN here because you'll probably notice ISBN numbers on the copyright page of genealogical source books.

Contracting with a printer and paying for the printing

As a business, you'll want to talk to more than one printer and get *competitive bids*. To assure that bids are indeed competitive, prepare your own bid specification sheet, listing all the options we discussed in TURNING CAMERA-READY ART INTO BOOKS (don't forget shipping and delivery). If the printer has their own form, fill it out, but also attach your bid specification sheet. You want to avoid any surprises.

Don't settle on the first printer you contact. Even if you are fairly certain you're going to use that printer, shop around. You'll be a more informed consumer and may pick up some good ideas.

Once you've settled on a printer, get all the details in writing. Again, no surprises.

Different printers have different payment plans. Some expect all the money at once; others divide it with portions due at camera-ready art delivery, blue-line approval, and book delivery. Make sure you understand the terms.

To recoup the cost of printing your book (and the other expenses involved), you need to market your book. If you can't afford to finance the printing yourself, you need prepublication orders, which means marketing.

Marketing your books

There are a number of targets in your marketing campaign. Some are potential customers, others are sources of publicity. You'll be preparing four types of publicity: in-progress announcements, order flyers (pre- and post-publication), announcements, and complimentary books.

> *"In progress" announcement.* Some genealogical periodicals have a section for announcing works-in-progress. You may hear from potential customers or get additional information for the book. Include the title, anticipated publication date, and your address in the announcement (use your name, not the publishing company name.)

> *On-line announcements.* Post a work-in-progress announcement in an appropriate on-line location.

Order flyers can be a simple letter or a trifold brochure. You may find it advantageous to offer a discount for prepublication purchases.

> *People who are in your book.* If your book mentions living descendants, each family should receive both a prepublication order flyer *and* a post-publication order flyer. Presumably you've kept in touch with them as the work progressed, and they are anxiously awaiting its release.

> *Researchers with whom you have corresponded.* Send an order flyer to every researcher with whom you have corresponded on this or a related family.

> *Other researchers.* As you work on the book, add to your mailing list the names of researchers who might be interested (based on a query, for example).

Write a two-paragraph announcement about your book. The first paragraph should describe the content (make it sound interesting), and the second should contain ordering information. Specifically mention the areas of residence of the families covered.

If the announcement is well written, you may get it published in its entirety as a book notice.

> *Genealogy columnists.* Send an announcement to any columnists in areas covered by the book. Some may write back and request a copy of the book to review, but this isn't really cost-effective.

> *Libraries and societies in areas mentioned in the book.* Send an announcement to every library or society in areas mentioned in the book and those further along the migration path. Libraries and societies rarely have the money to purchase family histories, but they often share such announcements either by posting them or publishing them.

Complimentary copies of the book are expensive. Choose carefully who receives them.

> *The Family History Library.* As discussed in WHAT TO WRITE; WHEN TO WRITE IT, this is the largest genealogy collection in the world. Having your book as part of the collection is worthwhile publicity.

> *Major libraries.* Donate books to one or more other large libraries— but be clever about it. Determine which publication publishes critical book reviews and donates the books to that library. Send the book to the *review editor*, not directly to the library. (Include the announcement.) If you have written a quality family history, the review may bring more orders.

> *Libraries in localities significant to the family.* The same procedure applies. Donate to the library by way of the book reviewer for the local genealogical society.

> *The Genealogical Helper.* The book review section of this high-circulation periodical is read by many.

Maintaining mailing lists

Keep one or more mailing lists to facilitate both publicity and order fulfillment. In this way the addresses are always convenient if you need them again.

Display advertising

Ads in periodicals are called *display advertising*. We mentioned in UNDERSTANDING TYPE AND FONTS that large sans serif font is called *display type*. This is what display type is for. If you place ads, choose the periodicals carefully. Often donating a book for review is a more effective use of your funds.

Fulfilling orders

In self-publishing, *fulfillment* is not the warm, fuzzy feeling you get when you finally open the box of printed books. It's getting rid of the darn things. Your first question on receiving the books may well be a dismayed, "Where will I put all these books?"

Your basic goal is to get them back out of your house as quickly, efficiently, painlessly, and economically as possible. Fulfillment usually comes in two phases: mailing a large number of books when the shipment first arrives and mailing a dribble of orders over time (often years) as other people learn of your publication.

The tasks in fulfillment are fairly straightforward.

➤ Purchasing shipping materials.

➤ Receiving the books.

➤ Creating labels and tracking orders.

➤ Packing the book orders.

➤ Delivering the books to the carrier.

Receiving the books

When discussing shipping with your printer, ask about options for delivery. Usually the books will be delivered by a freight company, but possibly by a parcel-delivery service. Find out if you must be there to sign for the delivery, and if the delivery time is predictable. Waiting at home for a freight delivery "sometime next week" can be a major inconvenience.

Delivery usually means depositing the boxes on your front porch. Most services will not put them inside the house or even in the garage. Furthermore, the boxes may be heavy and dirty. Be prepared. If you have one of those small collapsible luggage carts, put it by the front door.

The basic plan is to get the books in the front door, repackaged for shipping, and out the back door and to the carrier as quickly as possible. The checklist at the end of this chapter contains a comprehensive list of supplies you'll need for this day.

To process the books with as little frustration and back pain as possible, prepare a room with a large cleared table. The boxes will be dirty and possibly have brads or staples, so you may want to protect your furniture and flooring from dirt and scratches.

Opening and checking the boxes

Mistakes do happen. If there is one, you need to know right away. Open every box. Have scissors, pocket knife, or blade cutter ready for the task. Opening boxes can be rough on your hands, so you may want to wear gloves.

Count the books in the standard box and multiply it by the number of boxes. If one box is not a full box, adjust accordingly. The count should agree with the shipping invoice (and with the final bill from the printer).

Check one book in every box (you may need to remove the shrink wrap). Open the book and fan the pages. They should be right-side-up and in order.

Use packing tape to reseal all boxes that you won't need.

Shipping books to your customers

You have several options in choice of carrier and several options concerning service. The service option affects delivery time and rate. Investigate.

Ask at the post office for the postal bulletin on rates. The postal service offers two special rates related to books. They are slower than regular parcel post, but less expensive. Special Fourth Class Book Rate can be used for shipping all books. (You may include an invoice.) Library Rate can be used to ship books from a *publisher* (a good reason for a DBA) to a *library*.

For comparison, these are the rates in 1996 for a 1½ pound book (packages must be clearly marked as to type of rate):

Priority mail $3.00 (includes light-weight cardboard mailer)
Parcel post $2.63 to $2.95, depending on distance
Book rate $1.24
Library rate $1.12

Rates for parcel-delivery services vary by distance and speed of delivery. Do not use a shipping service that adds a fee to the basic rate.

Non-USPS carriers generally cannot deliver to a post office box. Orders you receive with only a PO Box address usually must be filled by mail. (Depending on the carrier, it may be possible to ship to boxes at commercial mail-box businesses.)

When making your choice, consider convenience. If the office is across town, take that into account.

Shipping supplies

Before the anticipated delivery date, assemble all needed shipping supplies in the work area. Shipping supplies are in two broad categories—general materials and items specific to each order.

If your book is small and lightweight, you can send it in a padded mailing bag. The bubble-lined bags are usually too lightweight for heavy books. The cellulose-lined bags are better. Shop around to get the best rate. Look at discount office-supply stores and in mail-order office-supply catalogs. Self-sealing bags are more convenient but more expensive.

If the book is thick and heavy, a box may be a better option. Look for one close to the correct size, because you will have to add packing material to prevent the book from sliding around. The packing material can be Styrofoam, popcorn, egg cartons, or clean wadded paper (not newspaper). Save any packing material that you receive in the year before completing your book and recycle.

You need packing tape and scissors, and possibly a sturdy stapler and plenty of staples.

After you complete all orders, you are going to take them to the post office or delivery service. You'll need something to carry them in. The emptied book boxes will not hold all of the repackaged books.

If you are mailing the books, the post office will provide convenient mailing baskets. They are white, about the size of a laundry basket, and have handles. And speaking of laundry baskets, they are a pretty good means of transport. (Just ignore the funny looks from the other people in line.)

The first cycle of order fulfillment will have a *lot* of books in it (you hope). Arrange for at least one friend or family member to help you take the books to be shipped.

Handling orders

Several days before the books are delivered, make a list of all orders. You'll find these tasks easier if you take advantage of computer software, but exactly what software you use and how much information you record is up to you.

Print label(s) with the publishing company name and address and the customer's name and address. If you are mailing the books, print the rate classification (Special Fourth Class—Books, or whatever) on the mailing label or a separate label.

If you are using a parcel-delivery service, follow their instructions for preparation of labels.

Assembling a package

You'll save lots of time on delivery day if you have already attached the labels to the bags or boxes, assembled the boxes, and put the appropriate papers with each bag or box.

If you are mailing the books, you may prefer to add the postage now to save time at the post office.

You may choose to include some kind of invoice marked "paid." Carefully slit the shrink wrap and slide it in, or tape it to the shrink wrap. Book review copies going to periodicals should have a cover letter and promotional information with them.

Put the book in the package along with any associated papers, seal the package, put it in the delivery basket, and check the name off the list.

Invoices

The standard practice in genealogy is to ship books immediately on receipt of payment, with two exceptions. Libraries and book vendors customarily do not pay in advance. For them you'll have to prepare an invoice. (Genealogical book vendors normally receive a discount on the sale price of the book.)

Mark a file folder "Pending Invoices." Keep a duplicate copy of the invoice in the folder until it is paid. If an invoice is more than 60 days old, send a reminder.

Storage

You probably did not dispose of all of the books on delivery day. Where are you going to store them? They are too heavy to put in the attic. If you put them in the garage or basement, do not set them on the floor. Protect them from damp and excessive heat.

The best plan is to get rid of them as quickly as possible. If you mailed the advertising on schedule, you'll probably receive some orders over the next few weeks. Keep the shipping supplies together in one box, handy for another fulfillment round.

Returns

Occasionally a customer will write and say that their book was defective. This happens occasionally. Gracefully replace it for them, but don't ask them to return it. The alternative is to open and check every book, which defeats the purpose of the shrink wrap.

Getting help

We can't emphasize enough that your best resource for the details of self-publishing is other genealogists who've been-there, done-that. Ask them to share hints on what *did* work—and what did *not* work for them.

There are many details involved in publishing. The best choices for you may be entirely different from the best choices for someone else, so ask as many people as possible for advice.

Checklist of fulfillment supplies

☑ Luggage cart for moving boxes

☑ Scissors, pocket knife, or blade cutter for opening boxes

☑ Gloves

☑ Printed return-address labels, shipping labels, rate labels

☑ Completed parcel-delivery forms

☑ Padded mailing bags or shipping boxes (and packing)

☑ Package tape and scissors

☑ Stapler and staples

☑ Postage

☑ Letters and flyers to accompany review copies

☑ Invoices

☑ Basket or box for finished packages

☑ Master order list to check off orders

Resources

The resources that follow are by no means a comprehensive list. Often only one among equals is listed because it is more used or more available. Many of the items have been standards for years and are listed because they can be found readily in libraries and second-hand book stores. Use the bibliographies and notes in these resources to identify additional resources in areas of interest.

Context

These books are a mixture. Some are finding aids and standard reference works. Others are listed simply as examples of the types of books in which you will find fascinating contextual information. Of these, some were found in libraries, but many were purchased at used-book stores. Don't neglect articles

American Historical Association. *America: History and Life.* Annual volumes indexing and abstracting current publications such as articles and dissertations. The combined series on CD-ROM is a powerful tool for finding sources on specialized topics.

Arbor, Marilyn. *Tools and Trades of America's Past: The Mercer Collection.* Doylestown, PA: Bucks County Historical Society, 1981. There are many small museums with specialized collections that focus on aspects of our ancestor's lives through the items they left behind. Visit the museums and use their publications.

Arksey, Laura, Nancy Pries, and Marcia Reed. *American Diaries: An Annotated Bibliography of Published American Diaries and Journals.* Detroit: Gale Research Company, 1983, 1987. Arranged chronologically, with name, subject, and geographic indexes. Coverage for Civil War, women, maritime, and westward migration is good. Many other bibliographies of published and unpublished diaries, letters, and manuscripts are at your library.

Billington, Ray Allen. *Westward Expansion: A History of the American Frontier.* New York: The Macmillan Company, 1949. Often used in college classes, it discusses the push, pull, and pathways as migration spread into new regions. Reach for this book each time your ancestors move.

Bowman, John S. *Civil War Day by Day.* New York: Barnes & Nobel, 1989. "Timeline" books can be helpful in identifying events and trends that might have affected your ancestor, but should not be used for unrelated "on this day in history . . ." comparisons.

Cappon, Lester J., Barbara Bartz Petchenik, and John Hamilton Long, editors. *Atlas of American History.* Princeton: Princeton University Press, 1976. In addition to political or topographic maps, atlases contain special or annotated maps, statistical information, and even articles.

CD Sourcebook of American History. Provo, UT: Infobases, Inc., 1992. An example of books and documents on CD-ROM with full-text-search capabilities available for home use.

Chesnut, Mary Boykin Miller; edited by C. Vann Woodward. *Mary Chesnut's Civil War.* New Haven: Yale University Press, 1981. Pulitzer prize-winning transcript of her extremely readable Confederate diaries, familiar to fans of the PBS series. Look for diaries of individuals whose circumstances were similar to those of your ancestors.

DePauw, Linda Grant and Conover Hunt. *"Remember the Ladies"— Women in America, 1750–1815.* New York: The Viking Press, 1976. Typical catalog for a touring exhibit. Informative chapters on "Love and Marriage," "Motherhood," "Sickness and Death," and other topics are beautifully illustrated with photographs.

Everyday Life books. Several publishers have everyday-life series written by a variety of authors and aimed for the school market. Many individual books have been written on the subject, also. The title usually begins with "Everyday Life . . ."

Fischer, David Hackett. *Albion's Seed: Four British Folkways in America.* Oxford: Oxford University Press, 1989. The title is a misnomer. He examines a variety of folkways for four regions of British immigration (Massachusetts, Virginia, Delaware Valley, and the backcountry). Evaluate his conclusions critically.

Hinding, Andrea, editor. *Women's History Sources: A Guide to Archives and Manuscript Collections in the United States.* 2 volumes. New York: R. R. Bowker, 1979. Half of our ancestors were female. Much was recorded by them. This is a finding aid to distaff sources, organized by location of repository.

Hume, Ivor Noël. *Martin's Hundred.* London: Victor Gollancz Ltd., 1982. An absolutely fascinating tale of the excavation of one of the oldest settlements in Virginia, it provides a wealth of information on Tidewater life in the early seventeenth century. Publications about archeology are an under-used resource.

Hurmence, Belinda. *Before Freedom: Forty-eight Oral Histories of Former North and South Carolina Slaves.* New York: Mentor, 1990. The Federal Writers Project produced many oral history collections.

Layburn, James G. *The Scotch-Irish: A Social History.* Chapel Hill: The University of North Carolina Press, 1962. There are many social histories of ethnic and religious groups available, from easy-to-read books in the youth section to pedantic tomes.

Library of Congress. *National Union Catalog of Manuscript Collections.* Hamden, CT: 1959–1992. Affectionately known as NUCMC (pronounced "nuck-muck"), contains card-catalog style descriptions of archives' manuscript holdings reported to the Library of Congress. This is how you locate a neighbor's diary or a store ledger. Electronic databases are rapidly becoming a more effective method of accessing this type of information.

McWhiney, Grady. *Cracker Culture: Celtic Ways in the Old South.* Tuscaloosa: The University of Alabama Press, 1988. Were Southerners really different from Northerners? Yep! The many contemporary observations on southern lifestyle may have you looking at your ancestors in a totally different way. Recent books on social history are more realistic than those from the first half of this century.

Medical and Surgical History of the Civil War. Wilmington, NC: Broadfoot Publishing Co., 1990–92. Illness and injury were a daily reality for the troops—even when there were no battles. These twelve volumes, edited by various individuals, contain case studies. The introduction to the index is a brief history of medical conditions during the Civil War.

Meyer, Richard E., editor. *Cemeteries and Gravemarkers: Voices of American Culture.* Logan, UT: Utah State University Press, 1992. Papers presented at conferences sometimes also appear in print. These dozen papers were presented at an American Culture Association conference. Topics include upland-South folk cemeteries, nineteenth-century rural cemeteries, and the "white bronze" markers of the late-nineteenth century.

Microsoft. *Encarta.* Annual releases. Encyclopedias on CD-ROM are a convenient starting point, especially if you are not seeking in-depth information.

Osgood, Herbert L. *The American Colonies in the Eighteenth Century.* Gloucester, MA: Columbia University Press, 1958. This multivolume series and its companion, *The American Colonies in the Seventeenth Century,* are a very readable history lesson. Use it to understand which events of history affected your ancestor.

Rothman, Ellen K. *Hands and Hearts: A History of Courtship in America.* New York: Basic Books, 1984. It wasn't always the way you think it was—or was it? Covers 1770-1920.

Rutman, Darrett B. and Anita H. Rutman. *A Place in Time: Middlesex County, Virginia, 1650-1750.* New York: W. W. Norton & Company, 1984. An example of a publication arising from research by academicians. These history professors examine the relationships between the people of this tidewater area.

Salmon, Marylynn. *Women and the Law of Property in Early America.* Chapel Hill: University of North Carolina Press, 1986. Extremely useful for understanding how women's lives were restricted by the statute and common law that "protected" them.

Schlissel, Lillian, editor. *Women's Diaries of the Westward Journey.* New York: Schocken Books, 1982; 1992 with new introduction. An early classic of the growing pool drawing on women's diaries. Discussion uses diaries of four women 1849-1862. An additional volume *Far from Home: Families of the Westward Journey,* edited by Schlissel, Byrd Gibbons, and Elizabeth Hampsten, has been published

Smith, Barbara Clark. *After the Revolution: The Smithsonian History of Everyday Life in the Eighteenth Century.* New York: Pantheon Books, 1985. Our national museums produce many interesting exhibits and publications. This one discusses the everyday lives of four socially different families from Massachusetts, Delaware, Virginia, and Philadelphia, focusing on items in reconstructed rooms at the National Museum of American History.

Stewart, George R. *American Given Names*. New York: Oxford University Press, 1979. What can the names that your ancestors gave their children tell you about the parents? "Historical Notes" describes the trends in name choices, "Dictionary" lists specific names and their meanings, "Notes" discusses nicknames and other items.

Stratton, Joanna L. *Pioneer Women: Voices from the Kansas Frontier*. New York: Simon and Schuster, 1981. One of the earlier books to chronicle history based on the recollections of female pioneers.

Szucs, Loretto and Sandra Luebking. *The Source*. Salt Lake City: Ancestry Incorporated, 1996. Use this text for background material on the who, what, when, where, why, and how of the records. Each chapter is written by an expert in that field. The first edition, published in 1984, was edited by Arlene Eakle and Johni Cerny.

Thompson, Roger. *Sex in Middlesex: Popular Mores in a Massachusetts County, 1649-1699*. Amherst: University of Massachusetts Press, 1986. Court records were combed for testimony related to adolescents, couples, and families. An example of a university-press publication.

Tunis, Edwin. *Frontier Living*. New York: The World Publishing Company, 1961. One of a series of easy-to-read pictorial history books, profusely illustrated by the author with pen-and-ink drawings of dress, housing, tools, and so on.

Ulrich, Laurel Thatcher. *A Midwife's Tale: The Life of Martha Ballard, Based on Her Diary, 1785-1812*. New York: Vintage Books, 1990. Winner of a Pulitzer Prize. Less a story of midwifery (there are few details on childbirth) and more a story of the daily rhythms, ebbs, and flows of the life of a New England farm woman. Her gardening and their meals are fascinating.

US Bureau of the Census. *Historical Statistics of the United States: Colonial Times to 1970*. Washington: US Government Printing Office, 1976. Want to know how many people lived in your ancestor's state in 1800? This is where to look.

US Geological Survey (USGS). Call 1-800-USA-MAPS to access their automated phone system to receive ordering information for USGS topographic maps.

William and Mary Quarterly. This quarterly contains many scholarly articles on history of interest to genealogists. Although based in Virginia, articles cover topics from other regions, primarily of the colonial period. (Box 8781, Williamsburg, VA 23187-8781.)

Copyright

Cogswell, Robert. *Copyright Law for Unpublished Manuscripts and Archival Collections*. Dobbs Ferry, NY: Glanville Publishers, Inc., 1992. Not as helpful as might be hoped.

Copyright Office. Library of Congress, Washington, DC 20559. (202) 707–9100 to order circulars via voice mail or call (202) 707–2600 for fax on demand. For Internet access to circulars and information: marvel.loc.gov (Telnet [login Marvel] or Gopher); or http://lcweb.loc.gov/copyright (World Wide Web). They have useful circulars available on copyright basics (circular 1), copyright notice (circular 3), and researching the copyright status of a publication (circular 22), plus form TX for registering a copyright.

Fishman, Stephen. *The Copyright Handbook: How to Protect and Use Written Works*. Berkeley: Nolo Press, 1992. One of several references written about copyright. Look for recent publications.

Dictionaries

American Heritage Dictionary of the English Language, 3d edition. Preferred by many writers, but possibly less useful for genealogists than Webster's.

Black, Henry Campbell, *Black's Law Dictionary*, 6th edition. St. Paul: West Publishing Co., 1990. Older editions are fine for genealogists. Includes almost all of the legal terms you are likely to encounter in your research (although some creative searching may be required).

Merriam-Webster's New Collegiate Dictionary, 10th edition. Not many significant changes from the 9th edition. Genealogists will find many "historical" terms, such as cordwainer and vara. Note also that they will answer by mail—free—up to three "specific questions about words and their origin, spelling, pronunciation, meaning, or usage" not only from scholars but from "professionals, students, and laymen alike." (Presumably that includes genealogists!) Send your question(s) with an SASE to Language Research Service, PO Box 281, Springfield, MA 01102.

Oxford English Dictionary. Defines historical use of terms in great detail. Originally issued in 1933 in 13 volumes, it has been reprinted and updated (including a CD-ROM edition). The recently published two-volume *New Shorter Oxford English Dictionary* provides a less-cumbersome alternative.

McCutcheon, Marc. *The Writer's Guide to Everyday Life in the 1800s.* (Cincinnati: Writer's Digest Books, 1993). Dictionaries focusing on a specialized vocabulary can be useful for identifying archaic terms in wills, letters, and diaries. This one, for writers of historical novels, is organized topically rather than alphabetically.

Documentation and evidence

Devine, Donn, "Do We Really Decide Relationships by a Preponderance of the Evidence?" *NGS Newsletter* 18 (September–October 1992): 131–133. Discusses relative terms of evidence.

Lackey, Richard S. *Cite Your Sources: A Manual for Documenting Family Histories and Genealogical Records.* New Orleans: Polyanthos, 1980. Long accepted as the standard reference for genealogical documentation, it is becoming out-of-date, but still good reading. Use Turabian and *Chicago* for additional examples.

Mills, Elizabeth Shown. *Evidence: Citation & Analysis for the Family Historian.* To be published in 1996. The new standard for documentation and evidence.

Stevenson, Noel C. *Genealogical Evidence: A Guide to the Standard of Proof Relating to Pedigrees, Ancestry, Heirship and Family History,* revised edition. Laguna Hills: Aegean Park Press, 1989. Written by an attorney and considered a standard, it is difficult to follow.

Examples: Books

The books below are recognized for both their presentation and their research. The more recent ones have won awards for their quality.

Davis, Walter Goodwin. *The Ancestry of . . .* Davis compiled sixteen slim volumes before 1963, each tracing the ancestry of one of his great-great-grandparents. His "organized" arrangement of the families within the book is no longer recommended.

Davis, Virginia Lee Hutcheson. *Tidewater Virginia Families.* Baltimore: Genealogical Publishing Company, 1989. 1994 NGS Award for Excellence.

Donaldson, Patricia, and Vernon Stiver. *Stöver-Stoever-Staver-Stiver: An Account of the Ancestry and Descendants of Johan Caspar Stoever of Pennsylvania.* n.p.: produced by McNaughton & Gunn, 1992. 1993 NGS Award for Excellence.

Ferris, Mary W. *Dawes-Gates Ancestral Lines.* Privately printed, 1943. Massive two-volume all-my-ancestors work. Early and excellent example of going beyond the vital statistics.

Rohrbach, Lewis Bunker. *Höffelbauer Genealogy 1585–1993: The American Families Helfelbower, Heffelbower, . . . Together with their German and Austrian Ancestry.* Camden, ME: Picton Press, 1993. 1995 Donald Lines Jacobus Award.

Smith, Dean Crawford. *The Ancestry of Emily Jane Angell: 1844–1910: With Lines from Angell, Ashton, Inman, Mowry, Olney, and Smith of Providence, R.I.; . . .* Boston: New England Historic Genealogical Society, 1992. Smith (with editor Melinde Lutz Sanborn), like Walter Goodwin Davis, is publishing a series of books, each tracing a portion of his ancestry. 1993 Donald Lines Jacobus Award.

Examples: Journals

The following journals all provide excellent examples of genealogies, both in terms of quality of research and presentation models. They are widely available in genealogical libraries.

The American Genealogist (TAG). A privately published journal begun by Donald Lines Jacobus and currently coedited by David L. Greene, FASG, and Robert Charles Anderson, FASG, (PO Box 398, Demorest, GA 30535-0398). Uses Register numbering system. Issues prior to 1996 used in-text citations; now uses footnotes.

National Genealogical Society Quarterly (NGSQ). The quarterly, coedited by Elizabeth Shown Mills, FASG, and Gary Mills, PhD, is a benefit of membership in the National Genealogical Society (4527 Seventeenth Street North; Arlington, VA 22207–2399). Uses NGSQ numbering system. Issues prior to 1996 used endnotes; now uses footnotes.

New England Historical and Genealogical Register (NEHGR or *The Register*). The quarterly, edited by Jane Fletcher Fiske, FASG, is a benefit of membership in the New England Historic Genealogical Society (101 Newbury Street, Boston, MA 02116). Uses Register numbering system. Issues prior to 1994 used in-text citations; now uses footnotes.

New York Genealogical and Biographical Record (NYGBR or *The Record*). The quarterly, coedited by Henry Hoff, FASG, and Harry Macy, FASG, is a benefit of membership in the New York Genealogical and Biographical Society (122 E. 58th St., New York, NY 10022). Uses Register numbering system. Issues prior to 1995 used in-text citations; now uses footnotes.

The Virginia Genealogist. Edited and privately published by John Frederick Dorman, FASG (Box 5869, Falmouth, VA 22403-5860). Uses footnotes.

Illustrations and artwork

Dover Books. 31 East Second Street. Mineola, NY 11501. A source for many books of inexpensive clip art. The books are found in many bookstores or can be ordered from their catalog.

Ledden, Larry. *Complete Guide to Scanning.* Westfield, NY: Family Technologies, 1994. Spiral bound. Best explanation available on what scanners are, how they work, and what a genealogist can do with one.

Library of Congress. Several divisions of the Library of Congress have documents, maps, and photographs of interest to the genealogist. Some of these are being scanned. Historical Image Collection (202) 707-6233; Map Division (202) 707-3300; Prints and Photographs Division (202) 707-6394. Visit their American Memory Web page, http://lcweb2.loc.gov/amhome.html, to learn more about it.

Shull, Wilma Sadler. *Photographing Your Heritage.* Salt Lake City: Ancestry Incorporated, 1988. Many helpful hints on cameras and photography.

US Bureau of the Census. TIGER mapping service. A project to provide a public resource for digital maps. Visit their Web page at http://tiger.census.gov.

Indexing

Hatcher, Patricia Law, and John V. Wylie. "Indexing Family Histories," *NGSQ* 81 (June 1993): 85–98. Also available as NGS special publication #73. Recommends some standards and explains the process of indexing with a word processor.

Mulvany, Nancy. *Indexing Books.* Chicago: University of Chicago Press, 1994. Although the most recent authoritative book on indexing, the author admits, "The discussion that follows is based upon the state of embedded indexing tools [indexing features of word-processing software] in the early 1990s." [page 255] The discussion indicates a complete lack of familiarity with the indexing capabilities of 1994 software (or even the software available in the early 1990s).

Wellish, Hans H. *Indexing from A to Z*. New York: The H. W. Wilson Company, 1991. An encyclopedic-format reference of interest to those who want to learn more about indexing in general, but does little to address the special needs of genealogical works.

Literature search

Family History Library Catalog™ (FHLC). The catalog of both book and microform holdings of the Family History Library (Salt Lake City) of The Church of Jesus Christ of Latter-day Saints, it is accessible on microfiche and CD-ROM at the Family History Centers (FHC) and many major libraries. The microfiche can be purchased. There are three sections: Locality, Author-Title, Surname.

Genealogical Books in Print. Springfield, VA: Genealogical Books in Print, 1985, 1992. The two-volume fourth edition was edited by Netti Schreiner-Yantis; the supplement by Bette A. and Kamm Y. Schreiner. Publishers (especially self-publishing authors) place listings in General Reference, Locality, and Family Genealogy sections.

Genealogical Index of the Newberry Library, Chicago. Boston: G. K. Hall and Company, 1960. The four oversize volumes of card-catalog images are organized by surnames. Although outdated, the massive size of the Newberry's collection still makes this a valuable source to check.

Genealogies in the Library of Congress. Edited by Marion J. Kaminkow. Baltimore: Magna Carta Book Co., 1972. There is also a *Complement* and two *Supplements*. Organized by surname. If copyright is obtained on a genealogy, the copy is placed in the Library of Congress.

National Society of the Daughters of the American Revolution Library Catalog. Washington: n.p., 1986. Presently three volumes. Includes many typescript "publications" by DAR members not available elsewhere.

New York Public Library Dictionary and Catalog of the Local History and Genealogy Division. Boston: G. K. Hall & Co., 1974. Organized by surname, 18 oversized volumes of card-catalog images.

Periodical Source Index (PERSI). An enormous project of the Allen County (Fort Wayne, Indiana) Public Library, identifying the primary topic of each article in each publication in its substantial genealogical and local history periodical collection. Presently almost one million entries in twenty-five volumes. A merged edition on CD-ROM and microfiche is planned.

Numbering systems

Crane, Madilyn Coen. "Numbering Your Genealogy—Special Cases: Surname Changes, Step Relationships, and Adoptions," *National Genealogical Society Quarterly* 83 (June 1995): 85-98. Supplement to Curran, discussing augmentations (not changes) to the accepted numbering systems.

Curran, Joan. "Numbering Your Genealogy," *National Genealogical Society Quarterly* 79 (September 1991): 183-193. Excellent explanation of numbering systems for genealogies. The standard reference. Also available as National Genealogical Society special publication #59.

Printers

Johnson Printing Service. 14030 Welch Road, Dallas, TX 75244. Developer of EcoFLEX™ binding.

Literary Market Place™. New Providence, NJ: R. R. Bowker, annual. Alphabetical listings of many printers and binderies. Available at many public libraries.

Professional genealogists

Association of Professional Genealogists (APG). *Directory of Professional Genealogists 1995*. The Directory lists research specialties of members. 3421 M Street NW, Suite 236, Washington, DC 20007.

Board for Certification of Genealogists (BCG). *'95 Roster*. The Board tests and certifies researchers in six categories. The *Roster*, which can be purchased, lists research specialties of those certified. PO Box 5816, Falmouth, VA 22403-5816.

Family History Library. Accredited Genealogist (AG) List. The AG program tests for research skills in the library. Send SASE and request the list for a specific geographic or topical specialty. 35 North West Temple Street, Salt Lake City, UT 84150-1003.

Publishing

Bowker, R. R. 121 Chanlon Road, New Providence, NJ 07974. Source for International Standard Book Numbers (ISBN) and publisher of *Books in Print*.

Cataloging in Publication (CIP) Division, Library of Congress, Washington, DC 20504. Form 607-7 is used to request a CIP number.

Poynter, Dan. *The Self-Publishing Manual: How to Write, Print, and Sell Your Own Book*, 8th edition. Santa Barbara: Para Publishing, 1995. A classic on self-publishing. Targeted to a broader audience, it still has many useful hints for genealogists.

Standards for genealogical publishing

Barnes, Donald R., and Richard S. Lackey. *Write It Right: A Manual for Writing Family Histories and Genealogies*. Ocala, Florida: Lyon Press, 1983. Typographically awful and outdated, but generally good advice.

Colket, Meredith B., Jr. *Creating a Worthwhile Family Genealogy*. *National Genealogical Society Quarterly* 56 (December 1968): 243-62. Although written many years ago, almost all of the advice remains sound. Lists a sampling of genealogies that the author considers worthwhile.

Fiske, Jane Fletcher, and Margaret F. Costello. *Guidelines for Genealogical Writing*. Boston: New England Historic Genealogical Society, 1990. Intended as the style guide for the *New England Historical and Genealogical Register*.

Worthy, Rita Binkley. *Write Your Family History*. Arlington: National Genealogical Society, 1988. Written as the guidelines for submitting to the NGS Family History Writing Contest, this booklet offers good advice on writing family history.

Style manuals, grammars, and typesetting guides

Bernstein, Theodore. *The Careful Writer: A Modern Guide to English Usage*. New York: Macmillan Publishing Company, 1977. Alphabetically arranged answers for common usage questions.

Boston, Bruce O. *Stet! Tricks of the Trade for Writers and Editors*. Alexandria: Editorial Experts, Inc., 1986. *The Editorial Eye* is a (high-priced) newsletter respected in the professional writing and editing community. This book is based on articles from earlier issues of the newsletter.

Brady, Philip. *Using Type Right: 121 Basic No-Nonsense Rules for Working with Type.* Cincinnati: North Light Books, 1988. Easy for the nonprofessional to understand. Lots of examples of both good and bad.

Chicago Manual of Style. Chicago and London: The University of Chicago Press, 13th edition. 1982, 14th edition. 1993. This book, subtitled "For Authors, Editors, and Copywriters," is for professionals. For normal matters of grammar and citation you may find Lackey, Mills, Sabin, Turabian, and Venolia easier to use. However, for those preparing camera-ready art, *Chicago* has much to offer. *Chicago* is conservative and widely accepted in genealogy. Virtually every chapter provides additional information on the topics covered in this book.

Craig, James. *Designing with Type,* 3rd edition. New York: Watson-Guptill, 1992. Designed as a textbook, this large-format book provides a good explanation of typography and can often be found in used-book stores.

Fowler, H. W. *A Dictionary of Modern English Usage.* Oxford: Clarendon Press, 1987. The classic for arbitrating questions of usage.

Gibaldi, Joseph. *MLA Handbook for Writers of Research Papers,* 4th edition. New York: The Modern Language Association of America, 1995. Section 4.8, "Citing CD-ROMs and Other Portable Databases," and section 4.9, "Citing Online Databases," are recommended *reading* (not just reference) for any genealogist using any information obtained in electronic form. The examples given are for bibliographic rather than note form, so use it as a guide on what elements to include in your notes.

New York Public Library Writer's Guide to Style and Usage. HarperCollins Publishers, 1994. More in the modern swing than *Chicago,* but still not as helpful for the seamless writing and publishing process as would be hoped. Do not use their guidelines for informal documentation, which are not acceptable in genealogy.

Plotnik, Arthur. *The Elements of Editing: A Modern Guide for Editors and Journalists.* New York: Macmillan Publishing Company, 1982. Defines and describes the role of an editor.

Sabin, William A. *The Gregg Reference Manual,* 7th edition. New York: McGraw-Hill, 1992. Especially useful for grammar, punctuation, and word usage, with many examples (available in wire-binding).

Safire, William. *Fumblerules: A Lighthearted Guide to Grammar and Good Usage.* New York: Dell Publishing, 1990. If you're worried about learning grammar again, start here.

Siebert, Lori, and Mary Cropper. *Working with Words & Pictures.* Cincinnati: North Light Books, 1993. Great ideas for combining text and graphics. Be sure and read the sidebars for the valuable information presented there.

Turabian, Kate L. *A Manual for Writers of Term Papers, Theses, and Dissertations,* 5th edition. Chicago: The University of Chicago Press, 1982. Designed for the nonprofessional, easy-to-use for citations, but consistent with *Chicago.* Available in paperback, it is an inexpensive alternative to *Chicago.*

US Government Printing Office Style Manual, also published as *A Manual of Style: A Guide to the Basics of Good Writing.* Washington: Government Printing Office, 1984, (produced by several publishers under slightly varying titles over the years). Readily available style manual.

Venolia, Jan. *Write Right!,* revised edition. Berkeley: Ten Speed Press, 1988. Sections on punctuation, grammar, style, spelling, and often-misused words offer advice on the elements of writing that confuse us most. The examples used to illustrate, which range from Mark Twain to Oscar Wilde to Vince Lombardi, will enliven your day.

Words into Type, 3d edition. Englewood Cliffs, NJ: Prentice-Hall, Inc., 1974. Many professional writers and editors have well-thumbed copies on their bookshelves.

Index

Major categories in this index include Binding, Book design, Computers, Context, Documentation, Editing and reviewing, Family history, Fonts, Grammar and punctuation, Illustrations, Index, Numbering systems, Page layout and formatting, Printing, Publishing, Research, Style, Typesetting, and Writing.